C000127998

INDONESIAN
SLANG
COLLOQUIAL INDONESIAN AT WORK

Christopher Torchia & Lely Djuhari

TUTTLE Publishing

Tokyo | Rutland, Vermont | Singapore

Published by Tuttle Publishing, an imprint of Periplus Editions (HK) Ltd.

www.tuttlepublishing.com

Copyright © 2011 by Christopher Torchia and Lely Djuhari

All rights reserved. No part of this publication may be reproduced or utilized in any form or by any means, electronic or mechanical, including photocopying, recording, or by any information storage and retrieval system, without prior written permission from the publisher.

Library of Congress Control Number: 2011921096
ISBN 978-0-8048-4207-5

This title was previously published as *Indonesian Idioms and Expressions* (ISBN 978-0-8048-3873-3).

Distributed by:

North America, Latin America and Europe
Tuttle Publishing, 364 Innovation Drive,
North Clarendon, VT 05759, USA
Tel: (802) 773 8930; Fax: (802) 773 6993
info@tuttlepublishing.com
www.tuttlepublishing.com

Asia Pacific
Berkeley Books Pte Ltd,
61 Tai Seng Avenue #02-012, Singapore 534167
Tel: (65) 6280 1330; Fax: (65) 6280 6290
inquiries@periplus.com.sg
www.periplus.com

Indonesia
PT Java Books Indonesia
Kawasan Industri Pulogadung
Jl. Rawa Gelam IV No. 9, Jakarta 13930
Tel: (62) 21 4682-1088; Fax: (62) 21 461-0206
crm@periplus.co.id
www.periplus.co.id

Printed in Singapore

15 14 13 12 11   6 5 4 3 2   1107TP

TUTTLE PUBLISHING® is a registered trademark of Tuttle Publishing, a division of Periplus Editions (HK) Ltd.

Contents

Introduction   5

Part 1: Life Forms   9
1. Creatures   10
2. Characters   27
3. Body Language   45

Part II: Power and Conflict   61
4. Authoritarian Rule   62
5. Money and Politics   79
6. Protest Fever   101
7. A History of Violence   118

Part III: Traditions   145
8. Faith and Fortune   146
9. A Matter of Taste   165
10. Family Affairs   186
11. Wisdom   204

Part IV: Modern Life   213
12. Around Town   214
13. Insults and the Underground   233
14. Hanging Out   251
15. Tech Talk   273

Sources   279

Index   281

Introduction

Diam seribu bahasa. Quiet in a thousand languages.

A rough translation might be: The silence is deafening. It evokes barely repressed anger, or the haughty indifference of a beauty with many suitors.

Nongkrong. This is a casual phrase, a reference to the Indonesian custom of hanging out, sometimes by squatting on the roadside.

Mengadu nasib. Tempt fate. Countless Indonesians do this, converging on Jakarta in hopes of finding something better in life. Some succeed, many don't.

These and other expressions offer one of the best windows onto the Indonesian culture. Slang, titles, proverbs, nicknames, acronyms, quotations and other expressions reveal its character, in the words of its people. This book of expressions looks at Indonesia with the help of its national language, *bahasa Indonesia.* It describes Indonesians and their fears, beliefs, history and politics, as well as how they live, fight, grieve and laugh.

Indonesian is a variant of Malay, the national language of Malaysia, and many of its expressions come from the Malay heartland of Sumatra island. Indonesian has also incorporated terms from Javanese, the language of the dominant ethnic group in a huge nation of more than 17,000 islands, most of them uninhabited. Hundreds more ethnic groups with their own languages are scattered across the archipelago, and many Indonesians speak *bahasa Indonesia* as a second language, or mix fragments of it into the local tongue. Still, schools in far-flung regions teach Indonesian, and its role as the language of government and the national media make it a unifying force in one of the world's most culturally diverse countries. Mindful of that variety, this book offers only a slice of how Indonesians talk.

Although Indonesian is officially a young language, it contains words from Sanskrit, Arabic, Chinese, Dutch, Portuguese and English, a legacy of the merchants, warriors, laborers and holy men who traveled to the archipelago over the centuries.

The Indonesian language was a nationalist symbol during the campaign against Dutch rule in the 20th century. Indonesians who fought against colonialism made it the national language in their constitution when they declared independence in 1945.

Two generations later, modern Indonesians love word play. The tongue slips and skids, chopping words, piling on syllables and flipping them. Indonesians turn phrases into acronyms, and construct double meanings. Their inventions reflect social trends, mock authority, or get a point across in a hurry. Colloquial Indonesian is constantly evolving, and often bears little resemblance to the "correct," written form of the language, a source of concern to some linguists. Such a divergence is common in languages worldwide, but the vast ethnic mix and breadth of linguistic influences in Indonesia deepens the trend.

Some expressions are easy to match up with idioms from other cultures. *Musang berbulu ayam* is a civet in chicken's feathers. In other words, a wolf in sheep's clothing.

This book divides Indonesian expressions into categories such as food and wisdom, politics and personalities. The format is the same in each chapter. An expression in Indonesian, or sometimes a regional language in Indonesia, is followed by a translation, an interpretation of the meaning, and usually a summary of the idiom's origin or background. Some translations are more literal than others, reflecting an effort to balance clarity of meaning with the flavor of the original words.

We are grateful to Tantri Yuliandini and Amalia Ahmad for their contributions, and to Sara Datuk and Johanna Wulansari Istanto for their valuable suggestions. Many thanks also go to Mia Amalia, Murizal Hamzah, Prof. Anton Moeliono and Dr. Jan-Michael Bach.

As journalists, we covered a chaotic period in Indonesian history in the late 1990s. The currency plummeted, students protested, riots erupted, and the president resigned, triggering euphoria over the promise of new freedoms and uncertainty over unleashed tensions that often spilled into violence.

Years later, the image of Indonesia as a nation on the brink of collapse has faded. Democracy has taken hold and Indonesia is a place of potential, even if corruption, terrorism and other problems persist. Away from the headlines, *bahasa Indonesia* tells a different story about Indonesia and its people.

CHRISTOPHER TORCHIA & LELY DJUHARI

PART I

Life Forms

Chapter One

Creatures

Indonesia teems with tame, predatory and mythical animals. Some stick to the jungles, some loiter in your living room. Others roam the underworld.

❀ Tikus kantor
"Office rat" = Thief.

A miscreant lingers in the office or on the factory floor until everyone leaves, then swipes valuables before scurrying away like a rodent.

Tikus negara (state rat) is a government worker intent on personal gain. A motorcycle policeman on the take pulls over a motorist who runs a red light or stop sign. The driver settles the case on the spot. He leans over and tucks a banknote into the cop's boot, which rests on the foot peg of his bike.

Rats are part of life in Indonesia. They rummage through garbage at street corners and crawl from drainage ditches. They gnaw on house foundations, chew window screens, scuttle in ceilings, slither around the water bowls of squat toilets, leave droppings beside bedside tables and munch through food containers. A newspaper columnist once proposed putting a bounty on rats, but the idea fizzled.

Rats are cunning and live in the same surroundings as humans, so they make good symbols of unsavory characters such as *tikus berdasi* (rat in a tie) and *tikus berjas* (rat in a suit).

Rats are also a scourge in the countryside, where they eat rice and other crops, inflicting huge losses on farmers. They multiply and spread disease.

✽ Bajing loncat
"Jumping squirrel" = A thief who waylays vehicles on long journeys.

Bajing loncat was the bane of the trans-Sumatra highway, a major artery stretching between Lampung province in the south and Aceh province in the north of the island.

Luggage-laden buses or cargo trucks formed convoys on the highway for safe passage through forests at night. Groups of *bajing loncat* hid behind trees at curves, or near potholes and bumpy stretches, and jumped onto the backs of slowing vehicles. They climbed up to bus roofs, or opened rear truck doors, and lobbed bags and goods onto the street. Then they leaped off, backtracking to collect the booty. Drivers and passengers realized their misfortune when they reached their destination.

You can travel the length of the trans-Sumatra road in two days, making regular stops. Jungle foliage and neat palm plantations line the road between towns of two-storey wooden buildings. The worst stretch of road is in the Palembang area in the south. You sometimes come across an overturned truck that blocks the road, delaying the trip for hours. Bandits lurk in places. Children converge on buses at rest stops and beg for money.

Bajing loncat is also a term for someone who jumps on the bandwagon. In early 2004, President Megawati Sukarnoputri criticized several former ministers in her Cabinet who had quit to run in the presidential election. She described them as *bajing loncat*, fickle people who pursued their own interests, not those of the nation. One of them, Susilo Bambang Yudhoyono, defeated Megawati in the election and became president.

❀ Kelas kakap
"Snapper class" = Top of the line

A red snapper fish is big and bold, and feeds on smaller fish. But *kakap*, which can refer to any large fish, also has negative connotations. *Penjahat kelas kakap* is a big-time gangster; *playboy kelas kakap* is a habitual womanizer.

The low end of the scale is *kelas teri* (*teri* is a small fish).

Ali Ghufron, an Islamic militant who claimed to have fought alongside Osama bin Laden in Afghanistan in the 1980s, and two other people were sentenced to death for organizing bombings that killed 202 people at nightclubs on Bali island on October 12, 2002. During his trial, Ghufron said he was *ikan teri* (small fry) and that U.S. President George W. Bush and his allies were the big fish who deserved punishment. Authorities blamed the attacks on Jemaah Islamiyah, a Southeast Asian terrorist network linked to al-Qaida.

Ghufron and the two other militants were executed in 2008. Their families said they believed they would be rewarded in heaven.

❀ Kutu loncat
"Jumping louse" = An opportunist

Someone who bounces from one job or scheme to the next, like a louse that dances in locks of hair.

Mati kutu (dead louse) is a cornered, powerless person.

Kutu buku (book louse) is a bookworm, or nerd. The term is complimentary because book lice are smart and eager to learn. Some Indonesian literacy campaigners hoisted huge posters with a cartoon image of a bespectacled louse, smiling and reading a book.

Lice are a nuisance in rural Indonesia. Farmers sigh with exasperation when they find lice squirming in grain sacks, but take the discovery in stride. Villagers, mostly females, sit on front porches on a lazy afternoon and pluck lice from the heads of friends and relatives in full view of passers-by. Lice-laced hair doesn't inspire revulsion. Villagers often crunch the lice in their teeth, and eat them. They like the mild, salty taste.

❀ Terlepas dari mulut buaya, masuk ke mulut harimau
"Released from the crocodile's mouth, enter the tiger's mouth" = From the frying pan into the fire

The tiger is a symbol of pride and power in Indonesia. At one time, powerful people were believed to become tigers after death. The symbol of a division in the modern military is the white tiger.

In parts of Central Java, people who walked through jungles to get home once murmured *eyang* (grandfather or grandmother in Javanese) to any tigers lurking in the undergrowth. They believed the tigers would spare them if they addressed the creatures as respected family members.

Poaching and depletion of habitats slashed the tiger population. For decades, poachers defied conservation laws, hunting tigers for fur, bones, teeth, claws and whiskers. Middlemen sold the body parts across Asia as good luck charms and in traditional treatments for ailments such as arthritis. Some people covet the tiger penis as an aphrodisiac. Tigers disappeared from Bali and the crowded island of Java long ago. Park rangers on Sumatra protect a dwindling number of the big cats, but forests where they dwell are shrinking because developers clear land for palm oil plantations and other industries. Tigers sometimes pad out of the jungle and attack livestock and even villagers.

Crocodiles are better off than tigers. The Sumatran city of Medan has the biggest crocodile farm in Indonesia. But demand for skins is high, and some rearing farms depend on eggs and young crocodiles seized from the wild.

Ancient beliefs held that the crocodile was the ruler of the underworld.

East Timor, a former Indonesian territory, holds the crocodile in high regard. A legend describes how a huge crocodile transformed itself into Timor island: A boy rescued a crocodile that was parched and stranded on land. The grateful reptile escorted the boy around the world for years until it was time for the crocodile to die. It arched its back, and the ridges and scales on its great body formed the hills and contours of the island that became a home for the boy and his descendants.

Jose Alexandre Gusmao, East Timor's first president and former guerrilla leader, wrote poetry in jungle hideouts and later in a Jakarta jail. One poem describes the legend of how the crocodile's back formed the mountainous backbone of Timor. The ridge gave shelter to separatist rebels fighting the Indonesian military.

After independence from Indonesia, East Timor adopted two saltwater crocodiles as mascots for its new army. One of the beasts had belonged to Col. Tono Suratman, former commander of the Indonesian military in East Timor.

Lidah buaya (crocodile's tongue) is the Indonesian name of aloe vera, the plant that yields a gel used in shampoo and cosmetic skin creams, and as a treatment for minor wounds and burns. The leaf of aloe vera is green and its serrated edges are reminiscent of the contours of a crocodile's body.

❀ Krakatau/Krakatoa

There is often more than one theory about the origin of an Indonesian expression or place name. Oral tradition, a dearth of written records, the passage of centuries and a diverse mix of ethnic languages obscure the truth.

Mystery surrounds the spelling and etymology of the volcano Krakatoa, in the Sunda Strait between Java and Sumatra. In 1883, the volcano erupted, killing nearly 40,000 people, darkening the sky with ash and sending shock waves around the world. Many victims died in tsunamis generated by the explosion. In his book ''Krakatoa: The Day the World Exploded,'' author Simon Winchester discusses the name:

> There is an early and linguistically alluring report by a French Jesuit priest, Guy Tachard, suggesting that it was an onomatopoeia. Tachard passed the island eighty years after the Dutch cartographers, and wrote in his log that "we made many Tacks to double the island of Cacatoua, so-called because of the white Parrots that are upon that Isle, and which incessantly repeat the name." It sounds improbable, not least because of the difficulty that any mariner might experience trying to hear the call of land-based birds from high on the windy deck of a passing ship.
>
> Others subsequently thought that Krakatoa, of the more common local form Krakatau, derives essentially from one of three words, *karta-karkata*, *karkataka* or *rakata*, which are the Sanskrit and, according to some, the Old Javan words mean-

ing "lobster" or "crab." Then there is a Malay word, *kelekatu*, which means "flying white ant." Since crabs and parrots belong on the island—or since they did, at least, until that dire August morning in 1883—any one of the two last lexical explanations seems reasonably acceptable. White ants only occur in the eastern part of the archipelago, rendering this theory rather less credible; though perhaps rather more credible than the notion, briefly popular in Batavia, that an Indian ship's captain had asked a local boatman what name was given to the pointed mountain he could see, prompting the local to reply *Kaga tau*, meaning "I don't know."

❀ Buaya darat
"Land crocodile" = Playboy, womanizer.

One who treats women as expendable.

To older Indonesians, *buaya darat* is a thief, or scoundrel. Philandering was tricky in the old days, partly because young women rarely met men without chaperones. Families arranged marriages, and some betrothed couples set eyes on each other for the first time on their wedding day. Marriage among distant relatives was common.

Another term for womanizer is *hidung belang* (striped nose). A lover kisses her man on the nose, leaving a smear of incriminating lipstick.

An untrustworthy person is *mulut buaya* (crocodile mouth). He inflicts wounds with words, not teeth.

❀ Seperti ayam melihat musang
"Like a chicken that sees a civet" = Dumbstruck.

Like a deer frozen in a car's headlights.

Civets eat fruit and seeds, but they're also predators. Farmers fear the furry, mongoose-like creatures will raid chicken coops at night.

A rare coffee (*kopi*) was produced with the help of civets (*musang*), which gobbled coffee berries and excreted the partly digested beans. Farmers plucked the beans from civet feces and washed off the dung. Roasting yielded a gourmet brand known as *kopi luwak*. *Luwak* is the Javanese word for civet.

Some said the process became a marketing scam, and that *kopi luwak* was just an exotic brand name. It's unclear how a civet's digestive tract would enhance the coffee taste. Perhaps its stomach acids gave the bean an unusual flavor. Or maybe a civet picked the ripest berries.

❀ Ayam bertelur di atas padi
"A hen that lays eggs in the rice field" = Snug as a bug in a rug. Content with life.

Ensconced in a pile of rice husks, a hen has nourishment and a warm, secure place to lay eggs. The husks are called *kulit gabah* (rice skins).

In some shops and supermarkets in Indonesia, eggs are kept in wooden boxes filled with rice husks to keep them from breaking. The husks are a substitute for Styrofoam. Eggs are available in sealed plastic trays, but some Indonesians prefer to touch the eggs in the bed of rice husks, and pick them out one by one.

If someone is suffering in what appears to be an ideal environment, the following applies: "The chicken that lays eggs in the paddy starves to death, the duck that swims in water dies of thirst."

Ayam tertelur di atas padi mati kelaparan, itik berenang di air mati kehausan.

Civets were linked to the SARS virus that was first recognized in China and killed nearly 800 people worldwide in 2003. Scientists said a virus in civets resembled the virus that infected humans with SARS, or severe acute respiratory syndrome. Civets and other wild animals are culinary delicacies in China, raising the possibility that the virus passed to humans through food.

Recent research suggested that a species of bat may have been the main source of the disease.

❋ Seperti kerbau dicocok hidung
"Like a water buffalo led by the nose" = Like a "yes" man.

Such a docile creature is like a lackey under a boss's thumb. A dumb, indecisive person who cannot think for himself.

❋ Musang berbulu ayam
A civet in chicken feathers.

A wolf in sheep's clothing (*serigala berbulu domba*) is an equivalent expression from ancient Greek times. The wolf version is more popular than the civet one in Indonesia.

Farmers keep one or two chickens in the backyard at home, putting the docile birds within easy reach if it's time to eat.

In villages, it's cheap to buy a live chick and feed it scraps, eat its eggs and later slaughter the bird for meat. Only city dwellers buy a slaughtered, fully grown chicken for supper.

The civet has an image like that of the fox: slick, cunning and adept at slipping into a place where it's unwanted. A chicken coop.

A powerful Javanese king sent his army to seize Malay land on neighboring Sumatra. The Malays knew they were too weak to win on the battlefield, so they challenged the Javanese to a fight between their strongest water buffaloes. The Javanese king dispatched his sturdiest beast to the contest, and the crafty Malays sent a famished calf with an iron spike bound to its nose. The calf thought the Javanese buffalo was its mother, and sidled up to it in search of milk. The spike gored the big buffalo, and the Malays kept their land.

The folktale ends with the Malays naming themselves *Minangkabau* (winning water buffalo) to commemorate their victory.

Today, the traditional headdresses of Minangkabau women, and the corners of thatched roofs of their traditional houses, arch upward like buffalo horns.

The Minangkabau region is the cradle of Malay culture. Millions migrated centuries ago to Malacca and other places in the archipelago. Their descendants reside in what is now Malaysia. Their language is slightly different from that in their ancestral homeland, Sumatra. Many expressions in Indonesian and Malay, the official language of neighboring Malaysia, come from the Minangkabau region.

❈ Seperti cacing kepanasan

"Like an overheated worm" = Somebody who has the fidgets, or is losing his mind.

Coldblooded worms get restless when they pop above ground. Their thin skins heat up and they try to wriggle back into the earth to escape the sun.

Politicians who waffle on policy are also *cacing kepanasan*.

The term describes someone who craves a cigarette and will light up anywhere, or lovers who become cranky and restless when deprived of each other's company.

Kebakaran jenggot (your beard is on fire) is another expression for an agitated person. It also implies anger or rage.

❀ Malu-malu kucing
"Shy cat" = Warning: appearances can be deceiving.

Don't judge a book by its cover. It's not easy to get close to a cat, but it quickly becomes clingy and affectionate when it warms up to you. A tongue-tied girl with a crush on a boy is too shy to say a word, but she opens up once he talks to her.

The complete saying is *Malu, tetapi seperti malunya kucing* (shy, but only as shy as a cat).

❀ Hangat-hangat tahi ayam
"Hot as chicken shit" = Fickle.

Steaming excrement exits the chicken, splatters on the ground and quickly loses its heat. If you launch yourself into a project with gusto and lose interest, then you are *hangat-hangat tahi ayam*.

The complete saying is *hangat, tapi hangatnya seperti tahi ayam* (It's hot, but only as hot as chicken shit).

❀ Seperti katak di bawah tempurung
"Like a frog under a coconut shell" = Someone with a narrow view of the world. Like a frog in a well.

A frog grew up under a coconut shell, and one day a fly crawled into the shell. It said to the frog: "What are you doing here? Go out and see the world."

The frog replied: "Go where? This is the world." The exasperated fly told the frog to jump. The frog did so, toppling the shell. He discovered that there was a world beyond his own.

"A frog that wants to be an ox," is *katak hendak jadi lembu*. He's too big for his boots. He has lofty dreams. Regardless of his talents, he cannot fulfill them because they are unattainable.

❊ Bagaikan pungguk merindukan bulan

"Like an owl that misses the moon" = Pining for your lover.

A swooning teenager writes this old-fashioned expression in a letter to the girl he adores. Youths say it in jest to lampoon a pair of lovers.

❊ Jinak-jinak merpati

"Tame pigeon" = A coy person, especially in courtship.

A woman beckons a suitor, but flutters away when he approaches. After a while, she gestures again. The ritual repeats itself.

The expression also refers to arranged marriages, which were common in Indonesia until the 1960s. *Jinak-jinak merpati* is a woman who agrees to the arrangement, but laments it in her heart.

The complete saying is *Jinak tetapi jinaknya merpati* (docile, but only as docile as a pigeon).

Pigeons are depicted as lovebirds. *Merpati ingkar janji* (when a pigeon breaks its promise) refers to a spouse who commits adultery.

❊ Cinta monyet

"Monkey love" = Puppy love. An adolescent crush.

Indonesians think monkeys are as foolish as starry-eyed lovers. People mimic the sounds and gestures of monkeys if they want to act stupidly. On television, comedians launch into monkey sounds to make someone look stupid.

Monkeys mesmerize onlookers in street shows, sometimes riding miniature bicycles. The animal usually answers to a common male name, *Sarimin*, and wears a cheap, glittery skirt. The handler bangs a small drum and calls: *Sarimin pergi ke pasar* (Sarimin goes to the market). The monkey mimics a woman putting on a hat, carrying a basket and taking produce from a seller while handing over money. Sometimes Sarimin passes the money back and forth with its owner or onlookers, making it look as though it is haggling over the price.

Lutung Kasarung is the nickname of a prince who fell under a curse that transformed him into a big, black monkey.

A Sundanese folktale from West Java begins with the prince's mother fussing about how long it was taking him to find a bride. He joked that he could find no one as beautiful as her. She said: "Do you wish your mother to become your bride? That's a despicable act. You're like a big monkey."

The gods agreed, and struck her son with a bolt of lightning. Black fur sprouted from his skin, and he turned into a monkey (*lutung*). A booming voice in the heavens said the boy was doomed to wander the forests (*kasarung* means "being lost somewhere") until he found true love. Only then would he recover his original form as a handsome prince.

During his travels, *Lutung Kasarung* met a princess who had been banished by her eldest half-sister in a power grab in a nearby kingdom. The older sister had cursed her sibling, transforming her into an ugly, deformed girl. The *lutung* fed the exiled princess, gave her a potion to restore her beauty and helped her regain her kingdom. His loyalty won her heart.

Another bolt of lightning flashed when she introduced the monkey to her family. The *lutung* turned back into a prince. The couple married.

A song from this story was a favorite of Indonesia's first president, Sukarno. Decades later, some Indonesians complained that the tale implied that a woman always needs a man's help to get out of a jam.

❄ Sepandai-pandai tupai melompat, sekali akan gawal juga
"However deftly the squirrel jumps, once in a while it falls down" = Even maestros make mistakes.

❄ Anjing menyalak takkan menggigit
"A barking dog won't bite" = All bark and no bite. All talk and no action.

A widely told story in Indonesia explains why a dog's nose is always wet. During the Great Flood, a dog tried to secure passage on Noah's Ark, but turned up late for boarding. There was only room on the open deck, and the shivering hound caught a cold. The dog's offspring and descendants inherited the sniffles.

❄ Bagai anjing menyalak di ekor gajah
"Like a dog that barks at the elephant's tail" = Like banging your head against a wall. A fruitless exercise.

This expression can refer to someone who lacks responsibility or credibility, and has little sense of value. The person tries in vain to impose an opinion or achieve a goal.

Other expressions about futility are *menggarami laut* (putting salt in the ocean); *menjaring angin* (netting the wind); and *bagai mencincang air* (like chopping water).

❦ Kuman di seberang lautan tampak, gajah di pelupuk mata tak tampak

"A germ across the sea can be seen, an elephant in front of the eyelid can't" = It's easy to spot the mistakes of others, but not your own.

❦ Bangkai gajah bolehkah ditudung oleh nyiru?

"Can a dead elephant be hidden by a flat woven basket?" = You can't hide a bad deed.

Or, "No matter how well you wrap it, a rotten thing will smell right through."
  Sepandai-pandainya membungkus, yang busuk berbau juga.

❦ Gajah sama gajah beradu, kancil mati di tengah-tengah

"When two elephants collide, the mousedeer between them dies" = When leaders fight, the little people suffer. Caught in the crossfire.

The tiny mousedeer is a cunning survivor. A staple of Malay folktales, it outsmarts bigger, ferocious creatures such as the tiger and crocodile. It's like Brer Rabbit, the "catch me if you can" protagonist of folktales that originated in Africa and were collected in the American South in the 19th century. Another equivalent is the crafty coyote of Native American tradition, and the mischievous Anansi the Spider, which dodges the fish and falcon in Ashanti tales from West Africa.

The mousedeer has big, piercing eyes and keen hearing. Its long canines resemble fangs. In some rural areas, it's a pest because it eats crops.

❋ Gajah mati meninggalkan gading, harimau mati mening-galkan belang, manusia mati meninggalkan nama

"A dead elephant leaves its ivory, a dead tiger leaves its stripes, a dead man leaves his name" = Man must build a good reputation. He is remembered only by his deeds.

❋ Nyamuk mati, gatal tak lepas

"The mosquito dies, the itch doesn't go away" = Memories are forever. You can never get over some things. Stewing in your own juice.

Indonesia is obsessed with *obat nyamuk* (mosquito medicine): oils, coils, sprays, lotions and electric mats.

Vendors sell traditional medicines billed as cures for the symptoms of malaria and dengue fever. They tout *jambu kelutuk*, a sweet, red-fleshed guava, as a treatment for dengue, and the leaves of *sambiloto*, a plant with anti-inflammation properties, as malarial medicine.

Dengue is widespread in Indonesian cities and rural areas during heavy rains. An outbreak in 2009 killed 1,300 people and sickened more than 150,000. Malaria is a threat in many areas outside major cities.

The mosquito has a foothold in folklore. A children's tale ends with the rain telling the gecko that it must let each animal do its job. If rain doesn't fill potholes in the road with water, then the mosquito won't have a home. And if the mosquito has nowhere to live, then the gecko won't have anything to eat.

❀ Cacing telah menjadi ular naga
"The worm has turned into a dragon" = Rags to riches.

Bagai cacing hendak jadi naga (the worm seeks to be a dragon) refers to a poor person who aspires to be rich.

Chinese revere the dragon as a symbol of prosperity. The beast also symbolizes wealth in Indonesian mythology, which tells of dragon-like creatures that rule the earth and the underworld.

The *naga* of Javanese lore is a dragon that rules the underworld and hoards immense treasures.

Batak lore from Sumatra tells of an upper world where the Gods rule, a middle-earth for men, and an underworld that is the home of a dragon called Naga Padoha.

The serpent was banished to the underworld after it lost a battle with the Gods. Carvings on the gables of traditional Batak houses depict the story of *Naga Padoha*.

Indonesia has the real thing: Komodo dragons, giant lizards armed with toxic saliva that serve as a major tourist attraction. Stories about these reptiles circulated among Chinese traders and Dutch sailors centuries ago. The carnivores are solitary, but they gather to feast on a big carcass. They eat snakes, rodents, wild pigs and water buffalo. Sometimes they eat their own. They are efficient eaters, consuming just about every scrap of their prey. They can survive for weeks without a large meal.

It is said that a Swiss baron disappeared during a tour of Komodo island in 1974. He was presumed eaten.

Chapter Two

Characters

Indonesia is home to all sorts: tailors and tycoons, street strummers and the king of pickpockets.

❀ Pak Ogah (Betawi)
Mr. No Way.

A children's puppet show on television in the 1980s featured a character called Pak Ogah, a layabout in Jakarta, home to the Betawi people. The Betawi are a mishmash of ethnic groups from around Indonesia, with bloodlines from China, the Middle East and the former colonial power, the Netherlands. In the show, Pak Ogah has a stock reply when asked for help: *Ogah, ah!* —No way. The syllable *ah* emphasizes his point.

Today, any Indonesian who says *Ogah* means: "No way! I won't do it!"

The literal translation of *Ogah* is "don't want." The forceful "No way" fits better because Pak Ogah speaks with conviction.

Pak Ogah was in a puppet show called *Si Unyil* (That Small Cute One). *Unyil* is from the Sundanese language of West Java. In Bogor, Bandung and other West Javan cities, bakeries sell *roti unyil*: small bread, or buns made from leftovers of dough from bigger loaves.

Characters like Pak Ogah played on a stereotype of the

Betawi as dumb, uneducated and out to make an easy buck. Most Betawi accept the stereotype as good-natured ribbing.

In the show, Pak Ogah sometimes agrees to do a favor, but requests a payoff:

Cepek dulu.

"First, 100 rupiah."

Cepek is 100 in Hokkien, a dialect from southeast China that immigrants brought to Indonesia generations ago. Betawi merchants and haggling customers in the capital commonly use the term because Chinese influence on commerce and culture is deep. Other Hokkien numbers are *jigo* (25), *gocap* (50), *gopek* (500) and *ceceng* (1,000).

Economic turmoil hit Indonesia when the currency plummeted in 1997, and people lost jobs and savings. Food distribution networks broke down in some areas. So-called Mr. Ogahs popped up at intersections, T-junctions and U-turns across Jakarta. They acted as traffic lights or cops, regulating the flow and bustle of commuters. Drivers rolled down windows and dropped 100 rupiah coins into their palms.

These street entrepreneurs later became known as *polisi cepek* (100 rupiah police).

Indonesia's economic crisis triggered riots and protests, and helped push authoritarian President Suharto from power. Although the economy slowly improved, Mr. Ogahs patrolled the capital. Panhandling thrived. A boss at the wheel of a pickup stopped at busy intersections, where grandmothers, mothers and young children hopped out and begged. Beggars "rented" babies from poor families for the day to woo sympathetic tourists. The begging squad's manager pocketed a hefty slice of the take, and sometimes drove his "employees" from satellite towns ringing Jakarta. He charged them for the ride.

The number of panhandlers ballooned if pests or dry spells damaged rice harvests. Begging also picked up when people gave to the needy near the end of Ramadan, the Muslim fasting month.

Street musicians (*pengamen*) wandered main streets with guitars, serenading people at restaurants or street corners. Sometimes they shook a rattle and rhythm out of a glass bottle containing a stone, or from flattened bottle caps nailed onto a stick.

Tunes ranged from Indonesian pop and rock to Top 40 songs to commercial jingles. Some buskers boarded buses and sang anti-government songs, which flourished after the 1998 fall of Suharto.

Iwan Fals, a craggy-faced singer with unruly, silver hair, drew a huge following with his guitar talent and odes to the poor. One of his songs tells of *Bento*, a fictional businessman who lives the fast life. Many fans believed the inspiration for *Bento* was tycoon Bambang Trihatmodjo, Suharto's second son.

Suharto's kids used their connections to amass fortunes while their father was in power, triggering resentment among down-at-heel Indonesians. Bambang kept a lower profile than his younger brother, Tommy, a playboy and race car driver who sometimes tooled around the steamy streets of Jakarta in a Rolls Royce. Tommy was jailed for 15 years in 2002 for ordering the killing of a judge who had convicted him of corruption. His sentence was reduced to 10 years on appeal, and he was released in 2006, partly because of good behavior. The outcome angered Indonesians who believe the rich and well-connected still manipulate the law.

❀ Malin Kundang
Ingrate.

In a folktale, Malin Kundang was the only son of a poor village widow in West Sumatra. When he became a young man, Malin sought permission to seek fortune far from home. His mother wept, but gave her blessing and he boarded a ship and sailed.

Years passed without news. His mother stood daily by the shore, awaiting his return.

Far from home, Malin worked hard. Smart, diligent and handsome, he became rich, bought a ship and married. One day, he docked in his hometown, and villagers marveled how the scrawny lad had become a wealthy merchant with a dazzling wife. His ailing mother rushed to the dock to welcome her son.

"My son, Malin! It's me, your mother," she exclaimed.

The haughty Malin saw only a stooped woman in shabby clothes. Ashamed that the sight might offend his wife, he ignored the old woman. He kicked her to the ground when she tried to hug him, and he commanded his crew to sail. Malin's stunned, tearful mother watched as the ship drew further from the shore.

"Malin, my son, how could you do that to your mother? You will become a stone!" she cursed.

A storm struck Malin's ship and it ran aground. Malin turned into a stone on the rocky beach.

Nowadays, exasperated parents complain if their children ignore their advice or commands.

"Don't be like Malin Kundang," they say.

Jangan seperti Malin Kundang.

West Sumatrans like Malin have a reputation for traveling long distances. The calling is *merantau*, which means to leave one's home, or wander about, in the Minangkabau language of the region. It's a rite of passage to manhood. It's difficult to find Minangkabau men who have not left home, at least for a while. Most plan to return eventually.

The term *merantau* is so widespread that most Indonesians know it. It is associated with men. In the traditional view, women only leave home under duress: to find a job in a hurry, or escape some personal crisis.

Nowadays, the tendency is to settle away from home for a

long time. This practice is *merantau Cino*, or migrating like the Chinese, whose vibrant roots stretch all over Asia and beyond. A short period is *merantau pipit* (sparrow-like travels) because the bird doesn't linger long in one place.

Minangkabau restaurants serve Sumatran-style food across Indonesia, as well as in Southeast Asia, Europe and elsewhere. They are called Padang restaurants after the name of the West Sumatran provincial capital. They say you can find a Padang restaurant on the moon: just walk a little, turn left and there you have it! The most famous Padang dish is *rendang*, meat simmered in spices and coconut juice.

Some Minangkabau men leave home because they feel constrained by West Sumatra's matriarchal system, which requires a husband to allow a brother of his wife (*ninik mamak*, in Minangkabau) to settle any family dispute.

Matrilineal customs require a man to give advice and money to his sister and her family. He helps her out, but has little influence over his own affairs. His role as husband is marginal. Sisters usually inherit their brothers' *rumah gadang* (big house) and other family assets.

A century ago, West Sumatran men were only allowed to marry women from the same village. Some sought brides elsewhere so they could be free of the irksome *ninik mamak*.

West Sumatran men who leave home stay loyal to their families. Their success is judged by how much money they send home to build houses for relatives, or mosques or schools in hometowns.

✿ Cewek
Girl.

Linguists say *cewek* came from *ciwe*, which means female genitals in the Hokkien dialect from China. *Cewek* took hold in the

1970s, and dictionaries define it as a young girl. Nowadays, it's a colloquial term for a woman.

Then the term *cowok*, the male equivalent of *cewek*, came along. Male Javanese names usually contain the vowel o. Hartono is a male name, while Hartini is female. Joko, Padmo, Handoyo and Suranto are all male names.

❀ Perek (acronym)
PERempuan EKsperimental
"Experimental woman" = Prostitute. Bimbo.

The word *perek* appeared in the mid-1980s when teenage girls turned up at Jalan Melawai, a street in Blok M, a jumble of bars, malls and hotels in Jakarta. The street became known as *Lintas Melawai* (*lintas* means cross or pass quickly) because crowds streamed back and forth. Women strolled, loitered outside shops, dined on *bakso* (meat balls) and *teh botol* (cold, bottled tea), and waited for men. Some wanted money; others settled for sexual experience. They looked for a type known as *Oom-oom* (*Oom* means uncle in Dutch), a sugar daddy who drove a flashy car and spent with abandon.

Perek is a common term for prostitute among the young, though many elderly people don't know it. It used to refer only to a promiscuous woman, not a woman who required payment for sex.

Other terms for prostitute:
- *WTS.* A term for *Wanita Tuna Susila* (woman without morals). It appears in newspapers, radio and television talk shows, government edicts and speeches. The male version is *PTS* (*Pria Tuna Susila*, or man without morals). *PTS* can also be the client of a male prostitute.
- *Pekerja seks komersial* (commercial sex worker). A neutral term

commonly used by feminists and social workers.

- *Kupu-kupu malam* (night butterfly). An insect with beautiful wings lures its prey.
- *Perempuan jalang* (wild, untamed woman). A rude expression.
- *Ayam* (chicken). This rude term is similar to chick, the old English slang for a young woman. Some sociologists say the term became popular in Indonesia in the early 1990s because of the alleged tendency of prostitutes to chatter, or cluck like hens. Indonesians often use the term for the benefit of foreign men who are on the prowl.
- *Cabo.* This term for prostitute comes from *Ca-bau-kan*, which means woman in Hokkien.

Players in the sex industry address each other with familiar nicknames. The regular term for pimp is *mucikari* or *muncikari*, but he's also *papi* (daddy) to his charges. A madam is *germo*, but also *mami* or *tante* (aunt, in Dutch). They oversee *anak asuh* (children in their care), young prostitutes who often come from poor villages and have no other source of income.

Young prostitutes who become financially indebted to their pimps and cut off from their families are *anak potong* (cut child). Hefty cuts of their wages end up in the pockets of managers.

Kelas kambing (goat class) and *kelas embun* (dew class) refer to prostitutes who don't charge much.

That's because *kelas kambing* once referred to the cheapest seats in a movie theater. The meat of *kambing* (goat) is cheaper than that of a cow or buffalo.

Kelas embun also offers the cheapest seats at an outdoor cinema: spectators have to sit on grass covered in dewdrops.

Prostitution is illegal in Indonesia, but many Indonesians have a sweep-it-under-the-mat approach to the profession. The sex industry flourishes. Giant prostitution complexes operate in major cities. In some places, clients look through one-way windows at rows of seated prostitutes before making their selection.

In the 1970s, Jakarta governor Ali Sadikin advocated regulation of the sex industry, rather than an outright ban. He pushed for *lokalisasi*, a policy that let brothel complexes pay taxes and operate under state supervision. He made some headway, but the project died. One regulated brothel in North Jakarta has become a plush Muslim center with carpeted, brightly lit prayer rooms. Muslim groups voice their opinions more forcefully than they did under authoritarian rule, and *lokalisasi* is unlikely to make a comeback soon.

In 2004, hundreds of prostitutes in the East Javan city of Surabaya held a mass prayer for the success of the presidential election. They wore Muslim headscarves called *jilbab*, and some shed tears as they read verses from the Quran.

❀ **Waria** (acronym)
WAnita-pRIA
"Woman-man" = A transvestite/transsexual.

Bencong is another popular term.

Many cross-dressers work as hairdressers and specialize in bridal makeup. Some sing on stage or patrol streets and bars as prostitutes. They await clients at *Taman Lawang*, a traffic roundabout in Jakarta where trees and bushes offer discretion. *Waria* operate on the fringes of society, but enjoy a degree of acceptance, occasionally appearing on television soap operas and advertisements. In the final days of 2005, a group of Muslim women rallied at a local parliament building in Sumatra to protest plans for a New Year's Eve transvestite concert sponsored by the government.

An older term for transvestite is *wadam*, a combination of *Wanita* and *Adam*. It hasn't been used much in the last couple of decades.

❁ Tante girang
Happy auntie.

A middle-aged woman who seeks a gigolo. Armed with cash and gifts, she lures young men into romantic liaisons.

Some well-off Indonesian wives indulge in pleasures of the flesh because their husbands ignore them. Their spouses are busy, the wives figure, so why not keep busy themselves?

Om senang (happy uncle) is a man who seeks stimulation from younger women for a price.

Both characters became prominent during the 1970s heyday of the economic boom in oil-rich Indonesia. Buoyed by the rise in global oil prices, the elite had lots of money to splurge on good times. Some people frowned on amorous adventures, warning of the deterioration of family values and neglect of children.

❁ Anak bawang
"Onion kid" = The runt of the litter. A nobody.

A shallot usually has a bulb that is smaller than the rest. It just seems to fill the gap.

In a school playground, kids slot into two teams for a game of tag. The youngest jumps up and down, eager to join. Her older sister smiles and tells the others: "C'mon let her into my team. But she can't be 'it.' She's only an onion kid." *Ayolah, dia ikut timku. Tapi dia gak bisa jadi. Dia cuma anak bawang.*

Bawang merah (red onion) is the fragrant Asian red shallot. *Bawang putih* (white onion) is garlic. *Bawang bombay* is a big white or yellow onion that takes its name from the Indian city known today as Mumbai. Onions were noted as a digestive and treatment for the heart in India more than 2,500 years ago, though the vegetable is believed to have come from central Asia.

❀ **Arema** (acronym)
AREk MAlang
Malang guys.

Men from the town of Malang in the East Javan highlands get raucous when the atmosphere heats up at soccer games. They are some of the rowdiest soccer fans in Indonesia, and are notorious for getting into fights before and after matches. *Arek* means child in Javanese.

Soccer crowds from Malang are also called *bonek*, an acronym from the Javanese terms *BOndo* (collateral, or investment capital) and *NEKad* (recklessness). They are rich in recklessness, but don't have much capital to fund their trips to other cities.

The *bonek* rally their soccer team, also called Arema, at out-of-town games.

❀ **BTL** (pronounced *beh-teh-ell*)
Batak Tembak Langsung
Batak shoots directly/immediately.

The Batak people of North Sumatra province have a reputation for straight talk. They don't mince words. This upfront attitude seems abrasive to some Javanese, who are known for skirting a sensitive subject in conversation.

According to folklore, the Batak speak loudly because they once lived in houses near lakes, on mountain slopes, and in other sparsely populated areas. Their houses were set far apart and they had to shout to get their message across. Some Batak live around Lake Toba, the largest lake in Southeast Asia. It was formed by a huge volcanic explosion.

The ethnic spectrum in the stereotype from refined to rough runs from the Central Javanese, to the Sundanese in West Java, to the East Javanese, to the Batak. The Sundanese break down into the Bogor people, who are considered *pasar* ("market," or rough), and people from Bandung, who are thought to be refined, a legacy of the Hindu kingdom of Pajajaran that reigned over West Java centuries ago. Bandung is also home to many universities.

❀ Bulai/Bule
Albino/white foreigner.

Javanese believe albino animals are sacred, and parade white buffalo (*kebo bulai*) in a show of thanksgiving every Javanese New Year. Like the Muslim calendar, the Javanese calendar is based on the cycles of the moon.

Bule is a colloquial term for white foreigner. It can be neutral, affectionate or derogatory. Some foreigners bristle at the expression because it dumps them into a racial category. Indonesians often shout "Halo *bule!*" and "Hello, mister!" at foreigners on the street. Many Indonesians have had little contact with foreigners, and yell because they don't know how else to attract attention.

Another old term for Caucasian is *belanda* (Dutch) or *londo* (Dutch, in Javanese). It doesn't matter whether the white person is Dutch or not. The terms emerged during Dutch rule in Indonesia, which began on Java in the 17th century and ended after Indonesian nationalists declared independence in 1945. In 1949, the Dutch acknowledged Indonesian sovereignty after several years of war.

A foreigner is *orang asing* (alien person). The term also applies to Indonesians who travel to distant parts of the archipelago, home to hundreds of ethnic groups. These out-of-towners look different and speak their own language. Those with very dark skin might be from remote Papua, at the eastern tip of Indonesia.

People with pale skin could be from North Sulawesi province, where Chinese influence is heavy.

A long time ago, most Indonesians rarely strayed from their *kampung* (village) and had little contact with outsiders. Trade, modern communications and the population shift to the cities changed that over the last few decades. Under President Suharto, millions of Javanese left their crowded island and fanned out across Indonesia under a policy called *transmigrasi*. The policy reinforced government control over outlying areas, but created tension between local populations and Javanese migrants who took land and power.

❀ Kumpeni
Company.

A derogatory term for Dutch people and other Westerners. It comes from *Perserikatan Kumpeni Hindia Timur*, which means Dutch East India Company in Malay. Established in 1602, the trading company planted its headquarters on Java and served as an instrument of Dutch power in the region, trading in spices such as nutmeg and cloves, as well as tea, silk and other products. *Verenigde Oostindische Compagnie*, as the company was called in Dutch, dissolved in 1798 and Indonesia fell under the direct administration of the Dutch government.

Javanese referred to the company simply as *Kumpeni*. Today, an Indonesian who wants to shirk a chore says:

"Relax. The Company is still far away."

Tenang. Kumpeni masih jauh.

The implication is that the Dutch aren't about to invade, so what's the rush?

❀ Raja
King.

The Hindi term pops up in many contexts: *raja jalanan* (king of the road), or a high-speed, reckless driver; *raja dan ratu sehari* (king and queen for a day), or a bride and groom on a wedding day; and *raja copet* (king of pickpockets).

Raja singa (lion king) means top dog. It also refers to syphilis, the king of sexual diseases. The expression predates the AIDS era.

Nearly 2,000 years ago, travelers from India reached the archipelago that later became known as Indonesia. They brought Hinduism, and great kingdoms spread the religion across Java and other parts of the archipelago. Today, Bali is the only island that is predominantly Hindu.

Sanskrit, the language of ancient India, influenced Indonesia: the word *bahasa*, or language, is from Sanskrit. Hindi, which shares the same alphabet as Sanskrit, also made its mark.

❀ Vermak Levis
"Jeans changer" = A tailor who specializes in altering Levis and other jeans.

Vermak comes from *vermaken* (change, or turn), one of many Dutch words that were picked up by Indonesians during the colonial occupation.

Not every tailor has needles strong enough to alter jeans. Those who do hang a *Vermak Levis* sign in their shops or offer services on the roadside, equipped with only sewing machines. Others attach sewing machines—the kind with the wheel and the foot pedal—to their bicycles and offer door-to-door service. These *Vermak Levis* are easily identified by the red Levis emblem on their signboards.

You might see signs that say *Permak Lepis*, especially if the tailor is a Sundanese from West Java. Sundanese have trouble pronouncing the consonants v, f and p, and sometimes mix them up.

🦋 **Golkar** (acronym)
GOLongan Keturunan ARab
Group of Arab descent.

Golkar, the ruling political party under Suharto, had close links to the military and was dominant down to the village level. Its loyalists controlled Parliament, making it a rubber-stamp assembly for the president. Although Indonesia is now democratic, *Golkar* remains a powerful political force. The name of the party stands for *Golongan Karya* (Functional Groups).

Some Indonesians joke that citizens with Arab blood are *Golkar*, or Group of Arab Descent. The acronym is lighthearted rather than derogatory. Arabs arrived in Indonesia well over a millennium ago and established themselves as traders and purveyors of Islam, which became Indonesia's dominant religion.

Arabic is richly represented in the Indonesian language. The Arabic word for book, *kitab*, refers to Islamic books in Indonesian. Many bookstores have signs that read *Toko Buku & Kitab*. *Toko* means shop in Indonesian, and *buku* means book.

Prominent Indonesians of Arab descent include two former foreign ministers, Alwi Shihab and the late Ali Alatas, as well as Munir Thalib, a rights activist who fell ill and died on board an Indonesian commercial airliner heading from Jakarta to Amsterdam in September 2004.

An off-duty pilot was sentenced to 20 years in jail for the murder after a court found him guilty of putting arsenic in noodles served to Thalib. Judges concluded that Thalib was killed because of his strong criticism of human rights abuses by the military. Thalib's widow said the murder was part of a broader conspiracy by state agents in a case reminiscent of state-backed killings in the days of dictatorship.

❀ Indak mati oleh Belanda (Minangkabau)
"Can't be killed by the Dutch" = Invincible. A superman. Knock him down and he pops back up like a rubber ball.

Few Indonesians know this old phrase, which comes from a game of playing cards during Dutch colonial times. The Jack, Queen, and King cards symbolized Western nobility, or the Dutch occupiers of Indonesia. You were unbeatable if you had aces up your sleeve.

Indonesians who lose a board or card game say they have died (*mati*).

❀ Si Kabayan
That happy-go-lucky guy.

Kabayan is a character from West Javanese folklore who wears a sarong across his shoulder. He is an eternally lazy villager, armed with excuses to avoid work. He adores his sweetheart, the shy Iteung. Everything else, including money, bores him.

Kabayan became the hero in a popular television series, and a movie about him—*Si Kabayan Saba Kota* (Kabayan goes to the city)—broke box office records for an Indonesian movie in 1989.

In the film, Kabayan heads to town, where the tough, commercial culture shocks him. A city girl attracts his attention. He tries his hand at running a company. But he balks at the pressure in the big city and returns to his village, where Iteung awaits him.

Kabayan got an image makeover in 2004 when state-run television broadcast a show called *Kabayan Reformasi*. This time, the villager is clad in jeans and a shirt, and Iteung is not a tongue-tied lass, but a strong woman with a mind of her own.

Today, an office worker grumbles about a colleague: "Uggh. I really like Ahmad but he often gets on my nerves. He's so Kabayan, you know. He does nothing but smile!"

Aduh, aku suka sama si Ahmad tapi dia sering bikin kesel. Kabayan banget, sih. Kerjanya senyum doang.

❧ Arjuna
The warrior-lover.

Arjuna is the third of five Pandawa brothers in the Mahabharata, an ancient tale from India about a monumental war between family lines. The Pandawas won the war. Arjuna was a great warrior, mastering the bow and arrow and every other weapon in the world.

Slender and soft-spoken, Arjuna symbolizes an ideal of male beauty that eschewed muscle-bound hunks. Indonesians marvel at his exploits as a lover. He is said to have had at least 41 wives and countless lovers. One affair was with Srikandi, who attended one of Arjuna's weddings and fell in love with him. She got him to become her archery teacher. One popular puppet show features Srikandi learning to shoot an arrow; she aims for Arjuna's heart.

Indonesia's female archers won the country's first Olympic medal, a silver, at the 1988 Games in South Korea. They were crowned "Srikandi heroes" (*Pahlawan Srikandi*) back home.

Pop songs, contemporary novels and films pay tribute to Arjuna. In 2002, rock band Dewa (God) released a hit single, *Arjuna mencari cinta* (Arjuna looks for love). The lyrics of the rock stadium anthem describe how he would scale the highest peaks and sail vast oceans to be with his love. The ending says true love might elude Arjuna.

In an Indonesian household, a mother worries about her daughter, who listens to love songs and jumps for the phone when it rings. She fears her infatuated child will end up hurt by her "Arjuna," slang for a crush or new boyfriend.

A girl tells her lovesick friend:

"Don't take that Arjuna seriously. Yesterday he was out with that girl. Tomorrow, he'll be with a different one."

Jangan ambil pusing dengan si Arjuna itu. Kemarin dia pergi sama cewek itu. Besok pasti sama cewek lain.

✿ Musuh dalam selimut
"Enemy under the blanket" = An unknown danger.

A close friend betrays you. The traitor seemed like such an intimate friend that you both slept under the same cover. In another interpretation, the blanket is a convenient hiding place for the betrayer.

"There's a crayfish under the rock," also warns of hidden menace. *Ada udang di balik batu.* The crayfish will snap off your finger if you shift that rock.

"Selling a gun to the enemy," refers to betrayal. *Menjual bedil kepada lawan.*

"Bifurcate like a monitor lizard's tongue," has a similar meaning. *Bercabang bagai lidah biawak.* The lizard's forked tongue implies two-sidedness, or allegiance to everybody and nobody.

❀ Kyai mbeling

"The naughty cleric" = An off-beat, off-the-wall Muslim leader.

Kyai is a title of a senior Muslim preacher. *Mbeling* is a crude Javanese term for naughty.

One example of *kyai mbeling* was Emha Ainun Najib, who wrote tongue-in-cheek essays about corruption during the rule of President Suharto. Emha had long hair and wore Western clothes instead of traditional, flowing tunics favored by preachers. Emha invited actors and musicians to perform at his gatherings. They penned *puisi mbeling* (naughty poetry), which needled the government. Known as *Teater Mbeling*, the group was careful to avoid direct criticism of the state. They spoke in allusions because the government often shut theaters or publications that it deemed subversive, and jailed their owners.

❀ Tong kosong nyaring bunyinya

"An empty barrel makes a loud noise" = A blowhard, full of hot air. All talk and no action.

A similar expression: *air beriak tanda tak dalam* (rippled water is shallow).

On the other hand: *Air tenang menghanyutkan* (calm water carries away). Quiet people are profound.

❀ Bagai api dalam sekam

"Fire in the hay" = A spoiler.

A walking timebomb.
A rebellious teenager, perhaps. Or a disgruntled employee.

Chapter Three

Body Language

From head to tongue to toe, body parts reveal a lot about how Indonesians feel and think.

Muka (Face)

❀ Setor muka
"Deposit face" = Show your face. Drop by. Pop in.

"I don't feel like going to my boss's party, but if it's only a short one, I'll go," says the party pooper.

Saya malas pergi ke pesta bos saya, tapi kalau hanya setor muka, ayolah.

The expression is popular in Jakarta. *Setor* usually refers to depositing money in a bank (*setor uang di bank*).

❀ Carmuk (acronym)
"Look for face" = To suck up/butter up.

Ambil muka (take face) also refers to the act of seeking someone's favor.

❀ Buruk muka, cermin dibelah

"Ugly face, break the mirror" = A bad workman blames his tools.

It's easier to assign blame than to accept your own faults. Indonesians often just say the first half of the expression, and drop the rest. *Buruk muka...*

❀ Muka tembok

"Wall face" = A thick-skinned person, impervious to curses, insults and admonitions.

Another term is *muka badak* (rhino face).

Kepala batu (stone head) is a stubborn person.

❀ Arang di muka

"Charcoal on the face" = Shamed. Insulted. Disgraced.

Don't humiliate others in public, whatever the circumstances. Humiliation tarnishes "face," or honor, like a smear of charcoal.

Many Indonesians think a daughter who gets pregnant out of wedlock has smeared her family's face with charcoal.

Jangan coreng mukaku (Don't smear my face) means: Don't humiliate me.

Malu means shy or ashamed or embarrassed, and implies a loss of face.

"I am so ashamed. I've lost face. Where could I put my face?" whimpers a husband whose wife has embarrassed him in front of his boss.

Saya malu. Saya kehilangan muka. Muka saya mau taruh di mana?

✺ **Mupeng** (acronym)
MUka PENGen
"Wanting face" = Horny. Turned on.

Young people use this expression to indicate sexual desire.

Nowadays, *mupeng* refers to desire for anything, including inanimate objects:

"Look at him and that latest WiFi laptop. He has such a wanting face."

Lihat dia dan laptop wifi terbaru. Mupeng banget.

Mata (Eyes)

✺ **Main mata**
Eye playing. Flirting/checking out/winking.

Mata ijo are green eyes, a sign of yearning. Indonesians associate green with greed. The term combines Indonesian (*mata*; eyes) and Javanese (*ijo*; green), an example of how ethnic languages mix with the national language.

A more common expression for greed is *mata duitan* (money eyes). It describes a man or woman who seeks a rich lover or spouse.

Mata gelap (dark eyes) indicate violent anger, or possession by an evil spirit. *Mata hati* is heart's eye, or conscience.

Someone who ogles an object of desire, often sexual, is *mata keranjang* (basket eyes). He shops with his eyes, just as a shopper with a basket peruses market produce. The term suggests that the basket-sized eyes of the beholder can hold lots of people in their gaze.

The expression sounds like *mata ke ranjang* (from the eyes to the bed), a possible reference to the come-hither look that lures sexual partners into the sack.

A troll with a voracious appetite in folktales on Java and Bali is *Buto Ijo*, green giant in Javanese.

Three kinds of *buto* symbolize the ills of the world: *Buto Ijo* represents thievery and corruption, *Buto Kala* (time giant) stands for lust, and *Buto Cakil* (fanged giant) is a symbol of rage.

Buto Ijo is a villain in a folktale about a girl called *Timun Mas* (Golden Cucumber). The giant gave a magical cucumber seed to an old couple, telling them it would yield a baby girl if planted. The giant bestowed the gift on the condition that he could eat the girl when she turned 17 years old. The couple planted the seed, and it grew into a big cucumber. Out popped *Timun Mas*.

When *Buto Ijo* returned for his prize 17 years later, the couple urged their beautiful girl to flee, and gave her a small bag to assist her escape.

With the giant in pursuit, *Timun Mas* drew a handful of salt from the bag and flung it, turning hard ground into water. The giant floundered across. Then the teenager tossed chili pepper seeds from the bag, and a thorny bush briefly entangled the giant. *Timun Mas* hurled some cucumber seeds, and a cucumber field sprouted instantly.

Tired and hungry, the giant sat down to chew on the cucumbers. Soon he gave chase again, and *Timun Mas* lobbed *terasi* (shrimp paste) from the bag. The paste turned the ground into quicksand that swallowed up *Buto Ijo*.

Timun Mas returned to her parents and lived happily.

Each ethnic group in Indonesia has its own set of monsters in its own language, and *Buto Ijo* goes by different names elsewhere.

Another giant, *Buto Kala*, overheard the gods talk about *amerta*, the elixir of immortality. He disguised himself as a god and joined the gods as they sipped the holy water. After *Buto Kala* tasted the magic water, a god realized he was an impostor and cut off his head. The immortal, empowered head fell in love with the moon goddess, Dewi Ratih. She refused him, and Buto swallowed her in a jealous rage. Ratih escaped through Buto's severed neck, but the stubborn giant wouldn't give up, and he chases the goddess to this day. Balinese and Javanese say an eclipse of the moon signals that he has swallowed her, but not for long.

Buto Cakil, a giant with fangs that jut from a protruding lower jaw, makes regular appearances in traditional puppet shows. A typical performance features a battle between a knight and giants led by *Buto Cakil*. The good knight slaughters *Buto Cakil* in a triumph of good over evil.

❀ Mata tidur bantal terjaga

"Eyes asleep, the pillow awakes" = When the cat's away, the mice will play.

The expression refers to a husband or wife who has an affair while the spouse is off guard. The saying was originally meant for a wife who cheated on her husband, but now it applies to both genders.

❀ Hilang di mata, di hati jangan

Lost in the eyes, don't lose in the heart.

Hopefully, absence makes the heart grow fonder. This expression warns against the dangers of out of sight, out of mind.

"Don't forget me, sweetheart," singers croon.

Hilang di mata, di hati jangan, sayang.

The expression is old. A more up-to-date version is *jauh di mata, dekat di hati* (far from the eyes, close to the heart).

Hidung (Nose)

✺ Potong hidung, rusak muka
Cut nose, ruin face.

Shame your family, and you shame yourself. The nose is similar to your family: one is in the center of your face, and the other is in the center of your life.

"Like having a child with big nose" (*seperti beranak besar hidung*) means you are conceited because you're always flaunting what you have.

Many Indonesians worry that their noses are small and flat. Some mothers pinch their babies' noses upwards so they don't suffer the fate of kids deemed to have ugly, flat noses.

Haji Djedje, an elderly paranormal with blow-dried hair and a love of colorful shirts, turned the flat noses of his clients into Roman ones. Supposedly aided by special powers, he massaged a nose with the tips of his fingers over the course of several visits to his clinic. He also applied a nose clip padded with two rolls of cotton wool. Djdje claimed the result—a pointed, assertive nose—needed a touchup after two years. He also sold lotion that lightens the skin. His client base included many transvestites, who made him the guest of honor at a cross-dressing show in Jakarta in 2002.

West Javanese believed the nose indicated character, saying: "You are how your nose is."

Jalma mah kumaha irungna.

West Javanese traditional puppets are divided into broad-nosed giants who are mean and evil, and pointy-nosed knights who personify goodness.

At a mass prayer in West Java during parliamentary elections in 2004, Indonesian Muslim preachers asked God to curse the *anfun kabir*, Arabic for *si hidung besar* (big nose)—those who will lead Indonesians astray. The preachers appeared to refer to abstract evil, rather than an individual or group.

Mulut (Mouth)

✵ Mulut manis mematahkan tulang
A sweet mouth breaks bones.

Gentle persuasion does more to sway people than hammering them over the head with a tirade. So turn on the charm. *Mulut manis* (sweet mouth) isn't always positive. It can imply empty promises:

> *Mulut manis jangan percaya, lepas dari tangan jangan diharap.*

"Don't believe in sweet mouth. Don't hope once you let go of hands."

Clasp your sweetheart's hands, or twist an adversary's arm, and you might get a promise. But once you turn your back or part company—let go of hands—all bets are off.

"Cheap in mouth, expensive on the scales" (*Murah di mulut, mahal di timbangan*) refers to someone who makes promises easily but doesn't carry them out.

"Different in mouth, different in the heart" denotes dishonesty. *Lain di mulut, lain di hati.*

Mulut bocor (leaking mouth) or *mulut ember* (bucket mouth) means you can't keep a secret. *Mulut gatal* (itchy mouth) is a chatterbox. *Jadi buah bibir* (become lip-fruit) is to become a subject of gossip or conversation.

Lidah (Tongue)

✽ **Bersilat lidah.**
"Tongue fighting, or tongue kung fu." = Argue.

Silat is a term for the hundreds of Indonesian martial arts. Many are associated with mystical powers and heavily influenced by Chinese, Indian and Persian fighting styles. *Silat* schools across Indonesia teach students how to fight with sticks, knives, swords and rope. Some practitioners emulate the tiger, crouching as they poise to strike. Fighters ensure an opponent is down for good with repeated blows that seem excessive to an unschooled observer.

The *Merpati Putih* (White Dove) school of martial arts relies heavily on *tenaga dalam* (inner energy). Students at the school, some in their early teens, punch dozens of blocks of ice, wood and concrete until their bruised knuckles turn crimson. The goal is to shatter a target with one blow, a helpful skill in hand-to-hand combat. *Silat* alleviated one student's asthma, possibly by building strength in her lungs.

Indonesian *silat* were once so secretive that no foreigners were allowed to learn them. Today, they are commercial enterprises. Traditionalists complain about efforts to turn *silat* into a competitive sport.

✽ **Lidah tak bertulang** (Minangkabau)
"Tongue with no bones" = Silvery tongue.

Someone who promises easily but doesn't follow through. The tongue bends or changes easily because it is boneless.

Panjang lidah (long tongue) is a gossipmonger.

❀ Jadi penyambung lidah
"Become a tongue extension" = Become a mouthpiece, or spokesman.

The term can be derogatory because it implies the "tongue extension" is a lackey. But it was also used to praise President Sukarno, a hero of the independence movement during Dutch rule, as a voice for all Indonesians:

"Brother Karno is the spokesman/tongue extension of the people."

Bung Karno adalah penyambung lidah masyarakat.

❀ Unjuk gigi
"Show teeth" = A show of force. Prove one's worth. Get one's back up.

Dogs, cats and tigers bare their fangs to show ferocity. The phrase implies guts and verve. A junior basketball player gets his chance to show teeth after spending most of his team's games on the bench.

"Only have teeth and tongue left" (*tinggal gigi dengan lidah saja*) is to have nothing left. Not even the shirt on your back.

"Sometimes teeth bite the tongue" (*gigi dengan lidah ada kala bergigit juga*) is an old-fashioned way of saying allies, spouses or relatives sometimes argue.

❀ Menelan air ludah
"To swallow one's spit" = Take back what you say or preach. Eat humble pie.

"What a hypocrite! He has to lick his own spit. How dare he say wives have to remain loyal to their husband, while he himself commits adultery!"

Dasar munafik! Dia harus menelan ludah sendiri. Beraninya dia berkhotbah istri harus setia dengan suami tapi sendirinya menyeleweng!

Menelan ludah also describes the helplessness of someone who pines for something unattainable, but can only stand and gulp.

A person whose boss rebukes him can't do much but swallow saliva.

Menjilat air liur is to lick saliva. It means to praise something that was previously despised. Opportunists do this a lot.

❀ Odol
Toothpaste.

Odol, a German brand of toothpaste, was once so popular in Indonesia that it became a generic name for toothpaste, just as the brand name Xerox is synonymous with photocopy. Odol is no longer available in Indonesia.

In the old days, there were two kinds of dentifrice: Odol and Gibbs of Britain. The latter took the form of a cake that had to be scraped onto a toothbrush. Odol succeeded because it was hygienic and easier to use.

The literal term for toothpaste is *pasta gigi*. It's rarely used in conversation, but it shows up in advertisements and written Indonesian.

Other brands that became generic names for products in Indonesia include Honda (motorcycle), Softex (sanitary napkins), and Aqua (bottled mineral water).

––––––––––

Old Indonesian literature describes a beautiful woman in the following ways:

Bibirnya seperti buah delima,
Her lips are like pomegranates,

Rambutnya seperti mayang mengurai,
Her hair is like the tips of a palm blossom,

Alisnya seperti semut beriring,
Her brows are like ants walking in a line,

Dagunya seperti lebah bergantung,
Her chin is like honey hanging down,

Betisnya seperti paha balalang,
Her shins are like the thighs of a cricket,

Lengan bagai lilin dituang,
Her arms are like molded candles,

Kulit seperti sawo matang.
Her skin is like the ripe sawo fruit.

The sawo fruit has a sweet taste similar to that of a pear. Its skin is usually brown.

Older Indonesian men relish these images, but the phrases are a relic of a bygone age for the younger set. Today, the glut of skin whitening lotions on the market suggests soft white skin (*kulit putih halus*) is more popular than the darker shade of old. Long, shiny, straight black hair is in, though many women dye or highlight their locks.

❀ Dia bertangan dingin

"He is cold-handed" = He has a knack for success. He's a real pro.

One theory about the origin of this expression is that the nerves in a cold hand are numb, allowing their owner to take unpopular steps without hesitation. An executive fires workers to make his business successful. *Bertangan dingin* suggests an uncanny talent for making money or succeeding in any endeavor.

❀ Paling jempol

"The best thumb" = First rate. Great. Number one.

An old-fashioned term used to describe places, objects and people. As in other cultures, Indonesians also stick up their thumbs (*acung jempol*) to indicate approval.

❀ Bagai inai dengan kuku

"Like henna with nails" = Fast friends. Like lips and teeth.

This old-fashioned expression mostly applies to platonic friendships.

Henna is an earthy pigment made from shrubs that is used to color nails, hands, feet, hair and beards. Its use in religious ceremonies and other celebrations of many cultures goes back centuries. The swirling, intricate patterns associated with henna in other parts of the world are rare in Indonesia, where the pigment is mostly used on nails. It is popular among unmarried, conservative Muslim women in villages who don't use nail varnish. They believe Muslim custom only allows henna because it is natural, and allows the nails to "breathe." Ablution waters can touch the nails before prayer.

Other sayings such as *bagai empedu lekat di hati* (like a gall bladder close to the heart) can be used for friendship and lovers. A less common saying is *bagai aur di tebing* (like bamboo near cliffs). Most of the expressions show that rural Indonesians associate nature and body parts with friendship.

❀ Hendak menggaruk, tak berkuku

"Want to scratch, have no nails" = You want to do something, but are powerless.

"Have no nails yet, but want to scratch," is a variation. *Belum berkuku hendak menggaruk.*

This means you're out of your league. You're a deluded upstart.

"Give nails, want to grab," means you're greedy. *Diberi kuku hendak mencekam.* The more power you have, the more corrupt you become.

❀ Banting tulang

"Smashing bones" = Do all in one's power, make every effort.

The phrase implies a continuous, even endless struggle.

If you exert yourself to the fullest, even your bones ache. This applies to a single parent who works and raises a child at the same time.

❀ Hancur badan di kandung tanah, budi baik dikenang jua

Though the body rots in the dirt, good deeds will be remembered.

❀ Buah hati, cahaya mata

"Fruit of my heart, light of my eyes" = Sweetheart.

Hati means liver, but translates as heart in an emotional context. *Jantung hati* (heart's heart) is also the object of one's affection, or a child.

Buah hati is a lyrical, whimsical way for Indonesian parents to describe their children:

"My darling children, the fruit of my heart," they say. *Anak-anakku sayang, buah hatiku.*

Panas hati (hot heart) means angry, or jealous.

"My heart grows hot listening to the gossip," she fumes.

Panas hatiku mendengar gossip itu.

In some restaurants, menus knock off the "h" in *hati* to clarify that a dish contains liver rather than heart. *Ati ayam,* for example, is chicken liver.

❀ Lari terbirit-birit

"Running very fast" = Running like the wind. Helter-skelter.

The Malay word *birit* rarely surfaces on its own in Indonesia these days, but the expression *lari terbirit-birit* survives. The *ter-* suffix suggests a repetitive, compulsive action. The expression evokes an image of a person with diarrhea dashing to the toilet for relief, though it applies to anyone who rushes around frantically.

❀ Burung

"Bird" = Penis.

In Indonesian villages, little boys used to wander around freely with naked bottoms. Their mothers scolded them:

"Put your bird away, zip it up or it will fly away."

Masukin burungmu, tutup retsletingnya. Nanti burungmu bisa terbang.

PART II

Power and Conflict

Chapter Four

Authoritarian Rule

Suharto, an army general, took power amid chaos and killing. For a generation, he crushed dissent and pursued political stability and economic growth.

✿ Gestapu (acronym)
GErakan September TigA PUluh
The September 30th Movement.

In the mid-1960s, Indonesia was in turmoil. Prices soared. Students and militias demonstrated. Tension between the military and the communist movement was high. In the midst of it all, President Sukarno tried to balance competing factions, but his power was waning. He was known casually as *Bung Karno* (Brother Sukarno), yet he had declared himself president for life in 1963.

Early on the morning of Oct. 1, 1965, junior army officers rounded up and killed six senior military generals and one lieutenant in an apparent coup attempt. A seventh general escaped by jumping over the wall of his house and hiding in the bushes.

In a radio broadcast, the rebels called themselves *Gerakan September Tiga Puluh*, but the military referred to them by the acronym *Gestapu*. The analogy with the Nazi secret police added notoriety to the plotters.

Maj. Gen. Suharto became the most senior figure in the military after its senior leadership was wiped out. He blamed the uprising on the Indonesian Communist Party. The military instigated a bloody campaign against the communists and their sympathizers, and hundreds of thousands of people were killed in nationwide purges. In some cases, mobs took advantage of the chaos to settle scores, and the ethnic Chinese minority was also targeted.

Decades later, the alleged coup attempt remains a mystery. Who were the ringleaders and who knew what, and when? Was the uprising the work of disgruntled army officers, or were communist political leaders involved? Did they plan to overthrow the president? Did Suharto know about the plot? An independent investigation was never conducted, and Suharto banned publications about the incident. Many of those involved in the events of 1965 have died.

Suharto's version of those events is enshrined in school history books, as well as films that were shown on television throughout his rule. Some Indonesians say the account should be reassessed. Even after the death of Suharto in 2008 at the age of 66, it remains a sensitive subject.

❀ Cukil mata
Poke out eye.

Reports in military-run newspapers after the alleged coup attempt in 1965 vilified the perpetrators. The papers published photographs of *cukil mata*, a device that communists allegedly used to wrench victims' eyeballs from their sockets. The contraption was originally designed to slice open the bark of a rubber tree and obtain the sap. Media also published photos of an electric chair—allegedly used for torture—that was found at the home of Dipa Nusantara Aidit, head of the Indonesian Communist Party. Aidit was later executed.

Many historians believe the military planted the devices to portray the communists as depraved and sadistic.

✵ Supersemar (acronym)
SUrat PERintah SEbelas MARet
Letter of Order of March 11.

In early 1966, Sukarno's power was evaporating. Led by Suharto, the military backed anti-government demonstrations by students. On the night of March 11, Sukarno signed a document called *Supersemar* that authorized Suharto to restore order.

Suharto said the document gave him broad powers, but mystery shrouds the contents of *Supersemar* because the original document disappeared. Copies were released, but opponents of Suharto speculated that they were fake.

Armed with *Supersemar*, Suharto banned the Indonesian Communist Party, instituted economic reforms and ended conflict with neighboring Malaysia. Indonesia, which had pulled out of the United Nations under Sukarno, rejoined the organization.

The acronym *Supersemar* alludes to Semar, a character from *Mahabharata*, a story from India that was written in Sanskrit. The tale about a dynastic struggle and war inspired Javanese folklore and traditional shadow puppetry. Semar is a comical figure, but is viewed as a deity of Java and the redeemer of its people. The allusion to Suharto's legitimacy as a leader was clear.

On March 21, 1968, the People's Consultative Assembly—the nation's highest legislative body—elected Suharto as president. Sukarno died under house arrest in 1970.

❀ Dinusakambangankan
To be exiled to Nusakambangan.

Nusakambangan is a maximum-security prison on an island of the same name south of Java. Jagged rocks jut from treacherous waters that ring its shores. Dutch authorities jailed dissidents on the island, and Suharto sent suspected communists to its cells. Indonesia's most famous writer, Pramoedya Ananta Toer, did time there in 1969 because of his links to communists.

Today, *dinusakambangankan* also refers to being sent to a nasty place, or receiving an unwanted job transfer.

In 2004, separatist rebels from Aceh province with jail sentences of at least seven years were transferred to Nusakambangan, a long way from home. Officials wanted to prevent them from spreading separatist ideas in the prisons in Aceh. The government began releasing rebels under a 2005 peace deal.

Diselongkan (to be exiled to Ceylon) was a fate of exiles under the Dutch. The colonial authorities banished troublesome Javanese princes to Ceylon, a Dutch colony at the time. The British took over Ceylon, which was renamed Sri Lanka after independence.

❀ Buru

Dutch colonizers also shipped troublemakers to Buru Island in the Banda Sea.

Most of the mosquito-infested island, dominated by two mountains, was covered in dense jungle. In the late 1960s, Suharto sent communists to do hard labor at the notorious site.

Writer Pramoedya Ananta Toer spent 14 years on Buru, where he was denied access to pen and paper for much of the time. He composed the *Buru Quartet*, works about a leader of the revolution against the Dutch, by telling stories to prisoners who helped him remember and write them down later. Pramoedya was released in 1979.

Pramoedya's 34 books and essays were translated into several dozen languages, and he inspired pro-democracy activists. In 2004, he was trying to compile an encyclopedia of Indonesia, but he hadn't written anything in a while. He was weak and his hearing and eyesight were fading. He had difficulty climbing to his third-floor study, which was stacked with books and clippings. Still, he called himself a "fighter."

He died in 2006 at the age of 81.

In the old days, Buru housed as many as 12,000 prisoners. Hersri Setiawan, a former political prisoner, wrote a book called *Kamus Gestok* that contains prison slang:

❀ Ingus gajah
"Elephant's snot" = Tapioca pudding, or fried dough bread.

The dish earned its name because of its gooey consistency and greenish color. The prisoners also called it *umbel* (snot, in Javanese).

❀ Sayur kepala
"Head Soup" = Prison gruel.

Inmates joked that you could spin the ladle around in the pot all you wanted, but you'd only hook one or two limp spinach leaves at best. The most likely outcome, they said, was seeing the reflection of your face in the broth.

Sayur usually means vegetable, but in this case it means soup or broth.

❀ Sayur plastik
Plastic soup.

For prisoners on Buru, soup made of young leaves of papaya fruit was *sayur plastik* because the stalks were so thinly cut that they were almost transparent, like some plastics.

❀ Naik Honda
"Ride a Honda" = Suffer from malaria.

The spasms of convicts with malarial fever resembled the bouncing motion of a ride on a Honda motorbike. During the crackdown on communists in the 1960s, Honda bikes from Japan were all the rage in Indonesia.

Inmates improvised treatments for the symptoms of malaria. They made medicine out of boiled roots and leaves, and administered a mix containing a soybean cake called *tempe bosok*.

Tempe is soybean cake, which is fermented. *Bosok* is Javanese for rotten. So *tempe bosok* is doubly rotten. Javanese eat *tempe* after letting it sit for one or two days, a process they say makes it tastier. They grind it up with chili or add it to vegetable soup.

❀ Sabun londo (Javanese)
Dutch soap.

Convicts described soap as Dutch, or foreign soap. The sweet smell of soap was a rarity in the filthy prison, and inmates thought only people as wealthy and privileged as the Dutch had the privilege of washing with it. Many inmates scrubbed away grime with sand or dried grass.

❋ **Laler ijo** (Javanese)
"Green fly" = Prison guard.

Prisoners yelled the codewords *laler* (fly) or *laler ijo* (a bigger, green variety of fly) to warn comrades in other cells that guards were in the vicinity. The Indonesian word for green is *hijau*.

The term was a potent insult because *laler* settled on human excrement.

Pickpockets in Jakarta used *laler* as a codeword for police. The term faded in the 1980s.

❋ **Ali-ali** (Javanese)
"Ring" = A torture weapon on Buru.

Guards attached bronze rings to the fingers, nipples or penis of a victim. They hooked the rings with wires to a generator, and cranked it up by hand to deliver electric shocks. *Ali-ali* was an effective way to extract confessions, true or false, from *antek-antek PKI* (Indonesian Communist Party cadres). PKI was the Indonesian acronym of the party: *Partai Komunis Indonesia*.

Another torture weapon was *ikan pari*, a whip made from the dried tail fin of a *sting-ray*. Guards fixed a wooden handle onto the tail, which was covered with poisoned spikes.

"Give him the ring!" wardens yelled. *Kasih dia ali-ali!*

"Give him the tail!" they said. *Kasih dia pecut!*

❋ **Tapol** (acronym)
TAhanan POLitik
Political prisoners.

The tens of thousands of people arrested for alleged links with the communist movement.

Tapol fell into three categories. *Golongan A* (Category A) were high-level communist planners suspected of plotting against the government. They were prosecuted. *Golongan B* were mid-level suspects, many of whom were jailed without trial. *Golongan C* were accused of sympathizing with the communists, but were not considered a serious threat. Thousands of civil servants fell into *Golongan C*, and were fired, passed over for promotions and transfers, or were docked pay. They were *Tapol kelas teri* (small fry political prisoners).

Accused communist supporters who were released from jail carried national identity cards that read *ET*, or Ex-Tapol. Those with an ET stamp had trouble getting jobs or bank loans.

After Suharto was ousted, successor B.J. Habibie released many *tapol*. The president who followed him, Abdurrahman Wahid, freed the rest.

The communist party remains banned in Indonesia, and former political prisoners still face discrimination. The Supreme Court ruled that former communists can run for office beginning in 2009.

❀ Orde Baru
New Order.

Indonesia's experiment with parliamentary democracy in the 1950s was chaotic. The country entered a new period of stability after the tumult of the mid-1960s. President Suharto developed strong ties with the West, and the economy improved. The military was heavily involved in all aspects of government. This was *Orde Baru*, also known by its acronym *Orba*. *Orde* refers to a system, or set of rules. Suharto's government disparaged the years under his predecessor, Sukarno, as the Old Order (*Orde Lama*).

Orde Baru lasted until Suharto was toppled in a 1998 upheaval reminiscent of the one that brought down Sukarno. By that time, state corruption and repression had tainted the New Order label.

❋ Pembangunan
"Development" = A slogan of the New Order government.

Suharto attracted foreign capital and steered Indonesia's economic growth rate into double digits. Resource-rich Indonesia profited from rising oil prices, and achieved self-sufficiency in rice production in 1984, though it later resumed imports.

Posters carried the slogan along with an image of a smiling Suharto as *Bapak Pembangunan* (Father of Development). He was usually clad in a farmer's *caping* (a coned, straw hat), holding aloft an ear of rice.

Suharto mentioned *Pembangunan* in speeches and orchestrated chats in public. The slogan showed up in schoolbooks and cinema advertisements before the showing of feature films. Development was also a theme under Sukarno, who sought to lift Indonesia out of its colonial-era poverty.

❋ Tinggal landas
"Take off" = A New Order slogan.

Suharto wanted Indonesia to ascend to the ranks of developed countries like an airplane taking off from a runway. The term was listed in the 1989 Gramedia Indonesian–English dictionary, one of the most widely available dictionaries in Indonesia. The dictionary describes how the 6th five-year economic development plan will enable Indonesia to "take off" and attain the status of an industrialized nation. The end of that plan coincided with the beginning of the economic crisis that helped end Suharto's rule.

A third, unrevised edition of the Gramedia dictionary came out in 2004, long after the demise of five-year plans. It included *Tinggal landas*, which is still used by local authorities in speeches and development plans.

❀ Semut hitam
"Black ants" = Hard workers.

Manpower Minister Sudomo promoted the black ant as a symbol of productivity in the 1980s. A huge drawing of a grinning black ant in a hard hat once stood in front of the Department of Manpower. The industriousness of the ant matched the government's creed of fast economic development. The rights of workers got short shrift. The government banned independent labor unions, and jailed many labor activists.

❀ Pahlawan devisa
Foreign exchange hero.

The New Order government said Indonesian migrant workers were heroes because they funneled revenue back into their country. Indonesia's leaders still use the term.

Hundreds of thousands of people leave Indonesia annually to seek work elsewhere in Southeast Asia, and in the Middle East.

Working abroad can be perilous for Indonesians who don't know foreign languages and cultures. Many are illegal immigrants, and don't have the resources to defend themselves if trouble looms. Most get menial work for little pay. Indonesian men work as plantation or construction workers, and women work as maids. Indonesians usually earn half the wages made by Filipino workers, who are better educated and skilled, and speak better

English. Indonesian migrant workers still make three times more than what they would earn in Indonesia.

These expatriate workers are usually called *TKI* (*Tenaga kerja Indonesia*; Indonesian workers), or *TKW* (*Tenaga Kerja Wanita*; women workers) because most of them are women.

Jalur TKI (TKI lane) signs at Jakarta's main airport direct workers to designated areas before they fly to their overseas destinations.

✺ SARA (acronym)
Suku, Agama, Ras, Antargolongan
Ethnicity, religion, race, social relations.

Suharto tried to suppress ethnic, religious, racial and class tensions. These four sensitive themes formed *SARA*, an umbrella term with a cheerful sound that was prominent in the government lexicon. Authorities urged people to preserve national unity, whatever their differences. It was a tough task in one of the world's most diverse nations, and bloodletting erupted now and then.

Jangan SARA ya, Indonesian officials said at rallies. They meant: "Don't provoke or bring up ethnic, religious, racial or class issues."

This blanket form of censorship kept a lid on free expression, but failed to dissipate the social tensions boiling within Indonesia.

Violence hit many areas in the power vacuum that followed Suharto's fall in 1998. But Indonesia never came close to the Balkans-style breakup that some feared.

🦋 Gotong Royong
Sharing burdens.

The architects of the New Order said common interests should outweigh individual ones. They said Indonesians could achieve social harmony by sharing burdens such as communal jobs.

Villagers turned out on Sunday mornings to clean sewers together, build a bridge or repair the road. People pooled donations for a cause, such as helping a poor family.

The phrase took root before Suharto came to power and is still around, though it is less popular. The government of President Megawati Sukarnoputri, who was defeated in the 2004 election, was named *Kabinet Gotong Royong*. Officials still say it to rally support for state projects.

Under Suharto, the government required students and civil servants to study *Pancasila*, the state ideology enshrined in the 1945 constitution. Pancasila espoused five principles: belief in one God, nationalism, unity, democracy and social justice. Hence the Sanskrit name: *panca* means five, and *sila* means principles.

The ideology served as an instrument of state control. Authorities made arrests, closed down a newspaper or banned a radio broadcast by declaring that Pancasila was under attack.

It was a staple in the classroom from elementary school through university. Teachers taught a blur of clunky acronyms and slogans related to Pancasila. Indonesian youths can still rattle off the acronyms without knowing what they all mean.

❈ **P4** (pronounced *peh-empat*)
Pendidikan Penghayatan Pengamalan Pancasila
Upgrading Course on the Directives for the Realization and
Implementation of Pancasila.

Kids in elementary and high schools studied the subject all year.
University students took 100 hours of P4. Civil servants had
refresher courses when promoted. Active or retired military
generals taught seminar classes called *Wawasan Nusantara*, a term
that comes from Sanskrit.

Wawasan is world view; *Nusantara* is a name for the archipelago that became Indonesia. *Nusa* means islands, *antara* means
adjacent. The term was used in the 14th century during the
Majapahit kingdom's golden rule of Hayam Wuruk. His prime
minister, Gajah Mada, is believed to have unified almost the
entire archipelago.

P4 teachers stressed rote memorization of the basic tenets of
New Order rule, including the importance of national security.

P4 is no longer required reading in universities, but it's still
compulsory in civic education classes at lower levels.

❈ **Darma Wanita**
"The dedication of women" = The name of a women's
group during Suharto's rule.

Today, many Indonesians associated the term with something
boring or pretentious.

Darma Wanita was a pet project of Suharto's wife, Siti
Suhartinah. She came up with the idea and pushed state companies to donate a percentage of their profits to it.

Wives of civil servants and military personnel were drafted
into *Darma Wanita*, a state-backed organization that held social

meetings, sing-alongs and supported husbands' careers.

Darma Wanita was heavily promoted in the media and in educational institutions. No more. Rusty signs advertising the women's group still hang outside some state buildings. They exist in a few state-owned firms and embassies, though it usually depends on the wife of the director or ambassador to keep the momentum going.

"Don't be so old-fashioned and Darma Wanita-like," career women say. *Jangan kaku banget seperti Darma Wanita deh.*

❀ Ekaprasetia Pancakarsa

The New Order government borrowed Sanskrit to make some concepts sound mystical and intellectual. Teachers ordered students to memorize long tracts, including the definition of *Ekaprasetia Pancakarsa*, as outlined in the 1990 state guidelines that were drawn up by lawmakers:

Ekaprasetia Pancakarsa is derived from Sanskrit. Literally *eka* means one or one and only. *Prasetia* means promise or resolve. *Panca* means five and *karsa* means strong desire. *Pancakarsa* thus means the oneness of resolve to implement the five wishes ... these five wishes are the desire to cause the five moral principles of the Pancasila to materialize. It is called the oneness of resolve because the will is very strong and unshakable.

❀ Ipoleksosbudmilag

This tongue-twisting acronym stands for the unity of ideology, politics, economics, society, culture, the military and religion. Indonesians who said it enough times found it catchy. Another slogan that flew off the Indonesian tongue was *Sishankamrata.*

This stood for *Sistem Pertahanan dan Keamanan Rakyat Semesta* (Total People's Defence and Security System).

❀ Cekal (acronym)
CEgah tangKAL
Travel ban.

Cekal means to grasp, or hold firmly. To reinforce the point, the acronym comes from *cegah* (prevent) and *tangkal* (ward off danger). The government banned many dissidents from traveling overseas, where they could stir up animosity toward the government back home.

The 1992 immigration law enshrined this policy. It said the justice minister, attorney-general, the military chief and finance minister had the right to ask immigration authorities to slap a travel ban (*cekal*) on an Indonesian or a foreigner. They didn't have to get permission from the courts. The law is still in place.

In 2007, the Constitutional Court revoked *Haatzaai Artikelen* (hate-sowing articles), laws that Indonesia inherited from Dutch colonizers after independence. The laws allowed the government to prosecute anyone who disseminated what was defined as "elements of hostility or hatred or contempt against the government or state." Critics dubbed the laws *pasal karet* (rubber articles) because the state had broad, flexible powers to define what was hostile.

❀ Alon-alon waton kelakon (Javanese)
Slowly, but surely.

A rhythmic expression often used to describe Suharto's style as president. He was methodical, and put on a show of humility.

Hasty or flamboyant conduct was not refined. The style suited the culture. Traditional Javanese dances are often slow, graceful and deliberate.

❋ Kalau inkonstitusional, tak gebuk

If anyone acts unconstitutionally, I'll clobber them.

Gebuk is a formal Javanese term for clobber, or thump. Along with many other Javanese words, it is accepted now as part of the Indonesian language.

Suharto made the threat while talking to reporters on a plane flying home from Germany in 1995. The threat applied to any Indonesians who engaged in what he deemed unconstitutional acts.

Suharto was furious because protesters had blocked his bus as he headed to a dinner appointment in Berlin. The demonstrators were young Germans and separatists from the Indonesian-occupied territory of East Timor.

Babi! Pembunuh! they shouted. "Pig! Murderer!"

Suharto's entourage was forced to take another route.

One target for clobbering was Sri Bintang Pamungkas, an alleged organizer of the protest in Germany. Pamungkas was a former engineering lecturer at the elite University of Indonesia. He was arrested in 1996 and sentenced to nearly three years in jail for insulting the president at a Berlin university.

He was released pending an appeal, but he formed an illegal party and declared that he would run for president. Pamungkas was arrested again, but Suharto's resignation in 1998 cleared the way for his release.

❀ Sadumuk bathuk sanyari bumi, den kaloni taker pati
(Javanese)
"Touch me on the forehead with the tips of your fingers, even for a handful of earth, I'll fight you with all of my body and soul" = Back off. Over my dead body.

Suharto cultivated an aloof leadership that elevated him above the fray. He was also direct, sometimes brutally so. He cited the "touch me" expression in the 1980s when debate swirled about his family origins. Some Indonesians said Suharto had aristocratic blood, and disputed his claim that he was the son of a farmer. The debate annoyed Suharto, whose origins were humble. The old Javanese expression was about defending honor and pride, and family.

The reference to land made it a favorite among independence fighters during the war against the Dutch. In that context, land stood for Indonesia.

The expression is long, so Javanese usually say just the first half.

❀ Rumongso bisa, nanging ora iso rumongso (Javanese)
"You feel you can, but you can't feel" = A warning against complacency and arrogance.

Suharto said this phrase on occasion. Javanese pride themselves on humility and knowing one's place in life. God is capable and confident, but human beings are not. They lose awareness if they claim they are smart or skilled. Somebody who says "I can do" (*rumongso bisa*) has a big head.

Chapter Five

Money and Politics

Politics was predictable in authoritarian Indonesia. Today, Indonesia is a rough-and-tumble democracy. Corruption has deep roots.

❊ Kuningisasi
Yellowing.

Yellow (*kuning*) is the color of the Golkar political party, which helped keep President Suharto in power for 32 years. During parliamentary election campaigns, Golkar bathed Java island in yellow paint. Party workers doused bridges, fences, sidewalks, bus stops and tree trunks in yellow. *Kuningisasi* (yellowing) symbolized the power of the Golkar machine. It dominated Java, Suharto's power base and home to a huge chunk of the country's electorate.

These days, political operatives don't get out the paintbrushes as often. But campaign supporters decorate jackets, ties, socks, bags and cars with party colors.

In 2004, a district head in Banten province on the western tip of Java printed school exercise books with a red cover and an image of the Garuda, a mythical bird of prey that is the national symbol and the namesake of Indonesia's national airline.

Red is the color of the Indonesian Democratic Party of Struggle, the party that backed President Megawati Sukarnoputri.

The press said the official, a Megawati supporter, had violated the neutrality required of civil servants by telling schools to buy the books. The official apologized and withdrew the books.

One opponent of *kuningisasi* was Pakubuwono XII, a sunan or monarch in the Central Javanese town of Surakarta. He objected when the mayor ordered a yellow paint job on his white palace grounds in 1997. The ruler filed a lawsuit, and a court said the fence, walls and tree trunks inside the palace compound should be restored to their original color.

But the mayor painted it yellow a second time. Under government pressure, Pakubuwono dropped his protest. In court, his lawyers declared that the palace was supposed to be white, and that tourists didn't want to see a yellow palace.

The ruler's lawsuit was a rare show of defiance toward *kuningisasi*.

Pakubuwono, who became ruler in 1945, had more pedigree than political power. His name comes from *paku* (nail, in Javanese) and *buwono* (the world, or universe). It meant that the ruler was the nail at the center of the universe, holding everything together.

His full name was Ingkang Sinuhun Kangjeng Susuhunan Pakubuwono XII. He died in June 2004 at the age of 79, leaving 36 children by half a dozen mistresses, as well as 60 grandchildren. Weeping mourners lined the streets as a horse-drawn carriage carried his coffin to the family cemetery.

Golkar lost its monopoly on power after Suharto was ousted in 1998, though it has regained some of its prestige and remains a powerful establishment force.

Kuningisasi is an example of the Suharto-era trend of tacking the suffix *-isasi* onto nouns to change them into verbs denoting a campaign.

Desukarnoisasi was a campaign to get rid of all objects, reference and teachings related to Sukarno, Indonesia's first president. Suharto muscled him out of power in the 1960s.

Bodoh is stupid. *Bodohisasi* is the process of making someone, or people, or a state, stupid. It's a campaign to fool people.

Bungkam is to hush, or gag someone. *Bungkamisasi* are efforts to get people to stay mum about a scandal. Usually, the misdeed involves sex or corruption.

Neonisasi is a project to jazz up a street with neon lights. The perception in small towns is that lots of bright lights symbolize modernity. Local newspapers talked about the installation of electricity in a village, and how *neonisasi* should follow right away.

❈ Membeli kucing dalam karung
"Buying a cat in a sack" = Acquiring something without knowing its worth.

For decades, Indonesian voters only chose a political party during parliamentary elections, and the party later selected the legislators. Party cronies and businessmen with deep pockets often got the jobs. Many lived on Java, and showed little interest in their constituencies on distant islands.

So the voters bought a sack, or political party, without knowing what cat, or legislator, was inside.

The one sure thing was the dominance of the ruling Golkar party, which won with the help of vote-rigging. In 1973, most political parties were dissolved, leaving a token opposition.

Voters were also cut off from the selection of the president. Loyalist legislators and a quota of government appointees, including military men, elected the president and his deputy. Suharto had the system sewn up. He won five successive ballots.

Things changed once democracy took hold. Ballots list the names of candidates for the legislature, allowing voters to pick the person they want. On July 5, 2004, Indonesians voted directly for presidential candidates for the first time ever, and a runoff vote followed on Sept. 20. The election was a milestone in the shift to democracy. The political tradition of "buying a cat in the sack" at the ballot box was over.

Membeli kucing dalam karung applies to more than politics. Stock analysts in Indonesia say it if they don't have enough information to assess the value of shares. Parents say it to remind a daughter to be cautious about a prospective husband.

Dutch colonizers introduced the "cat in the sack" expression to Indonesia. Their version was: *Een kat in de zak kopen.*

✤ Wejangan (Javanese)
Advice from elders.

Indonesian officials ask superiors for *wejangan* (advice) before making a big policy decision, or embarking on a business trip. Elders happily deliver, usually in long-winded speeches to a big crowd.

Indonesians from all walks of life seek guidance from respected community or family figures before deciding whether to buy land, move away from home or get a new job. The ritual can be private, at least in the communal Indonesian sense. A gathering of several dozen family members—cousins, aunts and uncles—is considered private.

Although the term *wejangan* is Javanese, it is understood by most Indonesians who believe asking for advice from elders is an obligation in life. Suharto encouraged the custom, reinforcing his authority with the cultural backing of ancient Javanese customs.

At most public gatherings today, someone humbly asks the

advice of elders. During the presidential campaign in 2004, candidate and former army general Susilo Bambang Yudhoyono spoke to a gathering of war veterans. Rather than appeal for their support, he said he was a young politician who had come to seek their advice.

Yudhoyono won the election.

❈ Ngeluruk tanpo bolo, menang tanpo ngasorake
(Javanese)
Attack without troops, win without subjugation.

In his heyday, President Suharto was a master at bottling dissent and preserving a veneer of harmony. He dispatched troublesome or prominent officials to provincial posts far from Jakarta, or to cushy jobs as ambassadors in distant capitals. The tactic removed agitators, or potential threats, without a showdown.

Suharto was also brutal. During his rise to power in the mid-1960s, Suharto's military instigated an anti-communist purge that killed hundreds of thousands. Over the decades, dissidents were jailed and beaten. In 1996, pro-government thugs attacked the party headquarters of Megawati Sukarnoputri, the chief opposition leader at the time.

Indonesia didn't seem like a police state to many visitors. Some political enemies operated as long as they didn't go too far, and their activities let the government claim that Indonesia was not a dictatorship. For most of his rule, Suharto didn't face a unified political opposition, partly because Indonesia enjoyed annual economic growth of up to 10 percent.

"Satisfied with food, clothes and board" (*cukup pangan, sandang, papan*) described the majority of Indonesians who followed the government line. Suharto barred political parties from organizing at the village level between elections, creating an apolitical population known as the "floating mass" (*massa mengambang*).

The term appeared in textbooks with a message for Indonesians: staying out of politics is good, let the leaders decide.

The system gave an overwhelming advantage to government loyalists who controlled village leaderships and persuaded or coerced voters without fear of rivalry.

❀ **5-D** (pronounced *lima-deh*)
Datang, duduk, dengar, diam, duit
Come, sit, listen, quiet, money.

The legislature and the judiciary were pliant tools of Suharto's government. Parliament was packed with loyalists who approved government-sponsored bills. Lawmakers showed up at the green-domed Parliament building, sat quietly, listened to a government proposal, said nothing and obediently cast "yes" votes. Some dozed through predictable proceedings, mouths agape.

The government televised parliamentary hearings in an effort to show the process was transparent.

Legislators signed their names in a book before the hearing to confirm their attendance, guaranteeing a payment in exchange for a pro-government vote.

This custom continues. The honorarium is *uang sidang* (hearing money), but it's no longer contingent on how a lawmaker votes. The legislators also get a clothing allowance so they don't look shabby during debates. Legislators once finagled money to have washing machines installed in their houses.

5-D is a spinoff of *3-M*, or *Mari Mangan Mulih* (going home after eating, in Javanese). It is rude for guests to rush home after eating their fill. To laugh it off, the culprits say: *Wah sorry, tiga-M nih.*

Wah and nih emphasize a point. *Tiga* is three.

5-D and *3-M* are just two examples in a sea of Indonesian acronyms designed to poke fun or make a snappy point.

❄ **Golput** (acronym)
GOLongan PUTih
"White group" = Fence-sitters.

Indonesian political parties love bright colors, and people who stay on the sidelines are *golput* (white group). They can be politicians who abstain from a sensitive vote in parliament, or citizens who don't vote in an election, whether out of anger or apathy. Some anti-government activists urged *golongan putih* to cast blank ballots during Suharto-era elections as a form of protest.

Indonesians use the term to avoid taking sides in any setting, whether a tense standoff among co-workers or a casual exchange of gossip.

"Do you believe my version of last night's events or my girlfriend's story?" a guy asks his best friend.

Kamu percaya ceritaku tentang kejadian malam kemarin atau cerita pacarku?

His mate demurs.

"Nah. I'll sit this one out," he says.

Nggak. Aku golput saja.

❄ **Politik dagang sapi**
"Cow trade politics" = Horse-trading. Backroom wheeling and dealing.

The expression comes from the Dutch *koehandel* (*koe* is cow; *handel* is trade).

Livestock traders from Padang, West Sumatra, do business discreetly. The seller and buyer communicate with hand gestures to make sure nobody hears the haggling and benefits from the inside information in a later deal. To guarantee secrecy, the trader hangs a *sarong*, or traditional cloth, as a screen and slips his hands behind it to indicate the price. Only the customer peeks.

In 2000, Muslim cleric Abdurrahman Wahid proved himself a master at cow trade politics by taking advantage of a system that let lawmakers and delegates select the president.

A shrewd dealmaker, Wahid cobbled together a coalition called *Axis Tengah* (Central Axis), rallying support from Muslim parties who wanted a man with strong Muslim credentials as president.

Wahid outvoted Megawati Sukarnoputri, head of a party that won the biggest share of seats in parliamentary elections four months earlier. Megawati had seemed assured of the presidency.

Wahid's maneuver stunned Megawati's expectant supporters in the streets outside Parliament. They burned tires and lobbed stones in central Jakarta until she urged them to calm down.

Megawati's turn at Indonesia's helm came in 2001 after Wahid stepped down following his parliamentary impeachment for incompetence.

❀ Tumbuhkan demokrasi, jangan democrazy
Let democracy grow, not democrazy.

The path to democracy was chaotic in the years after the 1998 fall of Suharto. Activists and political parties jockeyed for influence, and agendas were poorly defined. Student groups, especially in the sober circle of Yogyakarta, Central Java, reminded their friends to keep protests sharp and focused.

The expression was a favorite of Hidayat Nurwahid, head of The Justice and Prosperity Party (*Partai Keadilan Sejahtera*). The party drew support from urban, well-educated Muslim student groups, and did well in parliamentary elections in 2004.

Indonesia's first direct presidential election on July 5, 2004 was fair and orderly. Some 80 percent of the 155 million registered voters cast ballots. A run-off vote in September was also a success. Some 580,000 polling stations opened. Fishing boats carried ballot papers in some areas. In the remote Papua region, some people walked for a day to vote.

❈ Gitu aja, kok repot, prek
"Aah, it's nothing" = What's all the bother about?

A favorite expression of former President Abdurrahman Wahid, who often spoke in a mix of Javanese and Indonesian. *Prek* is a casual Javanese word that adds emphasis. Wahid's informal speech did not befit the traditional idea of a statesman. Some Indonesians disapproved of the president's turns of phrase. Others loved his casual style.

The appropriate, presidential uttering would be: *Begitu saja mengapa repot.*

Linguists think President Suharto spoke terrible Indonesian because he mixed the order of sentences, and had a heavy Javanese accent. He used *ken* instead of the customary *kan* as a verb ending, and said *daripada*—a term without meaning— instead of *dari* (from).

Officials of other ethnic groups in outlying islands tried to copy Suharto's speaking style in hopes of impressing dignitaries from Jakarta. His influence over Indonesia was so great that many of his Javanese expressions effectively became part of the Indonesian language.

President Megawati Sukarnoputri was known for long Indonesian sentences with redundant words. Sometimes she appeared to get lost in her own syntax. Her sentences started with a subject and had many clauses, but left out verbs.

Linguists say Susilo Bambang Yudhoyono, a former army general and security minister who was elected president in 2004, constructs his sentences with more care than any of Indonesia's previous five presidents.

Yudhoyono also gives speeches in English, which impresses investors and diplomats at international forums. He was not happy when his industry minister, Andung Nitimihardja, fumbled a comment in English when they visited an Indian software company in 2005. The *Jakarta Post* reported:

> Andung's muddled assemblage of apparently English words left the executives visibly perplexed and the audience silent for a long, uncomfortable moment, as everyone attempted to decipher the verbiage. President Susilo had a disturbed look on his face and turned and glared furiously at Andung.

❀ Coblos moncong putih
Punch the white snout.

This slogan was a hit ahead of parliamentary elections in April 2004. The political party of President Megawati Sukarnoputri poured funds into television advertisements that drummed the slogan into viewers.

Punch refers to the traditional method of casting a ballot in a voting booth, and the snout belonged to a bull, the symbol of Megawati's party.

Since the nation's first parliamentary election in 1955, Indonesians have used nails to scratch, or punch, their party choice on a ballot paper. From 2009, they used pens.

Coblos is an earthy word that means a bit more than punch. It's more like: "enthusiastically punch right through until you rip a big hole." Other words for punch are *tusuk*, *colok* and *cocok*. The latter, *cocok*, is an especially violent term associated with punching a hole in a bull's nose to insert a ring.

In the 2004 parliamentary elections, several of the two-dozen competing political parties used a bull as a campaign symbol. Megawati's party invented the slogan *Coblos moncong putih* to distinguish its bull—a black one with a white snout— from those of competitors.

Coblos moncong putih was so pervasive in the media that toddlers and teenagers shouted it at home, in playgrounds and in the streets. It didn't make an impression on Indonesians of voting age. Megawati's party lost a third of the votes it had won in elections in 1999. She was voted out of office in 2004.

❦ Wong cilik (Javanese)
Little people.

The vast population of poor and unemployed Indonesians. They are the majority in a nation of at least 235 million people, and crowd city slums and villages across the archipelago. They work in offices and street stalls, or on farms and construction sites. An anonymous mass, they can carry a candidate. Politicians want their votes.

Wong cilik is a common, informal term. *Wong alit* is a formal Javanese term for little people.

Ahead of the July 5, 2004 presidential vote, incumbent Megawati Sukarnoputri campaigned for reelection with the slogan:

Suara wong alit sampai wong elit.

"The voice of the small people and the elite."

The message was that her party was for both rich and poor. The slogan appeared on party flags and pamphlets, followed by glowing testimonies from economists, political analysts, religious leaders, business executives, as well as cocoa farmers, shoeshine boys and rickshaw drivers.

A conservative Muslim party scoffed that Megawati's party

would not fight for *wong cilik*, but for *wong licik* (scam artists), or corrupt business interests.

Wong is people in Javanese, and *licik* means cunning in Indonesian.

Megawati appeared flustered when she talked to *wong cilik*, and was uncomfortable speaking off-the-cuff in public. In campaign ads on television ahead of parliamentary elections in 2004, Megawati appeared in front of a group of poor Indonesians, but she wore clunky, flashy bracelets. She took a lot of flak for that, and her campaign pulled the ads.

Sukarno, Megawati's father and Indonesia's founding president, reportedly groomed her for leadership from an early age. He took Megawati to the beach when she was a kid, and made her deliver speeches in a voice louder than the waves. Decades later, she delivered fiery speeches with prepared texts to stadium crowds.

❈ Putra daerah
Sons of the region.

Development policy in democratic Indonesia called for a shift of power and responsibility from the central government to regional leaders, or *putra daerah*. The idea was to give local areas more control over their affairs after decades of tight, often corrupt management by the central government. The concept was called *desentralisasi* or *otonomi daerah* (regional autonomy).

This policy was hugely popular. Local authorities get more of a hand in collecting taxes and allocating resources. Provinces exulted in their newfound power, but many lacked professionals to implement reforms and cut red tape. They had enthusiasm, but not expertise. In some cases, local leaders ended up competing for power at the expense of real change. Corruption persisted.

❀ Lapor ayam hilang, kambing pun hilang
"Report a lost chicken, in the end a goat is lost also" = A goat is worth 15 times more than a chicken.

Some Indonesians complain that you have more to lose if you report a crime to the police.

Sometimes, authorities want money for typing up a report on a stolen item, coming to your house to look at the crime scene, or going out to look for the thief.

Indonesians say stealing chicken (*maling ayam*) is the most common crime in villages, where people keep chickens at home. The saying migrated from the countryside to the cities, and refers to any two-bit thief.

Another urban expression: steal underwear, get beaten up (*maling kolor, kena gebuk*). It means punishment can be severe even for a trivial crime.

Indonesians say the easiest thing to steal is cheap underwear drying on a clothesline in a backyard. Such misdemeanors can carry fatal consequences in a nation where mobs sometimes dispense justice. A crowd once caught a man who stole a box of underwear from a market. They beat him, poured gasoline on him and burned him to death.

❀ Ada gula, ada semut
Where there is sugar, there are ants.

When you have money, people gather around you. When you lose it, they dump you.

While some Indonesians associate the expression with the politics of money or power, the idiom can have a positive meaning. A good restaurant, for example, will attract lots of people.

✳ **KUHP** (pronounced *ka-ooh-hah-peh*)
Kasih Uang Habis Perkara
Give money and your case/problem will be gone.

KUHP is the title of Indonesia's criminal law code, but the acronym has a second, mischievous meaning. To cynics, *KUHP* was synonymous with graft in Indonesia's judicial system under authoritarian rule, and also today. The government promised legal reforms after Suharto's downfall in 1998, but wealth and power still influence verdicts. Also, some of Indonesia's 4 million civil servants bolster low salaries with payoffs from citizens eager to resolve legal or administrative tangles.

The original meaning of *KUHP* is *Kitab Undang-undang Hukum Pidana*, or Criminal Law Code. The book is based on Dutch law, a legacy of colonial rule that has remained largely intact since the declaration of independence in 1945. The government is revising the book. A separate tome outlines business law, another Dutch inheritance.

✳ **UUD** (pronounced *ooh-ooh-deh*)
Ujung-Ujungnya Duit
At the end is money.

A play on the acronym of *Undang-Undang Dasar 1945*, the state constitution that was drafted at the end of World War II. Indonesians gripe that it takes money to get anything done. Want to speed up your application for a driver's license, new passport or a business permit? Slip a bribe across the counter.

UUD is not always a slap at state corruption. Every school year, parents dole out cash for textbooks, uniforms, class outings and other extracurricular activities for their children.

"At the end is money," they moan. *Ujung-ujungnya duit.*

❦ **KKN** (pronounced *kah-kah-en*)
Korupsi, Kolusi, Nepotisme
Corruption, Collusion, Nepotism.

A catch-all term for the corruption and favoritism that contributed to Indonesia's economic plunge towards the end of President Suharto's rule. The phrase became popular after a currency crisis hit in 1997. The Indonesian rupiah plunged and prices soared. *Berantas KKN* (Fight KKN) was a protest slogan during student-led demonstrations against the president.

The chief beneficiaries of Suharto's rule were his associates and children, who built business empires with the help of their connections. Shortly before he stepped down, Suharto appointed his daughter as social affairs minister in a Cabinet reshuffle designed to dampen calls for reform. His opponents viewed the reshuffle as proof that Suharto wasn't capable of reform. Rumors spread that he was grooming his daughter to take his job.

―――――――

KKN has another meaning for university students: *Kuliah Kerja Nyata*, or field practicing. As a requirement for graduation, students at state institutions visit rural areas to build roads for villagers, and teach them about sanitation and administration.

❦ **Tutut** (acronym)
Tanpa Usaha Tapi Untung Terus
Without effort but always gaining profit.

A pun on the nickname of Siti Hardiyanti Hastuti Rukmana, Suharto's eldest daughter. The nickname came from her third name, HasTUTi.

Tutut had stakes in toll roads, plantations, construction, communications and other enterprises. After her father's ouster,

Tutut was implicated in a graft scandal, but the case was dropped. She remains a powerful businesswoman.

Some people joked that Tutut earned her nickname because she loved the sound of cars tooting horns on her toll roads. The nickname still has a negative connotation for many Indonesians, who use it to refer to someone who amasses cash without lifting a finger.

Siti Suhartinah, Suharto's late wife, was also criticized because of her fundraising for social and cultural projects that she sponsored.

People called her Ibu Tien, or Madam Tien, because of the old spelling of her name, SoeharTIENah. That became Ibu Tien Persen, a joking reference to an alleged 10 percent cut she received when her social foundations asked state companies for money. Company directors were afraid to say no. One of her projects was the Beautiful Indonesia in Miniature Park, or *Taman Mini*, a cultural theme park said to have been inspired by Disneyland. Ibu Tien died in 1996.

Prosecutors alleged her husband embezzled funds from tax-free charities that he controlled, but Suharto didn't stand trial because of health problems.

❀ Gerakan Cinta Rupiah
Love the Rupiah Movement.

The name of this government-backed campaign to shore up the Indonesian rupiah in 1998 was shortened to *Gentar* (shake). The snappy acronym didn't help the currency.

Some state officials and tycoons tried to restore faith in the rupiah by exchanging dollars or jewelry for local currency. Suharto's eldest daughter, Tutut, pioneered the trend, selling US$50,000 at a state bank. Her supporters handed out stickers and badges with rupiah slogans echoing the "I love New York" theme. Many Indonesians viewed the effort as a publicity stunt. Too little, too late. The rupiah kept falling.

❋ Maling teriak maling

"Thief cries out thief" = Criminals never confess. They just pin the blame on others.

"Maling teriak maling," reformist leader Amien Rais said after prosecutors summoned Suharto's children to answer questions about their wealth. Things turned out as Rais expected. Suharto's children said they were innocent and did their best to deflect the accusations.

Only Suharto's youngest son—Tommy Suharto—was convicted in a land scam. He went into hiding, and the judge who had sentenced Tommy was shot dead by assassins on motorbikes as he drove to work. Then the Supreme Court overturned the corruption verdict by a lower court. But Tommy was caught and jailed for the murder of the judge. In October 2006, Tommy was freed after serving two-thirds of his 10-year sentence, partly as a reward for good behavior. Critics said the early release showed that the Suharto family remained above the law.

❋ Gali lubang, tutup lubang

"Dig a hole to close another one" = Pay a debt by incurring a new one.

The salaries of many Indonesian civil servants barely cover living expenses. To make ends meet, they borrow money from an employee cooperative, the bank, friends, or family. They buy groceries and other goods on credit at an employee cooperative, and pay debt at the end of the month by having the sum deducted directly from their wages. The need to pay off creditors dampens the relief of pay-day.

❋ Gajinya, sih, kecil, sabetannya besar
The salary is small, but the gains are huge.

Gains are *sabetan*. Also, *sabet* means whip, and the expression implies extortion, or the use of force to get something.

The wages of civil servants are small, but some make extra cash on the side. A post that is wet (*basah*) offers the potential of additional income; a job that is dry (*kering*) doesn't allow room for corruption.

The Indonesian military supplements its budget with gains (*sabetan*) from civilian foundations and businesses, some of them illegal. Some elements are believed to be involved in smuggling. In some cases, the military has received funds and resources directly from foreign energy firms operating in Indonesia. Such funding schemes raise concern that the military doesn't always answer to the civilian government because it relies so heavily on its own sources of income, rather than the national budget.

Allegations of mark-ups on military equipment, and collusion between the military and its suppliers, have been common. In one case, mountain-climbing equipment worth millions of dollars was supposed to turn up at a warehouse. It didn't. The military could not account for it, nor explain why it needed the equipment.

In 2004, the Indonesian Supreme Audit Board told Parliament that the "wettest" government agency, or the one with the most suspect bookkeeping, was the attorney general's office. The board referred to frozen assets of convicts that disappeared, contracts for prosecutors' offices that were never built and other corruption allegations.

In 2005, scandal enveloped the Ministry of Religious Affairs. Officials at the ministry, which had a monopoly on organizing package tours to Muslim holy sites in Saudi Arabia, were accused of pilfering tens of thousands of dollars in pilgrims' funds. Pilgrims who paid hefty prices for the trip also complained of lousy food and accommodation.

❧ Wartawan Bodrex

Wartawan means journalist, and *Bodrex* is a common medicine for fever, colds and headaches.

Some *wartawan Bodrex* are jobless con artists who pretend to be reporters. They go to news conferences where hosts hand out envelopes of cash to secure upbeat coverage. *Bodrex* journalists huddle at the same table and stay mute throughout an event. Public relations staff study the names of journalists who sign in to make sure they're genuine reporters.

Business events are the favorite beat of *wartawan Bodrex*. The food and the freebies are better. Once a *wartawan Bodrex* loses his anonymity, his career as a freeloader is doomed.

Bodrex implies the pretenders are a pounding headache for news conference hosts. In a television ad for the medicine, star actor Dede Yusuf appears at the head of a company of *Bodrex* troops, ready to defeat disease. The image has come to signify the large number of fake reporters on the prowl.

An obsolete term for a fake reporter is *WTS*, or *Wartawan Tanpa Surat Kabar* (journalist without newspaper). An older meaning of *WTS* is *Wanita Tuna Susila* (woman without morals), or prostitute.

Some *wartawan Bodrex* work for low-end newspapers, and supplement their income by writing puff pieces for sources in exchange for payoffs. One journalist had his own fax machines at home so he could receive invitations to events without his office knowing about it.

Some media organizations ban employees from taking money, while others collect it and donate it to charity. Many journalists write their names in attendance books at news conferences and pocket the cash. Sometimes they complain that it's not enough.

The practice is known as *journalisme amplop* (envelope journalism) because the money is usually given in white, blank envelopes to *wartawan amplop* (envelope reporters).

Indonesian journalists often tip sources. Few people frown on this culture of handouts; it's a natural expression of thanks, especially to *wong cilik* (little people) such as pedicab drivers and market vendors.

Terms for tip in Indonesian are *uang transpor* (transport money) and *uang taxi*, *uang rokok* (cigarette money), *uang kopi* (coffee money), *uang sirih* (betel nut money), *uang minum* (drinking money).

Bribes are *uang pelicin* (slippery money), *uang semir* (shoe polish money) and *uang pelumas* (oil money). Another term is *salam tempel*, which translates roughly as a "sticky handshake." It suggests the furtive passing of cash from palm to palm.

❈ Emas berpeti-peti, kerbau berkandang-kandang
"Gold in many boxes, buffaloes in many stables" = Riches in abundance. Be careful how you handle them.

Don't flaunt your money, but know when to display it. If you're well-off and live in a humble neighborhood, don't buy a fancy car because thugs will vandalize it. Wear your best clothes when you have to impress your boss.

The full saying is:

"They can fill many boxes with gold and many stables with buffalo."

Emasnya bisa penuhi peti-peti dan kerbaunya penuhi kandang-kandang.

In the old days, gold and buffaloes were the most common symbols of wealth.

✿ Utang emas boleh dibayar, utang budi dibawa mati

"You can repay debts in gold, but you take your debt of deed to your grave" = Good deeds will always be remembered.

This saying reminds people not to labor only for material possessions, but to dedicate time to helping others.

✿ Duduk sama rendah, berdiri sama tinggi

"Sit at the same low level, stand at the same high level" = Everybody is equal before the law.

Indonesians sigh at the pervasive corruption in their court system.

"Justice can be bought," they say. *Keadilan dapat dibeli.*

Opportunities for corruption are so common at all levels in *mafia peradilan* (the court system's mafia) that it feels like an organized racket. You might pay when the police arrest you, when prosecutors file charges and when you try to bargain down a sentence. Some tycoons in trouble have allegedly tried to pay for the reversal of a conviction.

Alap-alap pengadilan (court thieves) co-opt justice with money. They are defendants, go-betweens and anyone else who takes out a wallet. *Alap-alap* is a kind of hawk that preys on mice.

Sometimes you work things out directly with a judge or

another court official. At other times, you go through your lawyer or a *makelar*.

Makelar, which means broker in Dutch, is a go-between who relays messages or offers bribes to judges, and seeks information from them.

Some go-betweens are so casual that you can overhear them bargaining with judges and clients on their mobile phones in the hot, sticky halls of courthouses.

❀ Ninabobok
Lullaby.

It can also refer to deceiving, or lulling someone into a false sense of security. *Ninabobok* was popular among pro-democracy activists who warned that politicians who touted reform during election campaigns might renege on promises once in office.

"Don't be lulled into a false sense of security by those campaign promises," the activists said.

Jangan dininabobokkan oleh janji-janji kampanye.

Bobok is a child's word for sleep. Mothers sang:

Ninabobok, kalau tidak bobok digigit nyamuk.

"Lullaby. If you don't go to sleep, you'll be bitten by mosquitoes."

The composer of the lullaby is unknown. One theory about the origin of *nina* in *ninabobok* is that it comes from *menina*, which means little girl in Portuguese.

Bobok siang (daytime nap) is a slang term for a love affair.

Chapter Six

Protest Fever

Street demonstrations swelled in the last months of Suharto's rule. The protesters wanted the ouster of the president, an end to corruption, and democracy.

✺ Demo
Street protest.

Demonstrations helped end President Suharto's rule in 1998, and they flourished during the chaotic transition to democracy. Protesters slapped on headbands, waved banners, chanted until they were hoarse, tied up traffic and tangled with police. Indonesia has tolerated most peaceful *demo* since the fall of Suharto, who viewed free expression as a threat to his authoritarian rule.

Demo is a noun or a verb.

"Let's demonstrate!" a protester cries. *Ayo demo!*

Since the upheaval of 1998, the term *demo* has been mainly associated with street protests. It also appears in other contexts. A celebrity chef cooks up a recipe in a mall or on television in *demo masak* (cooking show).

A formal term for demonstration is *unjuk rasa* (show of feelings). Newspapers use it, as do student speakers at a rally. The expression dates to protests against Dutch colonial rule, and against foreign debt in the decade after independence. Military-backed *unjuk rasa* in the 1960s put pressure on President Sukarno, Suharto's predecessor.

In the 1960s, farmers and activists who demonstrated for land reform faced *unjuk otot* (show of muscles): violent crackdowns by police and security teams hired by landowners.

The term *demo* took off in the 1990s because young Indonesians who swarmed into the streets thought the English slang was hipper and snappier than the staid *unjuk rasa*.

Aksi, another word for demonstration, also refers to political street theater.

"When will you take action again?" a reporter asks student leaders. *Kapan aksi lagi?*

Protes, the Indonesian version of protest, is another option. Authorities disliked it because of its strong connotations of opposing the state.

During the Suharto era, only die-hard opponents demonstrated, risking harassment, imprisonment, beatings and torture such as electrocution.

Some fought for the rights of villagers who were evicted from land so that state or private developers could build projects such as a huge reservoir and a car-racing track.

Then came demos that shook the foundations of Suharto's power. Once democratic reforms took hold, any issue was worth a street march: students protested against corruption, poor pedicab drivers demanded permits to work in city streets, Muslim activists demonstrated against the U.S. war in Iraq, and transvestites rallied against negative television coverage of their lifestyle.

Some demonstrators rode around town on bus roofs, raising a ruckus. Others benefited from *bisnis demo*, the rent-a-mob racket. *Kampung demo* (demo villages) produced recruits—mostly laborers, farmers or the unemployed. A *korlap* (an acronym for *KoORdinator LAPangan*, or field coordinator) paid them a small fee and threw in lunch. He hired buses to transport them to the

demo site, and handed out *atribut demo*—signs and T-shirts emblazoned with slogans. Happy with pocket change and free grub,
some demonstrators yelled rehearsed chants without knowing
much about the cause.

Some political and business figures commissioned protesters
to back their interests. Rowdy crowds outside courthouses or in
courtrooms served as tools to sway public opinion, or pressure
judges, prosecutors and witnesses.

**FORKOT. BEMI. SMJ CEKAL. FKSMJ. BEM UI. BEM
UNPAD. BEM UNPAR. FAM. GERAM. HMI-NPO.**
These are acronyms of student groups that became prominent
at the end of Suharto's rule, and during the democratic reforms
that followed. Activists rarely got an early start. They joked that
waking up was as much of a hassle as harassment by state security
forces. They discussed politics until dawn, pooling cash to buy
snacks and cigarettes. When eyelids grew heavy, they gulped
down coffee, passing the cup around the circle.

Under Suharto, a former army general, the military enjoyed
dwi fungsi, a "dual function" of securing the nation, and playing a
political role. The armed forces had a quota of pro-government
legislators in Parliament. The military guarded the nation's bor-
ders, and also policed the country.

Students joked that they too were *dwi fungsi*, pursuing democracy as well as the demands of their libido. Romances blossomed
during the street protests in Suharto's last days as president.

A Sampling of Slogans

Students unleashed a barrage of slogans at demonstrations. They
invented their own, or borrowed from the struggle against Dutch
colonialists in the last century. Nationalists declared indepen-

dence at the end of World War II and took up arms. The Dutch gave up their claim to their former colony in 1949.

A sampling of street slogans:

❀ Reformasi
Reform.

The rallying cry of huge protests against Suharto. By April 1998, the word was on banners, posters, newspapers and wall graffiti. Students painted it on their faces and bodies. They shouted four syllables, staccato-style: "REH! FOR! MAH! SIH!"

Reformasi started out as a yearning for openness (*keterbukaan*), a moderate appeal for more freedom of expression, including the right to stage protests. Then it became a demand for outright *demokrasi*, a radical overhauling of Indonesia's authoritarian system.

For idealists, *reformasi* evolved into an all-encompassing remedy for Indonesia's ills. People wanted reform of the law, economy and education; free elections and abolition of the military's influence on politics; reduction in the prices of staples such as rice and cooking oil; elimination of corruption; trials for those responsible for kidnapping students and other activists. The list went on.

At first, the broad concept unified groups with different agendas. Even its main target, Suharto, tried to harness its appeal. On March 1, 1998, he said in his last State of the Nation address that the government was conducting economic *reformasi*. But, Suharto acknowledged, the situation was not improving. He was silent about the groundswell of protests and riots around the country.

The goal for many protesters was personal. *Reformasi* meant: Get rid of Suharto.

The term *reformasi* got global exposure, retaining its original form in international media reports. It spread to Malaysia, where a political reform movement was also underway. At a regional summit in Kuala Lumpur in November 1998, U.S. Vice President Al Gore hinted at the need for political change in Malaysia with a reference to *reformasi*. The comment infuriated his hosts.

Indonesia's first direct presidential election in 2004 was a *reformasi* milestone. The first vote and a runoff were peaceful.

Many problems remain, including poverty, corruption, environmental damage and sectarian tension in some areas. Protests continue, but they are less of a national pastime.

❀ Gugur satu, tumbuh seribu
One falls, a thousand others grow.

The slogan is a line in a mournful song called *Gugur Bunga* (Fallen Flowers). Musician Ismail Marzuki wrote it in honor of fallen independence heroes during the fight against Dutch colonizers. An arts center in Jakarta is named after Marzuki, whose statue stands at the gate.

The phrase took on fresh political meaning on May 12, 1998, when students held an anti-government protest at the prestigious Universitas Trisakti in Jakarta. Security forces opened fire from a highway overpass, killing six students. The deaths shocked Indonesia and triggered rioting that killed hundreds of people in the days that followed. Many were looters trapped in burning shopping centers. The unrest helped topple Suharto.

The media invoked the phrase *gugur satu, tumbuh seribu* to say the Trisakti students had not died in vain.

The expression also surfaces in daily language. Mothers might say it to children whose hearts have been broken in a romantic affair. The mothers mean: there are plenty of other fish in the sea.

The verb "die" takes different forms in Indonesian. *Gugur* often applies to a hero who falls, or perishes honorably, on the battlefield. Newspapers used the more neutral *tewas* if a rebel from Aceh province or a combatant in some other conflict zone died in battle. The military preferred potent terms in reports on rebel deaths.

"We've succeeded in paralyzing a separatist," they said. *Berhasil melumpuhkan seorang separatis.*

Meninggal is the version of die that applies to most people. *Mati* (die) is for animals, though it can be used in a casual way for people.

❀ Bersatu kita teguh, bercerai kita runtuh
United we are strong, scattered we fall.

This rallying cry, an echo of the American revolutionary cry, helped define a national identity during the struggle for independence. It countered Dutch efforts to play off Indonesian factions against one another. It was also invoked during the political reforms and upheaval under Indonesia's first president, Sukarno. Decades later, the slogan inspired unity among students in the campaign to topple Suharto and pursue *reformasi* after his fall.

The phrase ties in with the national motto *Bhinneka Tunggal Ika* (Unity in Diversity, in old Javanese), a call for cohesion among the Indonesian people. The motto was penned by Empu Tantular, a 14th century scholar in the Hindu kingdom of Majapahit, which dominated virtually the entire archipelago. Today, the motto appears on a banner in the talons of the Garuda, a mythical bird of prey that is the country's national mascot.

Many public places—government offices, schools, and even tiny barber shops—have pictures of the president on the right, the vice president on the left, and the Garuda in the middle.

Padamu negeri, kami berjanji,
To you, my country, we pledge,

Padamu negeri, kami berbakti,
To you, my country, we devote ourselves,

Padamu negeri, kami mengabdi,
To you, my country, we serve,

Bagimu negeri, jiwa raga kami,
For you, my country, our body and soul.

A patriotic song that Indonesian kids memorize at state and private schools, and sing at obligatory flag ceremonies every Monday morning. State-run television wraps up at midnight with a broadcast of the slow, somber song by an orchestra and choir. Activists coopted the verse, bellowing the lyrics at street rallies. The song is so familiar and evocative that many protesters wept when they sang it.

Composer Kusbini wrote the song, *Bagimu Negeri*, as a tribute to the independence struggle in the 1940s. Kusbini was also a noted musician of *keroncong*, a guitar-based music with Portuguese roots. His friends called him *buaya keroncong* (*keroncong* crocodile).

On its own, *buaya* can be derogatory slang for a womanizer or a trickster. In Kusbini's case, it was a compliment. He attacked his guitar with the gusto of a crocodile attacking its prey.

❀ Turunkan harga
Reduce the price.

Another crowd-rousing slogan in the last months of Suharto's rule. After years of growth, the Indonesian currency plunged, the economy shrank, and the International Monetary Fund stepped in with a multibillion-dollar bailout. Loyalty to the president eroded. The slogan became a rallying cry in early 1998 after the government raised prices of staples, including milk, rice and cooking oil. An activists' group called Voice of Concerned Mothers (*Suara Ibu Peduli*) warned that malnutrition threatened many children.

Some activists indulged in the Indonesian love of acronyms and invented another meaning for the slogan. *Harga* (price) became an abbreviation for *Harto dan keluarga* (Suharto and family).

So *turunkan harga* also meant "Down with Suharto and family!"

One of the most confrontational rallying cries was "Hang Suharto" (*Gantung Suharto*).

Suharto's corruption trial was called off in August 2000 after judges accepted his doctors' diagnosis that he had suffered brain damage because of strokes.

❀ Revolusi sampai mati
Revolution until death.

After Suharto's ouster, many students discarded their headbands and rolled up their banners. Plenty felt there was work ahead. Indonesians had toppled a dictator, but had a hard time maintaining the *reformasi* drive. The military was still powerful in politics, corruption was widespread, and Suharto was a free man.

The student movement lost steam, and fewer people turned up at rallies. Many who did were a harder breed who thought the slow, evolutionary pace of *reformasi* should be replaced by a speedier *revolusi* (revolution). Their cries became radical.

"Revolution until death!" they shouted. *Revolusi sampai mati!*

The phrase is a line in a catchy protest song, and an offshoot of *Merdeka atau mati!* (Liberty or death!), a motto of Indonesia's anti-colonial struggle that comes from the American independence movement.

"Give me liberty or give me death!" the American patriot and orator Patrick Henry said in a 1775 speech. Some Indonesian patriots wrote the phrase in English on walls in Jakarta.

In the 1920s, young Indonesian nationalists studied in Europe, showing interest in the histories of the American and French revolutions.

Merdeka atau mati was a popular graffiti on walls and train carriages in 1945, the year that Indonesia declared independence from Dutch rule. Sukarno, an independence leader who became Indonesia's first president, said it at the end of a speech on June 1, 1945 to Indonesian leaders. That day is now commemorated as the birth of Pancasila, Indonesia's state ideology. In those days, Indonesian nationalists greeted each other with a cry of *Merdeka!* (Liberty!). Today, elderly war veterans salute each other with this greeting.

Students in the late 1990s borrowed slogans of their forefathers, invoking the idea that they were fighting for the soul of the nation, as well as against the government of the day. Indonesians already knew the old mottoes, which popped up in songs and poems.

Indonesians who grew weary of constant rallies joked that protesters shouted "Revolution until death!" because they yearned to be eternal students, on the streets forever. Indonesian students can take a long time to finish undergraduate degrees. The rules tightened in the 1990s with the announcement of a deadline of seven years. Akbar Tandjung, a former Suharto ally and ex-parliamentary speaker, finished his degree in a decade because he was busy with his 1960s passion: student activism.

Tandjung protested against communism, high prices and expensive projects such as the construction of monuments and a stadium. The demonstrations in which he took part helped topple President Sukarno.

In 2002, Tandjung was sentenced to three years in jail for corruption. The Supreme Court overturned the conviction in 2004.

❀ Turun gunung
Go down the mountain.

Student protests gained legitimacy when alumni, lecturers, professors and even rectors gave support. Ensconced in their ivory towers, such respected figures chose to *turun gunung* and join the raucous masses.

Student leaders duly introduced them to the crowd, handed them a microphone and told them to speak from a makeshift podium. Many scholars liked the spotlight. Others found it awkward.

The dean of Universitas Indonesia, a top university where students wear canary yellow jackets, was once given the mike. He wasn't the fiery, rabble-rousing type and didn't last long. Students politely took the mike and handed it to Amien Rais, a reformist leader with honed rhetorical skills.

Professors and other academics rarely joined rallies before 1998. Some rectors expelled students if they took to the streets.

❋ Intel
Undercover agent of the security forces.

Under Suharto, plainclothes officers infiltrated anti-government rallies and yanked protesters out of a crowd. Activists feared and loathed *intel*. Sometimes it was easy to spot *intel*, especially those with short, military-style haircuts. The crackle of a police radio tucked under a jacket gave away a clumsy one. Students jumped the hapless agent, swinging fists. The terrified infiltrator pulled a pistol and fired warning shots to ward off the mob. Sometimes, frenzied protesters pummeled the wrong man.

Intel operate in post-authoritarian Indonesia, and their image has softened. Their methods are less heavyhanded, and protests have become smaller, less frequent and more peaceful. Many Indonesians regard *intel* with respect because of their role in the fight against Islamic militants.

During pro-democracy protests, students also referred to undercover agents as *kijang satu* (small antelope one). They lifted this nickname after hearing *intel* communicate with uniformed handlers with the radio codeword *kijang satu*.

Brazen students said the military were *monyet* (monkeys). To police clad in bulky body armor and visor-equipped helmets, the swarms of puny protesters were *semut* (ants) or *kancil* (mousedeer).

❋ Provokator
Agitator.

From the French *agent provocateur*, one who incites others to do things that could invite punishment.

During a rambunctious student rally, somebody hurled a rock at police or a building, and dozens of projectiles followed. Police unleashed tear gas, baton charges, rubber bullets and, on occasion, live ammunition. Student leaders sometimes blamed *provokators* in their midst: alleged state agents who lobbed a stone and then fled, giving authorities an excuse to crack down. State officials were quick to slap the *provokator* label on anti-government figures.

———————

Another term for agitator or troublemaker is *tukang kompor* (stove worker). This character brings things to a boil. The expression also refers to someone who gossips about private lives.

Lempar batu, sembunyi tangan (throw stones, hide hands) is about more than the custom of stone-throwing at protests or riots. It sums up any effort to sabotage an undertaking, and shirk responsibility.

✵ Tinggal gelanggang colong playu
"Run away from the forum/pit" = Shirk responsibility.

An event takes place in an open forum, and you shouldn't abandon your role and walk away.

In 1998, Suharto faced growing calls for his resignation. At first, he said he would serve the rest of his five-year term until 2003 because the highest legislative assembly, which he controlled, demanded that he stay. He said he could not run away from his responsibilities (*lari dari kewajibannya*).

Many supporters said Suharto should have the chance to pull the country through its crisis. They said he would not abandon his responsibilities (*tinggal gelanggang colong playu*). Citing the same phrase, his opponents said: Dump him. He won't live up to his promises.

Suharto finally relented, handing power to his protégé and former technology minister, B.J. Habibie, on May 21, 1998.

❁ TOPP
Tua, Ompong, Peot, Pikun.
Old, toothless, wrinkled, senile.

Suharto said this acronym in a self-deprecating way. His message was that he was unworthy of the office of president because he was old and ordinary. Many people thought Suharto was insincere, and that he was trying to undercut pressure to resign by appearing humble. Also, the acronym signaled that he was still very much in power, or on *TOPP*.

Indonesian politicians often put on a show of modesty, claiming they were unworthy of election. It was never their wish to hold power, but the wish of the people, they said. To acknowledge political ambition was crass. This custom is still widespread, but less so than in the Suharto days.

❁ Lengser keprabon (Javanese)
Abdicate from the throne.

On May 14, 1998, Suharto said he was prepared to quit (*lengser keprabon*) if he lost the trust of the people. It was unclear whether Suharto meant it, or was putting on a show of humility. *Lengser keprabon* is a theme from Javanese folklore about kings and dynastic struggles.

Using other Javanese terms, Suharto said he would become a sage (*ngadeg pandita*) and would guide the country from behind the scenes (*tut wuri handayani*).

The latter expression was the credo of the national teachers' association. In traditional Javanese culture, it is better to guide students from the background, rather than barking orders up front.

These expressions allude to Abiyasa, an elderly king from the mythical country Astina who abdicated from the throne and advised his children.

The story is from the *Mahabharata*, an epic tale from India that influenced folklore in Indonesia. Suharto used mythology to convey power and legitimacy in the tradition of Javanese kings.

Many Indonesians were reluctant to openly refer to Suharto's possible fate with words like *turun* (resign) and *jatuhkan* (topple).

Like their president, Indonesian officials hedged their bets until the end and spoke in allusions. In a May 16, 1998 interview on private television, Cabinet Minister Sarwono Kusumaatmadja said: "If the tooth is rotten and has holes here and there, why should we bother to fill it. Just pull it out."

Kalau gigi sudah sakit dan berlobang di sana-sini, buat apa kita harus repot-repot menambalnya, cabut saja.

Everyone knew he was speaking about Suharto. It was a daring comment. The uneasy channel directors cut the interview and went on a commercial break.

Suharto resigned five days later.

❈ Ngono ya ngono, ning aja ngono (Javanese)
"Do whatever you want, but don't overdo it" = Don't let differences undermine group harmony.

Suharto said this many times. Some Javanese used the term in Suharto's defense after he resigned under pressure. They watched as students fought police near the former president's home to press demands that he be tried on charges of corruption and human rights abuses. Some Indonesians felt the students had gone too far, and that Suharto should be left alone for the sake of harmony in their troubled country.

❄ **Mikul dhuwur, mendem jero** (Javanese)
"Carried high, buried deep" = Remember good deeds, and be silent about the bad.

Parents, or the dead, are usually the subject of this expression. A child who disapproves of his parents' conduct should praise them, not sully their reputation. Some Javanese parents urged their children to forgive Suharto, who had once enjoyed a paternal image. Student activists ignored the wisdom of *mikul dhuwur mendem jero* after Suharto resigned, demanding that he be put on trial. Their campaign was unsuccessful.

While in power, Suharto followed the wisdom of the expression. As an army general in the 1960s, he accumulated power and undermined President Sukarno, yet later refrained from besmirching the name of his predecessor. Suharto recognized that Sukarno was a nationalist symbol for many, and that overt criticism could alienate Indonesians. Still, Suharto tamped down pro-Sukarno sentiment, barring Indonesians from displaying his image or holding big commemorations on the anniversary of his death.

❄ **Kos** (or **Kost**)
One-bedroom lodging.

After an afternoon of street protest, many activists returned to *kos*, one-bedroom lodgings rented monthly by students or working singles. The kitchen and bathroom are shared.

Kos also refers to the lodger.

"I'm a paying guest in one-bedroom digs," a student says. *Saya kos*.

A slang equivalent is *saya ngekos*. "I am renting one-bedroom digs."

Kos comes from the Dutch *in de kost*, meaning "boarding in a family home."

Kos are in renovated houses with several rooms furnished only with mattresses, with tenants sharing communal bathrooms and kitchen; rows of specially built terraced houses; or plush serviced residences with cable television, 24–hour food service, private bathroom and pool.

An *Ibu kos* oversees the lodgings. Some apply strict rules at women-only accommodations, barring male visitors from stepping any further than the front porch.

Today, most *kos* are relaxed. Despite the lack of privacy, they're the first taste of freedom for students, many of whom are leaving home for the first time. They gossip, play guitars and make love. Politics was a big topic of discussion in the late 1990s, but student activism has faded.

Nasib Anak Kost (The fate of the Kost Children) was a 1990s hit by Indonesia's P-Project pop group, which came from the student city of Bandung. The lyrics are about sharing food and a bathroom, without money or privacy.

———————

Indonesia's first president, Sukarno, wrote about living *indekost* while studying at a Bandung university in the 1920s. His days were full of lively meetings with fellow students and independence activists. His arrival energized his *ibu kos* (lodging mother, or landlady), Inggit Ganarsih. She served cakes and coffee to Sukarno's friends during all-night discussions.

Sukarno, whose first marriage was annulled, had a love affair with Inggit. She was married and in her early 30s when she met Sukarno, who was 12 years younger. She left her husband, the owner of the boarding house, and married Sukarno. Inggit supported Sukarno during his student days by selling traditional herbs and face powder.

Sukarno became infatuated with a younger woman, Fatmawati, and asked Inggit to allow him to take a second wife. Inggit refused and they divorced. Fatmawati, who married Sukarno, sewed the Indonesian red and white flag that was hoisted when nationalists declared independence in 1945. She also gave birth to Megawati Sukarnoputri, who became president. Sukarno, who later left Fatmawati, had at least six wives.

Chapter Seven

A History of Violence

Soldiers and separatists, militias and terrorists. Mobs running amok. Indonesia is no stranger to upheaval.

✿ Konfrontasi
Confrontation.

Indonesia's first president, Sukarno, had testy ties with the West. He labeled his 1960s campaign against Malaysia: *Konfrontasi*. Sukarno regarded his newly independent neighbor as a front for British colonial meddling in Southeast Asia. Indonesian troops and militias infiltrated Malaysian territory on Borneo island, but didn't make much headway against British and Commonwealth soldiers. Fighting ended after Sukarno lost power.

When hostilities between Indonesia and Malaysia ceased in 1966, the two countries with similar languages agreed to craft a unified spelling system. The new spelling system finally took effect in 1972. Some differences in spelling, as well as pronunciation and vocabulary, remain.

Decades after *Konfrontasi*, the Indonesian language is full of Western influences. *Volatilitas* means volatility, *solusi* is solution, *tiket* is ticket, *globalisasi* is globalization. There's *demokrasi*, *tradisi*, *kriminal*, and *polusi*. *Krisis total* becomes an abbreviated *kris-tal*.

Some borrowed terms anger Indonesian linguists who say they defile the Indonesian language, a symbol of national pride during the struggle against Dutch colonizers. The experts say the uncontrolled influx of English into Indonesian makes it hard for Indonesians who don't know English to communicate.

Indonesians sometimes garble the spelling and pronunciation of English words that they adopt, or give them different meanings. *Isu* is from the English issue, but it means rumors or gossip in Indonesian.

✻ Pagar betis
The fence of shins.

Indonesia invaded the former Portuguese colony of East Timor in 1975. The military bombed rebel hideouts in the jungles and mountains, and conducted other large-scale operations against pro-independence forces. One of them was a tactic called *pagar betis*. Soldiers forced thousands of civilians to march through the undergrowth in an effort to flush hidden rebels into the open or push them into Indonesian forces. Dutch colonial troops are said to have used the same tactic, and today *pagar betis* is a slang term for a line of student activists who keep order at street demonstrations.

Pagar betis has also long referred to relatives who form a human corridor for newly weds entering a reception hall, especially in traditional Javanese weddings.

———

As many as 200,000 East Timorese and thousands of Indonesian troops died in the 24-year conflict. It ended in 1999 when East Timorese voted for independence in a United Nations referendum, triggering deadly violence by militias linked to the Indonesian military. The U.N. administered East Timor until it became independent in 2002.

❀ Kerikil di sepatu
A pebble in our shoe.

This is how Ali Alatas, foreign minister under Suharto, described East Timor. His point was that the tiny, half-island territory was a minor irritation for Indonesia despite the international outcry over human rights violations there.

On Nov. 12, 1991, Indonesian soldiers with M-16 rifles opened fire on pro-independence supporters who had gathered for a funeral at Santa Cruz cemetery in Dili, East Timor's capital. Hundreds were killed or injured, and witnesses said soldiers bayoneted some victims. Some people escaped by jumping over the cemetery walls. Indonesia blandly described the massacre as *peristiwa* (an incident). The killings at Santa Cruz stirred international criticism of Indonesia, and Alatas was dogged by questions about East Timor on overseas trips.

❀ Maubere (Tetum)
A boy.

Portuguese colonizers often addressed any East Timorese male as *maubere*, rather than by name. The use of *maubere* became a symbol of colonial arrogance. But the territory's independence movement turned the word into a symbol of a people's struggle against Indonesian occupation. *Maubere* became the namesake of many activist groups. Jose Alexandre Gusmao, the guerrilla leader who became East Timor's first president, wrote a poem with the title *Maubere*.

Ami isim Maubere, klamar mos Maubere goes the refrain of a protest song in East Timor's Tetum language. "My body is Maubere, my pulse is Maubere."

Bapak is the Indonesian word for father, but can mean Sir

or Mister. East Timorese shortened it to *bapa* to make a catchall term for any Indonesian male.

❊ Xanana (pronounced *Za-na-na*)

Sha Na Na, the American rock and roll band, inspired the nom de guerre of Jose Alexandre Gusmao, the rebel who became president. Gusmao, a former teacher, radio reporter and poet who rose through rebel ranks as leaders were killed, was a fan of the group during its heyday in the 1970s.

Gusmao was captured in 1992. Imprisoned in Jakarta, he communicated with Kirsty Sword, a former ballet student from Australia who worked as an undercover messenger for East Timor's independence movement. Sword's codename in the separatist underground was Ruby Blade. She chose Ruby because it reminded her of the cloak-and-dagger plots common to Agatha Christie novels, and Blade because it was similar to her surname. Gusmao was released in 1999, and soon after the separatist leader married the clandestine courier. Her name is now Kirsty Sword Gusmao.

One of Gusmao's field commanders was *Falur Rate Laek*, or Pigeon Without a Grave in Tetum. Another was *Lere Anan Timur*, or Child of the East, a reference to the area of East Timor where he operated.

Americo Ximenes, who became head of East Timor's military academy, had the nickname *Sabica besi kulit*. *Sabica* is a covering. *Besi kulit* is iron skin. His men declared that whatever he wore served as armor, shielding him from bullets.

Some of Gusmao's lieutenants wore berets, sunglasses, bushy beards and thick mustaches. They bore some resemblance to Che Guevara, whose stenciled image adorned some buildings in

East Timor. Traditional animist beliefs may have been the main influence on the guerrillas' appearance. Warriors did not shave their beards or cut their hair because they believed it would render them vulnerable to the enemy. Also, there probably wasn't much incentive to keep themselves shaven and groomed while conducting a guerrilla war.

The Indonesian military said guerrillas were *GPK*, or *Gerombolan Pengacau Keamanan* (Security Agitator Gang).

❋ Pat ujeun nyang han pirang, pat prang nyang han reuda (Acehnese)
No rain ever stops, and no war ever ends.

Aceh, a province on the northern tip of Sumatra, is accustomed to conflict. In 1873, Dutch colonial troops invaded Aceh and war dragged on intermittently for decades. A century later, separatists in the staunchly Muslim province took up arms against the Indonesian government. In 1989, President Suharto imposed martial law in Aceh, and the military under his successors continued the battle.

A lot was at stake in Aceh, a region rich in oil and gas, and the central government feared separatist success could encourage secessionists in other regions. Then the tsunami struck on Dec. 26, 2004, and the trauma and devastation prompted the adversaries to seek peace. Under an accord, Acehnese separatists dropped their demand for independence in return for wide autonomy.

Rebels drew inspiration from the glory of Sultan Iskandar Muda, who ruled Aceh in the 17th century and held sway over much of Sumatra and parts of the Malay peninsula. His land became a center of trade and Islamic learning.

Hasan di Tiro, the elderly leader of the rebel movement,

claimed he was a direct descendant of the sultan. Di Tiro lived in exile in Sweden from the 1970s until 2009, when he returned to Acheh after Indonesia granted him amnesty. He died a year later.

Rebels based in Sweden used an English name for their group: the Acheh/Sumatra National Liberation Front (ASNLF). They spoke Malay, Acehnese or English, and usually refused to speak Indonesian. The rebels in Aceh spoke Indonesian sometimes and accepted the Indonesian name for their group, *Gerakan Aceh Merdeka* (*GAM*), or Free Aceh Movement.

Separatist fighters preferred spellings of their region—Acheh, or Atjeh—that came before the 1972 spelling system introduced during Suharto's rule.

Many rebel leaders and spokesmen liked people to address them as *tengku*, a Malay term for a respected Islamic figure or someone related to the sultan's family. Some civilians in Aceh grumbled that you just had to hold a gun to be called *tengku*.

❀ Hom (Acehnese)
"Don't know" = Who knows? No idea. Beats me.

Hom was a survival mechanism for Aceh's civilians, who got caught in the conflict between the military and separatist rebels. Human rights abuses were frequent. Indonesian security forces swept through villages and interrogated the locals.

"Who killed this man?" the soldiers said. *Siapa yang bunuh lelaki ini?*

The villagers claimed ignorance. *Hom*, they said.

Who burned down this building? *Hom.*

Who set off these bombs? *Hom.*

Some villagers knew the answers. Maybe they supplied the rebels, or helped them hide, or served as lookouts. Others had no part in the conflict. All knew they could face abuse or even death if they admitted involvement, or rebel retribution if they cooperated.

Kande, an Acehnese band, sang about the dilemma of civilians in a 2003 number called *Hom*. The group wasn't popular outside Aceh, though national television stations broadcast *Kande* tunes in reports on the conflict.

The band named itself after a traditional lamp holder from Aceh, a symbol of light and hope for the province's people.

Indonesia used to crack down on music that it deemed subversive by jailing musicians, producers and consumers. The government toned down its approach after the end of authoritarian rule. It urged musicians and producers to shun anti-state songs. The effort was a failure.

❀ Disekolahkan

"To be schooled, or sent to school" = To be shot to death.

Indonesian soldiers sometimes said this phrase to intimidate local residents, according to civilians in Aceh.

In 2003, a military tribunal in Aceh sentenced three soldiers to several months in jail for raping four girls. One girl testified that the soldiers had warned the victims that they would be "sent to school," or killed, unless they succumbed to the sexual assault.

The military said its goal was to "reeducate" or "school" suspected rebels or sympathizers so they could become good citizens of Indonesia. Detainees took a three-month program called *pembinaan* (guidance lessons). They learned Indonesian history and ideology.

State-run schools taught Indonesian history as well as state ideology, and were a potent symbol of Indonesian influence in Aceh. Rebels sometimes occupied them, held hasty press conferences and staged flag ceremonies for the cameras. They slipped away before the military arrived.

During a big operation in May 2003, Indonesia sent tanks, warships and jet fighters to Aceh. In an apparent response, suspected separatists torched dozens of schools across the province. In the past, rebels had admitted burning school libraries containing Indonesian history books.

Guerrillas had their own version of history. They said an Anglo-Dutch treaty in the early 19th century recognized Aceh's sovereignty, and that the Dutch had no right to hand over the province when Indonesia became independent. They referred to the central government in Jakarta as *Kolonialis Jawa* (Javanese colonialists).

Another civilian term for shot to death was *disukabumikan*. *Suka* means like and *bumi* is earth. The sardonic expression, which translates literally as "made to like earth," suggested the victim wanted to be buried.

A similar term was *dibalikpapankan*, or "to be on the other side of the board." *Balik* is other side and *papan* is board. In a Muslim grave, several wooden boards lie on a corpse, which is wrapped in a white shroud.

✸ Kameng gampong nyang keunong geulawa (Acehnese) "It's the village goat that takes a beating" = The innocent take the rap.

A wild goat tramples a fence and munches on a vegetable patch before trotting up the mountain slope. The tethered goat on the premises gets saddled with the blame.

The Indonesian translation of this expression—*Kambing kampung yang kena pukul*—is the name of a 1999 Indonesian movie drama about Aceh's conflict by first-time filmmaker Aryo Danusiri. He saw a parallel between the domestic goat and villagers trapped in the conflict. Rebels conducted raids and withdrew to jungle sanctuaries, and the frustrated Indonesian military rounded up civilians in their wake.

❀ Tameng hidup

"Live shields" = Human shields.

In Aceh, rebels and the Indonesian military accused each other of deterring enemy fire by forcing women and children onto the frontlines of firefights. The tactic was reminiscent—on a far smaller scale—of the "fence of shins" that the Indonesian military used in East Timor.

It was difficult to confirm charges that combatants used civilians as cover. Each side also claimed to inflict heavy casualties. The propaganda war was as vigorous as the shooting one.

❀ Operasi Shock and Awe

In April 2003, the Pentagon announced a "shock and awe" campaign of bombing to stun Iraqi forces into surrender. A month later, the Indonesian military borrowed the term to describe its latest campaign in Aceh.

"Our shock and awe campaign has started," military commanders said. *Operasi shock and awe kami sudah mulai.*

On the first day, the press assembled as Indonesian jet fighters blasted a suspected rebel weapons cache on a hillside. Smoke billowed from palm-fringed rice fields and abandoned plantations. The results were inconclusive.

The Indonesian military adopted the U.S. military program of "embedding" journalists with units in the field. The journalists were dubbed the Sangabuana Group (*Kelompok Sanggabuana*), a reference to the West Javan mountain where they received basic training. Military brass used the English term "embedding" in conversation, but not in official writings.

The military drew on punchy rhetoric from the bloody crack-down on the Indonesian Communist Party in the mid-1960s. Commanders said they want to annihilate (*basmi*) and crush (*gan-yang*) rebels in Aceh.

Ganyang is an old standby for any Indonesian group that wants radical change. *Ganyang Malaysia!* was a popular slogan when President Sukarno tried to destabilize the neighboring nation in the 1960s. In 1998, student protesters shouted *Ganyang Suharto!* during protests against Sukarno's successor.

❈ Cunguk (Sundanese)
"Cockroach" = Spy. Snitch. Shady character.

This term from West Java once referred to an agent of the Dutch colonial government, and was common among pro-indepen-dence groups in the 1940s. The expression may have migrated to Aceh because of links with the House of Islam (*Darul Islam*), an Islamic rebellion with West Javan roots that fizzled in the 1950s. *Cunguk* survived in Aceh as a label for an Indonesian military spy. It also turned up in activist talk during nationwide protests against President Suharto in 1998.

Acehnese words for spy or traitor are *pang bayak*—a moniker from Dutch colonial days—and *cuak*, which is more common today.

A *cuak* reported to the Indonesian military on villagers' activ-ities or rebel movements, and sometimes took part in arrests and interrogations. Similarly, Dutch armies recruited local guides to root out rebel hideouts in dense forests. In Aceh, the Dutch relied heavily on Indonesian soldiers from other parts of their Southeast Asian colony.

GAM rebels in Aceh had their own spies, some of whom were believed to hold posts in the provincial government. These spies were called *cantoi*, which means "small but troublesome" in Acehnese. A local newspaper, *Serambi Aceh*, borrowed the term for the title of a comic strip, *Gam Cantoi*. The strip poked fun at the conflict, and one character was a village head stuck between the military and the rebels. Both sides extorted money from him.

Concerned about rebel infiltration, Indonesian authorities required provincial officials to take oaths of loyalty to the state. Civil servants in Aceh attended flag ceremonies and signed documents pledging fealty.

Businessmen who were the targets of guerrilla extortion said rebels knew the value of construction projects such as roads. The separatists demanded 10 percent of the value of a deal as a "tax." Authorities surmised that the rebels had spies in the public works department.

———

Pang Laut Ali was the bodyguard of Cut Nyak Dhien, a female separatist commander in Aceh who fought the Dutch. Pang Laut betrayed his ailing chief, and she was detained. Some speculate that he surrendered her on condition that she receive medical treatment and remain in Aceh. Others say Pang Laut sold her out for personal gain.

The Dutch exiled her to West Java, where she died in 1908. Adopted as nationalist hero after her death, Cut Nyak Dhien was called Mother Queen (*Ibu Perdu*) and The Queen of Jihad (*Ratu Jihad*).

Insurgents' Idioms

❀ **Boh Jantung** (Acehnese)
"Fruit of the Heart" = Rocket-propelled grenade launcher.

Rebels said the grenade resembled *jantung pisang* (banana heart), the heart-shaped, red and purple flower of the banana tree. They cherished the grenade launcher, a prized weapon in their arsenal. The peace accord in 2005 required them to turn in their weapons.

❀ **Fatima**
M-16 rifle.

Fatima is a common female Muslim name. Male rebels joked that the rifle was like a woman: you needed one nearby at all hours.

❀ **Kacang kuning** (yellow bean) was a policeman.
Kacang hijau (green bean) was a soldier.

The names referred to the color of the uniforms of Indonesian security forces. Police uniforms were the color of ocher, or soybeans.

❀ **Lembu**
"Cow" = Slang for a military truck.

Like the animal, it was big and slow. Rebels tried to blow up trucks with bombs concealed under bridges and in roadside paddy fields. Sometimes, casualties were unintended: children came across the explosives, and triggered them by accident.

❀ **Inong bale** (Acehnese)
Corps of widows.

Rebels formed a female military wing, *inong bale*. Many female fighters were young. Some lost their husbands in the conflict, and others were unmarried.

Members of *inong bale* served as eyes and ears, collecting information as they loitered in coffee shops, food stalls and open markets.

Rows of female fighters in boots, camouflage uniforms and Islamic headscarves sometimes paraded in front of journalists who visited rebel strongholds. Many women worked in rebel field kitchens or clinics. The tradition of Acehnese women taking up arms to avenge slain husbands is said to date from battles against the Portuguese centuries ago, as well as later struggles against the Dutch.

In May 2003, the military detained a group of girls who said they were tricked into joining rebel weapons training. The girls said they were lured to remote villages by promises that a party would be held. Rebels appeared and coerced them into taking part in a two-week training session. Whatever the truth, the girls had little idea of how to march or hold a gun.

❀ **Tipu Aceh!**
Aceh's fool!

A reference to the frustration of Indonesian soldiers who interrogated villagers about rebel movements. Sometimes the tips were faulty and the troops went on a wild goose chase.

The phrase comes from an Acehnese lyric:

Aceh Tipu, Gurindam Baruih.

"Aceh's dupe, Barus's verse."

In some parts of Sumatra, Acehnese have a reputation as first-class grifters. Baruih is Acehnese for Barus, the Sumatran hometown of renowned intellectuals such as Hamzah Fansuri, a mystical poet in the 16th century.

People from Barus are said to be experts in *gurindam*, rhyming couplets that contain nuggets of wisdom.

According to lore, Indonesian soldiers in Aceh muttered the term as they combed villages and forests for their elusive foe.

"What a waste of time and energy. We're Aceh's fools!" they barked.

Habis waktu dan tenaga. Tipu Aceh!

❀ Menciduk
"To scoop out (water)" = To arrest.

The verb *menciduk* comes from *ciduk* (a dipper). In a conflict, *menciduk* means to scoop out or arrest someone in a hideout. It implies a stakeout, often in a big operation targeting many suspects. Newspaper and official reports described dawn raids in which troops in Aceh made arrests, or "scooped out water." Sometimes, deadly firefights erupted.

❀ Dia dibon dulu
"We're taking him out on loan" = This guy is coming with us.

Indonesian police and soldiers said this when they detained a suspect, either on their own or with the help of civilians. *Bon* is the Dutch word for receipt for goods or services rendered. Security forces give a *bon*, or verbal IOU, to anyone who detains a suspected agitator. Or a soldier turns up at a house, picks up someone and tells the family: *Dia dibon dulu*. The *bon* is an empty promise, and the detainee might get roughed up in custody.

Security forces used the term in Ambon, provincial capital of the Maluku islands, during violence between Muslims and Christians soon after the end of authoritarian rule in 1998. Police and soldiers were supposed to keep the adversaries apart, but picked sides in some cases.

Dia dibon dulu was first used in the 1960s for communist prisoners who were taken from their cells to testify in other court cases. Many did not return, and the term assumed a sinister meaning: removal for summary execution.

Security authorities picked up a prisoner in his cell and yelled out for the benefit of the other inmates: *dia dibon dulu*.

The expression was linked to a case in early 1966, when more than 20 prisoners from the Wiraguna prison in Yogyakarta, Central Java, were taken away at midnight. Their bodies were later found in caves in a nearby mountain.

✸ Bunuh Acang/Bunuh Obet
Kill Acang/Kill Obet.

Common expressions during fighting between Muslims and Christians in Maluku province, known as the Spice Islands during Dutch rule. Violence erupted in 1999 and subsided three years later. Thousands died and many fled their homes.

After the first bout of killing at Christmas 1999, the government sponsored a local television advertisement to promote dialogue between the two camps. The ad depicted two boys, Acang and Obet, urging reconciliation and friendship.

Acang is a nickname for Hasan, a common Muslim name. *Obet* is short for Robert, a Christian name. Both are affectionate names for children.

An Indonesian child with a lisp pronounces Hasan as *acang* (dropping the h, pronouncing s as a c and ending with a nasal sound).

The same child finds it hard to pronounce the r in Robert. *Obet* is easier.

In the advertisement, Acang and Obet were firm friends before fighting started. Then the city divided, and they could no longer play together. Amid the smoke of bonfires, they sought each other out, and embraced.

But when fighting broke out again, the two camps adopted the names as their war cries.

"Down with the Muslims!" Christian mobs shouted during sectarian combat. *Bunuh Acang*!

"Down with the Christians!" Muslim rioters yelled. *Bunuh Obet!*

The local government dropped its television advertisement.

On urban battlefields, Christians wore red clothing, and Muslims wore white, and named their strongholds after these colors. Muslims feared to tread in Christian "red villages" (*kampung merah*), and Muslim "white regions" (*kampung putih*) were no-go zones for Christians.

Some say Christians first wore red because many Christians in Maluku traditionally supported the Indonesian Democratic Party of Struggle, a political party whose flag color was flaming red. Another theory is that fighters thought red symbolized bravery.

Muslims favor white tunics because white is a symbol of purity.

❀ **Lepas panah**

Let go of arrow.

❀ **Bakar batu**

Bake stones.

These are the Indonesian names of traditional ceremonies that end bouts of tribal violence in Papua, Indonesia's easternmost region. The hundreds of ethnic groups in Papua have names for these ceremonies in their own languages, but many understand the Indonesian-language terms.

An eye for an eye, many Papuans believe. If a clan member kills a man from another clan, revenge is justified. The clan of the victim takes up arms. Ancient traditions hold sway, and police and judges don't have much say.

Once the bloodletting has run its course, it is time to make peace. The peacemaking ritual lasts three days, and whole clans and allied tribes show up for the festivities. When the adversaries are cool enough to talk, they negotiate the payment of a traditional fine (*denda adat*) to the first victim's family. The perpetrator usually hands over cash, but can also pay with food or livestock.

Sometimes, more fighting erupts because rivals can't agree on the amount of the fine.

The Nduga and Damal tribes in Timika, a town in the mountains of Papua, held a ceremony for several days in June 2004 to end violence that killed two people on each side.

Tribal elders wore boar tusks in their noses and brightly colored feathers on their heads, and smeared war paint on their faces. Participants slaughtered two wild boars for a feast, and fired arrows into the air (*lepas panah*) in a sign that peace was at hand.

They shared meat, carrots and tubers baked under hot stones

(*bakar batu*), and vowed to stop the bloodshed.

At one stage, warriors from both tribes paraded in battle costume and took turns yelling as they ran up and down a field. A contingent of police and soldiers stood by to make sure things didn't get out of hand.

❋ Apel
Roll call.

In colonial days, Dutch officers conducted roll calls after summoning troops onto a parade ground. Overseers did the same with Indonesian workers before a day's slog on a rubber plantation. They called out names to find out who was absent.

The Indonesian military preserves the term: *apel bendera* (flag roll call), *apel besar* (big roll call), and *apel paripurna* (roll call for all the troops).

Apel tujuhbelasan (17 roll call) is the name of the flag ceremony on Aug. 17, the anniversary of the 1945 declaration of independence from colonial rule. Troops wear spick-and-span uniforms and brandish polished weapons on parade grounds.

Some prison inmates had *apel pagi* (morning roll call) and *apel petang* (evening roll call). Today, teenagers refer to a romantic date as *apel*.

❋ Juklak (acronym)
PetunJUK PeLAKsana
Directions to carry out tasks.

Military officers bark *juklak* at subordinates. Civilian workplaces picked up the term, and many office managers hand out *juklak* to the staff.

The military expression became widespread in government circles after Suharto, a military man, came to power in the 1960s. It set a stern tone in his administration.

Under Suharto's predecessor, Sukarno, government supervisors gave orders at a *brifing*, a variation on the English "briefing." Despite his political aversion to the West, Sukarno peppered speeches with Dutch, French and English terms.

❀ BKO (acronym, pronounced *beh-kah-oh*)
Bawah Kendali Operasi
Under the operational control.

This term refers to auxiliary soldiers sent into a region to help operations run by the local commander. Civilians use the military term to describe a job transfer. An Indonesian journalist whose editor in Jakarta dispatched her to the unsettled province of Aceh sighed:

"Oh, no! I'm being *BKO-ed* to Aceh for three months."
Aduh, aku di-bko-kan ke Aceh untuk tiga bulan.

Indonesian journalists accompanied military units for several months during intense news coverage of a crackdown on rebels in Aceh province in 2003.

❀ Organik
A term for locally based troops.

If a conflict becomes too hot, the military high command in Jakarta sends *non-organik* battalions from other regions, or combat troops from the army's elite strategic reserves (Kostrad) and special forces (Kopassus).

Troops from out of town stir up attention when they roll into an area, and they post slogans on the walls of their barracks such as:

"Don't forget your wives and children."

Jangan lupakan istri dan anak.

"Remember! Remember!"

Ingat! Ingat!

These are appeals to soldiers on the move to be faithful to their families.

✺ Keluarga Besar Kopassus
We are the big family of Kopassus.

This 1980s slogan adorned caps, bags and car bumpers when Kopassus, the military's special forces, enjoyed a fine reputation. At that time, most Indonesians did not know about the excesses of the military because of controls on the press, and they tolerated or approved of their government anyway. The military later lost its luster when its role as a pillar of authoritarian rule, and involvement in corruption and human rights abuses, came under intense scrutiny.

Kopassus comes from *KOmando PASukan KhuSUS* (Special Forces Commando).

✺ PBB (pronounced *peh-beh-beh*)
Pasukan Baris Berbaris
Marching troops.

Boy scouts, civil servants and other groups conducted many flag-raising ceremonies during the Suharto era. The custom continues today, with students goosestepping, yelling orders and running the national flag up a pole on a parade ground.

School children raise the flag every Monday morning. Civil

servants used to do it every Monday, but have scaled back to every 17th day of a month. On the Aug. 17 anniversary of independence, elite students from across Indonesia fly *bendera pusaka* (the sacred flag) at the state palace in front of the president.

The flag was sewn by Fatmawati, a wife of founding President Sukarno, and flown at the declaration of Indonesia's independence in 1945. Guards at the presidential palace brought out the flag in a wooden box every Aug. 17. In 2004, they did not do so for the first time. The faded, tattered flag is now kept in a museum.

❋ **Satgaskam** (acronym)
SATuan tuGAS KeAManan
Security task force.

These toughs include nightclub bouncers, security guards and militia members who sport army fatigues and bandannas in red and white, the national colors.

Political parties, religious groups, thugs, businessmen and celebrities have *satgaskam*, who act as parking attendants, keep a crowd in line or protect the head of the organization during large outdoor events.

❋ **Banser** (acronym)
Barisan ANsor SERbaguna
The multi-function helpers front.

The security force of the youth wing of Nahdlatul Ulama, Indonesia's biggest Muslim organization with a claimed membership of 40 million. The young men wear military fatigues when they are out in force, guarding congresses and other large gatherings.

Jusuf Hasyim, the former head of the group's youth wing and uncle of former president Abdurrahman Wahid, said the security force was formed to confront communism in the 1960s. Hasyim's force was named Banser because the word sounded like Panzer, the World War II-era German tank. It evoked force and power.

Many Indonesians aren't aware of the depth of disgust in other parts of the world toward the Nazis. Indonesian children might wear a T-shirt with a swastika, but their aim is not always to shock. They just don't know what it means.

Ansor is the Indonesian spelling of *ansar*, or "helper" in Arabic.

It came from helpers who aided the Prophet Muhammad when he fled Mecca, his birthplace, to escape persecution after preaching revelations from God and speaking against the polytheism of his fellow citizens.

❀ Kekaryaan
Work, achievement.

The name of the policy backing *dwi fungsi* (dual function), a Suharto-era doctrine allowing the military to take part in politics. *Kekaryaan* gave civilian work to a military official.

Under Suharto, active military officers became governors and took other civilian posts in the government. The policy started in the 1950s and expanded in the 1980s. The military's involvement strengthened state authority, and *dwi fungsi* also kept a lid on ambitious generals by shifting them into civilian jobs where they were less of a threat.

The military's involvement in civilian government exacerbated corruption, and the phenomenon was gradually phased out after the fall of Suharto. Vestiges of the military's influence over politics remained strong. Two former army generals ran for president in 2004.

Kekaryaan no longer exists as a policy. But some office workers refer to job-juggling as *kekaryaan*.

❀ Aman
"Safe" = Free from the threat of chaos and danger.

In military jargon, *aman dan tenteram* (safe and peaceful) refers to a secured or protected area, whether in a combat zone in a guerrilla stronghold or a Jakarta university that hosted student demonstrations. It means the military has pushed out militants or activists, and citizens in the area are presumably safe.

In troubled areas such as Aceh or Ambon, journalists asked the military:

"Which areas are secured?"

Daerah mana yang sudah diamankan?

In the 1960s, the state viewed undesirables as anyone suspected of links to communists; in the 1980s and onwards, separatists posed a big problem; and from 2000, terrorism emerged as an additional concern.

❀ Oknum-oknum
"Individuals" = Undesirables.

A government term for people linked to a disturbance, a security threat, separatist movements, organized crime or terror groups.

The military has used the word to deflect accusations that their institutions orchestrated a disturbance or some other illegal act.

"But it could be rogue individuals in the military," they have said.

Tapi itu mungkin oknum-oknum militer.

Oknum is believed to come from *ukuum*, which means individual in Arabic. Centuries ago, a Portuguese priest, Francisus Xaverius, traveled to Indonesia to spread the gospel. He decided to translate the Bible into Malay, which had Arabic influences. He translated the Holy Trinity as *Satu Allah, Tiga Oknum.* (One God, Three Individuals).

❀ Pasukan siluman
Invisible troups.

A term for shadowy groups, possibly rogue elements of the military, that were blamed for much of Indonesia's unrest in recent years.

Their alleged motive was to destabilize the nation toward the end of Suharto's rule and in the turbulence that followed.

The theory was that "invisible troops" wanted to portray civilian leaders as ineffectual in order to justify a military coup, or at least bolster military influence in affairs of the state. They were accused of instigating riots by Indonesia's poor, shootings or students, mysterious killings of Muslim preachers and shamans on Java, bombings of churches, sectarian violence in the Maluku islands and ethnic conflict in Kalimantan. There were numerous reports of fit men in crew cuts starting riots and speeding off in trucks once the mayhem was underway.

Indonesia is rife with rumors and conspiracy, partly because many violent episodes were never investigated. The speculation about *pasukan siluman* was widely believed in Indonesia, but was never proven.

A government term of these mysterious forces is *OTK*, which has two meanings:

Orang tak dikenal (Unknown persons/group).

Organisasi Tanpa Bentuk (Amorphous organization).

Mob violence in Indonesia is often spontaneous, rather than planned. The word "amok" comes from the Malay *amok*, a reference to a wild, frenzied attack. Crowds often dispense street justice to suspected thieves. In 2006, a Javanese mob killed a young boy and two men accused of stealing a motorcycle. The victims were beaten with clubs and machetes, and then doused with gasoline and set afire.

❀ **Petrus** (acronym)
PEnembak misTeRiUS
The mysterious shootings.

Several thousand people were killed in Jakarta and other major cities in the *petrus* shootings of 1983.

Most were criminals who were seized at night and shot. Corpses were left in streets, apparently to deter potential law-breakers. The brutal campaign led to a drop in crime. In his 1989 ghostwritten autobiography, Suharto described the killings as a "treatment, firm actions" to rid society of delinquents.

He said the killings were "shock therapy"—he used the English term and the Indonesian *terapi goncangan*. The president said he approved of the killings, but he did not admit authorizing them.

Human rights groups called for an investigation, but none was conducted.

Indonesia approved a panel to investigate state-sponsored killings and kidnappings during the Suharto era. The goal was to heal the nation's psychological wounds by finding out the truth, but little progress has been made. Also, the families of some victims feared perpetrators could escape prosecution just by apologizing for their acts. The panel was modeled on South Africa's truth-and-reconciliation commission, which was set up after the end of apartheid.

❈ Jemaah Islamiyah
Islamic Community.

An al-Qaeda-linked terror network accused of carrying out a string of deadly bombings in recent years.

The name of the group was a source of tension between some Indonesian Muslim leaders and supporters of the U.S.-led war on terror. Muslim leaders objected to U.S. condemnation of the group by name, fearing the label reflected badly on the majority of law-abiding Muslims. What if world leaders demanded the destruction of a terrorist group called "The Catholic Church," they argued. Catholics would be up in arms!

Some Muslims urged Indonesia to use another name for JI. They suggested "JI led by Abdullah Sungkar," a reference to the group's late founder. But *Jemaah Islamiyah pimpinan Abdullah Sungkar*, and its acronym JIAS, were a mouthful. JI stuck.

The suspected spiritual head of Jemaah Islamiyah is Abu Bakar Bashir, a Muslim cleric who was released in 2006 after serving two years in jail for his role in a conspiracy that led to the deadly bombings on Bali in 2002.

Prosecutors based accusations that Bashir headed the terrorist group in part on a 40-page manifesto. Bashir said the document, written mostly in Indonesian with some Arabic terms, was riddled with linguistic errors. Bashir, a fluent Arabic speaker, said he would not have made such mistakes.

❀ Detachment Eighty-Eight

The English name of an Indonesian counter-terrorism unit that was inaugurated in 2004. It's also called *Den 88*, a snappier version.

Members of the unit have undergone U.S.-funded training in hostage rescue, bomb disposal and crime scene investigation. In a major triumph, the unit killed Malaysian bombmaker Azahari bin Husin in a raid in East Java in November 2005.

U.S. and Indonesian officials say the name *Detachment 88* came from a linguistic misunderstanding over what Washington calls Anti-Terrorist Assistance, or ATA. To the Indonesian ear, the pronunciation of ATA sounds a lot like "eighty-eight."

Some Indonesian police officers linked to the unit didn't know the origin of the English name, and could only speculate. One said 88 is a lucky number, and another said the number 8, on paper, resembles the shape of a pair of handcuffs.

The number 8 is lucky in Chinese culture. The brushstroke of 8 is an unbroken line. The Chinese hope that luck and fortune will also be eternal.

PART III

Traditions

Chapter Eight

Faith and Fortune

Hinduism and Buddhism arrived in ancient times. Then Islam took over. Christianity made inroads. All mixed with home-grown beliefs and superstitions.

❋ Islam Warni Warni
Multicolored Islam.

A term for the diversity of Islam in Indonesia, which has a reputation for religious tolerance. That religious moderation has come under pressure in recent years from growing conservative influence, outbreaks of sectarian violence and terrorism by Muslim extremists.

A group of Muslims made this phrase the centerpiece of a 2002 campaign for religious moderation. They aired a TV ad showing party scenes from a Muslim circumcision, mixed with footage of women, some bareheaded and others with Muslim headscarves. The tagline was:

Islam warna-warni, tak cuma satu. Banyak ragam saling menghargai.

"Islam is multicolored, not only one. Many varieties, each respecting the other."

Muslims opposing a pluralist approach to Islam said the message insulted their religion. They said: *Islam hanya ada satu. Hanya ada satu Allah. Yang warna-warni itu ummatnya.*

"There is only Islam. There is only one God. Its many colors lie in its people."

Bowing to pressure, television stations pulled the ad. Such pressure from conservative Muslim groups is common, but the government is secular. The country's two biggest Islamic groups—Nahdlatul Ulama and Muhammadiyah—are considered moderate. Extremist views thrive in a small number of Islamic boarding schools called *pesantren*. The vast majority of religious schools are law-abiding.

At least 85 percent of Indonesia's population of more than 235 million are Muslim, making it the world's biggest Muslim country. Christians are the second-largest religious group, followed by Hindus and Buddhists.

Traders first brought Islam to the Indonesian archipelago via India. It combined with Hindu, Buddhist and animist beliefs. The Sunni branch of Islam took hold, and Sufi holy men also established roots. People absorbed Islam and expressed their faith in different ways across the vast region, which has hundreds of ethnic groups.

Today, some pray five times a day, send their children to Islamic boarding schools and pool resources to go on a pilgrimage to Mecca. Other Indonesian Muslims are less rigorous. For example, some Sasak people on Lombok island in central Indonesia observe *waktu telu* (three time) Islam. They only fast for three days during the holy month of Ramadan. They don't pray as much as other Muslims, they don't go to Mecca, and they don't mind eating pork.

Islam KTP refers to Muslims who do not adhere to religious customs. *KTP* is short for *Kartu Tanda Penduduk*, the Resident Identity Card that all Indonesians must carry. The card lists the religion of its holder. So *Islam KTP* means you're Muslim on your ID card, but that's about it.

❀ Jihad
Struggling/striving.

Moderate Muslims say Islamic extremists have co-opted the Arabic word, using it to justify attacks on Western and secular interests. Militants cite Quranic verses as proof that they have a divine mandate to carry out a violent jihad. Books by two men who were convicted in deadly bombings on Bali in 2002 have sold well.

"I Oppose Terrorists," is the title of one of the books, an autobiography. *Aku Melawan Teroris.*

Author Imam Samudra, who was executed in 2008, said the original perpetrators of violence were the United States and its allies. The view resonates among some Indonesian Muslims, who suspected a broad assault on their religion.

Moderates, in turn, have embarked on their own *jihad*: to correct what they view as a distortion of Islam and a misinterpretation of holy texts. They say, for example, that Islam does not condone suicide bombings, and that *jihad* refers to a struggle for a just cause such as spiritual improvement. *Jihad* is not just about "holy war," they say, and any violent *jihad* should be conducted in self-defense.

❀ Anjing menggonggong, kafilah berlalu
"The dog barks, the caravan passes by" = Do what suits you, and ignore the yaps of the critics.

The Arabic *kafilah*, or caravan, referred to a group of nomads or people who go on the *hajj*, the annual pilgrimage to Mecca, Islam's holy site in Saudi Arabia.

When he started preaching, the Prophet Muhammad is said to have kept his composure despite the jeers of skeptics in his hometown, Mecca. The expression compares the critics to dogs. Another story says people in Mecca used to unleash their dogs to harass Muslims who passed their homes.

Muslims say it is *haram*, or unlawful, for a dog's saliva to come into contact with a person. The "contaminated" body part must be washed seven times before the body is deemed clean enough for prayers.

❦ Serambi Mekkah
Veranda of Mecca.

A nickname for Aceh province, on the northern tip of Sumatra island. Indonesian pilgrims once traveled by ship to Mecca, stopping at the Acehnese port of Sabang before crossing the Indian Ocean on the way to the Middle East.

The explorer Marco Polo wrote about an Islamic kingdom, possibly in Aceh, on the north coast of Sumatra in the late 13th century.

Triggered by an earthquake, the Indian Ocean tsunami on December 26, 2004 inflicted the most destruction on Aceh, wiping out coastal towns and villages and killing more than 130,000. Some survivors said the tragedy was a divine punishment for those who had strayed from the path of Islam. As evidence of the power of faith, they pointed to sturdy mosques that withstood the waves while entire blocks of homes around them were swept away.

In the aftermath of the disaster, powerful aftershocks frazzled residents who feared more killer waves.

"Water is rising!" they shouted. *I ek!*

Parents snatched their children and a small bundle of clothes, and rushed to higher ground, on foot or by car or motorbike. There were no more tsunamis, and the panic was unfounded.

Some people said false alarms were raised by thieves who waited until everyone had abandoned their houses before ransacking the empty homes.

Many Acehnese words are one syllable, which prompts jokes that Acehnese are lazy or efficient. It depends on how you want to look at it.

U is coconut, so the clear sweet coconut juice (coconut water) is *i u*. Many tsunami survivors in isolated areas survived on little food for weeks as aid groups raced to supply them with instant noodles, rice and mineral water by helicopter. The Acehnese survived by eating coconut flesh and coconut juice. When that ran out, they chopped the top part of the palm branches and chewed the inner bark. They said it tasted similar to milky, soft wood.

———————

The collection of stories about the words and actions of the Prophet Muhammad are called *hadith*, or *hadis* in Indonesia. Many Indonesian Muslims know the following phrases attributed to Muhammad:

❀ Surga ada di bawah telapak kaki ibu
"Heaven lies under the soles of a mother's feet" = Respect your mother because she makes sure you have the best in life, and the afterlife *(akhirat,* **in Arabic).**

A man who wanted to wage holy war approached the Prophet Muhammad to ask for his permission. Muhammad asked if he had a mother. The man said he did. Muhammad urged him to take care of his mother instead of fighting because heaven lay under the soles of her feet.

Another man asked Muhammad whose word he should follow. Muhammad said: "Your mother. Your mother. Your mother and then your father."

In Indonesia, boys and girls who misbehave get a reprimand and a warning to listen to their mother. After all, heaven lies under her feet.

✸ Luruskan syaf, rapatkan barisan

"Straighten the line, tighten the formation" = Unite. Become one voice and let nothing interfere.

The Prophet Muhammad said this phrase before prayers. He said a straight line makes for a perfect prayer. If the line isn't straight, he told the faithful, Allah will make you fight each other.

At prayer time in a mosque, a prayer leader takes a position at the front and others form neat lines spanning the room. The worshippers stand so close that their shoulders touch.

Children are told that this keeps the devil from disturbing the concentration of the faithful.

Indonesian politicians borrowed the expression. Sukarno, the nation's founding president, said it to hammer home a message of national unity. His daughter and former president, Megawati Sukarnoputri, also said it.

Politicians deliberate together and "tighten the formation" in order to issue a single statement from their camp, rather than a bunch of conflicting opinions.

✸ Orang ketiga setan

The third is Satan.

The Prophet Muhammad warned that an unmarried man should not be alone with a woman who is not closely related to him. If that man is with an unrelated woman, a third individual or entity will also be present: the devil, who represents lust.

This view mirrors the Muslim concept of *muhrim*, a system of bloodline ranking that maintains a single man will not be tempted if he is alone with a sister or other close relative.

Today, Indonesian parents sternly recall the Prophet's words when they warn their children to resist temptation. The phrase is also a joke among teenagers:

"Don't canoodle together. The devil will turn up," they say.

Awas berdua-duaan. Nanti ada orang ketiga setan!

Berdua-duaan means being alone together.

Islam's Satan is *al-Shaitaan* (the transgressor in Arabic), or *setan* in Indonesian. The Quran says Satan disobeyed the divine command to bow before God's human creation, Adam. God banished the demon, but gave him temporary respite from punishment. Since then, Satan has constantly tried to tempt people away from God's path.

❊ Bagaikan titian rambut dibelah tujuh

"As narrow as a bridge made from a strand of hair split seven times" = A tough task.

The phrase comes from a story attributed to the Prophet Muhammad. Times were tough: his wife had died and he had endured the jeers of non-believers. God granted him a trip on a winged horse, Buraq, along with an escort, the Archangel Gabriel. Muhammad flew to several towns in one night and went to heaven, where he received the first order from God to pray five times a day. Muhammad saw a bridge that linked heaven to the earth.

Muhammad was told that the bridge was hair-thin and razor-sharp, and that it would broaden beneath the steps of the faithful. However, infidels would lose their balance and topple into the abyss because the bridge would become "as narrow as a strand of hair, which is split seven times."

The number seven is prominent in Islam. Heaven has seven levels, as does hell. But paradise has eight gates while hell has seven doors, a sign that you have a greater chance of going to heaven than hell. It means God shows more mercy than wrath. Pilgrims throw seven small pebbles (to thwart the devil) at each of the seven stone pillars in the last ritual of the *hajj*, or annual pilgrimage to Mecca—Muhammad's birthplace.

They also walk seven circuits around the Ka'ba, a square stone block that serves as a focal point that Muslims worldwide face when they pray to God.

❈ Jaga silaturahmi
"Guard the ties of families" = Keep in touch with family and friends.

The Prophet Muhammad said people who wanted God to bring them fortune and make them live long should cultivate family relationships.

In Indonesia, *silaturahmi* refers to visiting or keeping in touch with family, friends and business associates. It comes from the Arabic *silah* (rope, or tie) and *rahmi* (womb).

Indonesians send gifts of ornately decorated hampers of food and even fine china at the close of some Muslim celebrations. The goal is to promote *silaturahmi*, or lubricate a business relationship.

❈ Gus Dur

The affectionate nickname for Abdurrahman Wahid, a Muslim cleric and former president. Dur is short for AbDURrahman.

Gus, which comes from *si baGUS* (the good), is an honorific title given to sons of the head of a religious boarding school, or *pesantren*. The head is *kyai*, a learned man in religion matters.

Usually, a Gus becomes *kyai* when he grows older. Gus Dur's nickname stuck because of his relaxed style of leadership. During his tenure as head of state, people called out to Gus Dur without using the title of president.

Kyai haji is a head who has gone on a pilgrimage to Mecca. *Kyai khos* is a venerated leader of a religious school who is deemed to have special spiritual abilities. Some say the 20 or so *kyai khos* in Indonesia can predict the future. During elections, Muslims in East Java, a deeply conservative area, pay keen attention to their words.

Kyai is mostly used in Java, and other regions have different names for this Muslim teacher.

Ustadz is the title of a teacher in a religious day school (*madrasah*) or a boarding school (*pesantren*) or a Quranic study group. In the Middle East, that title is reserved only for university professors. Most Indonesians don't speak Arabic, and some with a smattering of Arabic pose as wise and holy men. They call themselves *ustadz*.

There are thousands of *pesantren* across Indonesia. Some have as few as 10 students, while the biggest has 15,000 pupils.

The schools have a strict regimen of worship and scripture study, with little exposure to the outside world. One subject is *Kitab Kuning* (Yellow Books). The books consist of Islamic teachings on law, philosophy and other matters that were written by Arab scholars in the 14–15th centuries. The original set of books was published on yellow paper.

❀ Klenteng

The onomatopoeic name of a Chinese shrine in Indonesia. It sounds like bells during worship. *Klenteng! Klenteng!* they toll.

The term *klenteng* is usually followed by another name that defines it as Taoist, Buddhist or Confucian. The authoritarian government of President Suharto banned Taoist and Confucian practices, and Chinese shrines were known during that time as *wihara*, an Indonesian term for a Buddhist temple. The country officially recognizes Islam, Protestantism, Catholicism, Hinduism and Buddhism, and the government relaxed controls on worship after the fall of Suharto in 1998.

The guardians of *klenteng* went to extraordinary lengths to avoid persecution during the Suharto years. They didn't put up signposts. They hid ornaments. If you asked where a *klenteng* was, many people shrugged their shoulders and said they didn't know. But they would point the way if you asked for directions to *rumah abu* (ash houses), or crematoria. *Rumah abu*, considered harmless by the government, were a codeword for *klenteng*.

❀ Gereja-gereja liar
Wild churches.

A term used by some Muslim groups to refer to unauthorized Christian churches in shopping malls and other business districts. These makeshift places of worship don't have permits. Many consist of one room with a pew, folding chairs and a tape recorder. Today, there are fewer *gereja-gereja liar* because of growing Muslim pressure.

Christians say it can be difficult to get permission to build new churches. They complain that rules requiring approval from local leaders to build a house of worship are enforced more strictly for Christians than Muslims. Muslim critics who are concerned about Christian proselytizing say churches should not operate in Muslim-majority areas or in commercial districts. Muslim mobs have sometimes ransacked *gereja-gereja liar* as well as regular churches.

Siti Suhartinah, the wife of former President Suharto, was born a Roman Catholic and was involved in gathering donations for the construction of churches.

Tensions between Muslims and Christians erupted in violence in some areas after Suharto's authoritarian rule collapsed in 1998. Ethnic and economic factors exacerbated the problem. For the most part, the faiths get along.

❀ Dukun
Shaman.

Indonesians from all backgrounds consult *dukun* to cure ailments, secure good fortune and send messages to the supernatural realm. Five-star hotel managers summon *dukun* to bless their premises.

In 1999, a staffer at the bureau of an international news agency in Jakarta was working late one night when he glimpsed what he thought was a man in a *peci*, a traditional cap of black felt. Then the mysterious man vanished. Days later, a second staffer was working alone when she briefly saw the man in the *peci* out of the corner of her eye. The spooked staff concluded that bad spirits were on the prowl in the office. A sorcerer was summoned to exorcise them. The *dukun* said a couple of prayers and sprinkled holy water around the premises. He concluded that there were plenty of spirits in the women's bathroom. After the exorcism, the interlopers were not seen again.

To guarantee good business, some company owners hire *dukun* to meditate (*semedi*) at graveyards, caves and volcanoes or other sacred sites. Some shamans do it in the nude. Often, clients participate.

Former President Suharto is said to have had many *dukun* as advisers. They allegedly gave tips on the best time or date to launch a policy or project, and fended off perceived efforts to harm him with black magic.

Muslim clerics try to wean Indonesians off mystical beliefs, and oppose *dukun* who treat the sick without modern medical training. Some Islamic leaders say shamans exploit the poor and uneducated, though the elite are also faithful clients. Paranormals administer potions and amulets, and burn incense in rituals that blend Muslim, Hindu and Buddhist practices.

The combination of religious and mystical beliefs is known as *kejawen* on Java. Not all Muslims are "white" or "pure ones" (*putihan*) who pray five times a day and strictly observe Muslim rituals. Many are "red ones" (*abangan*) who preserve home-grown, centuries-old beliefs.

Some *dukun* are charlatans who cast curses on a client's enemy in an attempt to ruin his business or make him ill. The spell is more effective if the shaman has a lock of hair, or a possession, of the victim.

In 1998, panic and violence swept East Java after a wave of mysterious killings of Muslim preachers and people said to be sorcerers. Villagers said the assassins, labeled "ninjas," dressed in black clothing. Fear spread, and mobs lynched dozens of suspected killers. One man died because a crowd found a black cap in his pocket and concluded he was a ninja.

Superstition thrives among the young. Rather than have plastic surgery, some popular singers and actors wear *susuk*, small pieces of gold or diamond surgically inserted in their lips or chin. These magical charms are said to enhance beauty and sensuality.

A frame shaman (*dukun bingkai*) is a person who sells frames for pictures. He is so named because he makes miracles with plain pictures.

Javanese lore brims with spirits:

Tuyul, a bald, pesky, child-like imp that steals money and other valuables. It floats, and is invisible. On Java today, people often blame the *tuyul* if something is missing. Some really believe it, while others are just joking.

Tuyul is a favorite character in Indonesian television comedies and films. One 2003–04 series was entitled *Tuyul Millenium*: the main character was a kind, modern and funny *tuyul* called Ucil. He didn't steal, and relied on his smarts to outwit his foes: Tuyul Samson, a fat imp in a green and gold vest, gold headband and pink trousers, and Jendol, his small, thin sidekick.

Kuntilanak, the ghost of a woman who has a hole in her stomach because she died in childbirth. Seeking her child, she roams the land and kills young men in the real world.

Pocong, a ghost that dwells in graveyards. Indonesian Muslims bury the dead in *kain kafan*, a shroud of unbleached cotton tied in a knot at the top of the head. The *pocong* has similar attire because it wakes up in the graveyard.

Jin, a supernatural being that grants wishes and protects people and their possessions. It has Arab origins, and is known as a genie in the West. A favorite among businessmen and lawmakers.

Leak is a term for a Balinese magic similar to voodoo. The good *leak* cures illness. The bad kind hurts people. Balinese believe those who practice *leak* transform themselves into animals, cloth, wood, cars, airplanes or motorbikes, and all manner of shapes and images. The bad *leak* feeds on animal corpses and assumes the form of a grotesque monster, or demon.

❀ Mengadu nasib
"To tempt fate" = Try your luck.

People from villages and small towns go to Jakarta to tempt fate.
The Indonesian capital teems with millions. The success stories
of workers who return to home villages over the Muslim holiday of Idul Fitri, or the end of the fasting month celebrations,
spur others to tempt fate in the big city. Many find frustration,
and unemployment. No one gives them the time of day. They
get lonely. They get mugged. Life is harsh.

No wonder that a joke evolved out of Jakarta's nickname,
the mother city (*ibu kota*):

"The mother city is crueler than the stepmother."

Ibu kota lebih kejam dari ibu tiri.

The notion is that stepmothers are cruel to the children in
their care. So Jakarta must be really bad.

❀ Alamat
An omen or sign.

Alamat dia sakit is an old-fashioned way of saying: "It's a sign he's
going to be sick."

Alamat also means street address.

Malays once believed that a movement of the body was a sign
that something was about to happen. If your left eyelid twitched,
then someone close to you was going to travel far. If your right
eyeball moved, it was a sign that you would cry over love. If
your ears twitched, a fight was imminent. If you moved your left
arm, fortune would befall you. Some older Indonesians in West
Sumatra know these superstitions, but young people have never
heard of them.

❀ Ada air, ada ikan

"Where there is water, there are fish" = Count on good fortune. Think positively, and things will turn out fine.

A fool wanted to learn the Quran, but he was so dumb that the teacher didn't know how to begin. So he told the student:

"Where there's water, there are fish."

The dunce returned to his village, where someone asked him what he had learned.

"Where there's water, there are fish," the fool intoned. His questioner laughed, then mocked him with another question: "So, are there fish in the water of a coconut?"

Unfazed, the fool repeated what the teacher had told him.

A villager passed him a coconut and suggested he break it open to look for fish. The idiot recited the phrase one more time before cracking the shell. He found fish inside.

❀ Kejatuhan durian runtuh

"Get hit by a falling durian" = A windfall. Unexpected luck.

Grown in Southeast Asia, the durian is a football-sized fruit with a pungent smell and thorny skin. People hate it because of its overwhelming odor, or love it for its heavenly taste. It is said to be an aphrodisiac. In 2003, an Indonesian foundation introduced durian-scented condoms as part of a safe sex campaign.

"When the durians are down, the sarongs are up," goes a Malay saying. *Kalau durian jatuh, sarong turut naik.*

A sarong is a traditional fabric that can be worn around the waist.

Just as New York City is called the Big Apple, so Jakarta had a fruity nickname: The Big Durian. You love it or hate it. The nickname was for English-speaking tourists; Indonesians didn't know it. Some foreigners also said Jakarta was The Big Smoke, a reference to the urban smog. Many Indonesians have never heard of the name.

Another phrase for winning big is *kejatuhan bulan* (get hit by the falling moon).

❈ Sudah jatuh, tertimpa tangga pula
"Fallen down, then hit by a ladder" = Get hit when you're down. To suffer one misfortune after another.

❈ Untung
"Lucky" = It could have been worse.

Indonesians look on the bright side when adversity strikes. *Untung* is consolatory, whether in the wake of a destructive mudslide during the rainy season, or in the mundane inconvenience of a traffic jam. If a pickpocket swipes your cellular telephone on the bus, relax and tell yourself:

"What luck! He could have taken my purse!"
Untung! Bisa saja dia ambil dompetku.

Many Indonesians believe misfortune breeds benefits in the long run, and that God inflicts setbacks to test, rather than punish, his human flock.

❈ Celaka dua belas!
"Bad luck twelve times over!" = Condolences.

Celaka is bad luck, and *dua belas* (twelve) adds emphasis. The number refers to the double six, the tile with the most dots, or points, in dominoes. In one popular game, the player with the most points left loses.

On Java, the number nine (*songo* in Javanese) is associated with good fortune. *Wali songo* (nine saints or holy men) are the teachers who spread Islam on Java in the 15th and 16th centuries following the decline of the Hindu kingdom, Majapahit.

———————

Indonesians, especially Javanese, think giving a humble name to a baby will distract evil spirits. The family of Lely Djuhari, the coauthor of this book, observed this custom. At birth, Lely's father was grandly named Muhammad Siradj, which means Muhammad, The Light of Truth. Sickness struck Muhammad time and again during childhood. His mother, who had lost one child to illness, switched her son's name to Udin. That name sounds humble to Indonesian ears and comes from *din*, an Arabic word that means religion, or Islam. Soon, Udin recovered his health.

Some ethnic Chinese in Indonesia also believe evil spirits won't bother kids with lowly, down-to-earth names. Many parents address their children as *akaw* (dog, in the Hokkien dialect from China).

Some farmers avoid using some words for fear of ruining, or jinxing, a harvest. They substitute lice for a host of animal names. Paddy field louse (*kutu sawah*), for example, replaces buffalo(*kerbau*).

Farmers might say "louse" to downplay expectations of a successful harvest. The louse is a tiny, useless creature, while the buffalo is big and productive.

This custom is roughly similar to the English expression "break a leg," a substitute for wishes of good luck before a challenge or big event.

✻ Sumur pengantin
Bridal well.

A well on the left behind the house.

An open well in this position is thought to bring good luck in Javanese culture. Traditionally, a "bridal" well is made for newly weds who move into their first house. Urbanization has rendered this phrase quaint.

The Javanese consider the well sacred because it is a source of water and therefore life. Many villagers rely on wells for water.

✻ Sebagai anjing terpanggang ekor
Like a dog with its tail on fire.
In panic. If misfortune strikes, desperation sets in.

✻ Hidup seperti roda pedati, ada kalanya di atas dan ada pula kalanya di bawah.
Life is like the wheel of a horse-drawn cart, sometimes you're up and sometimes you're down.

A modern version of the expression removes the cart (*pedati*), and sticks with *roda* (newly translated as tire).

An equivalent phrase is: There are high and low tides (*air pun ada pasang surutnya*).

✻ Panjang umur
Long life.

Wish someone long life when you congratulate them on their birthday.

You can also use the expression when someone you are chatting about pops up all of a sudden. In this context, it means: "Talk of the devil!"

It comes from a belief that a person who is a popular subject of discussion is blessed and will live long.

❋ Seperti kacang lupa akan kulitnya
Like a peanut forgetting its shell.

The peanut is someone who turns his back on his origins, and those who helped him make his fortune early in life.

A successful businessman attended a fund-raiser for an international program for exchange students. He had spent a year abroad as an exchange student when he was 17, an experience to which he attributed his later success. He arrived late that evening and reneged on a promise to donate money so students could go on the same scholarship.

"Huh, he's just like a peanut forgetting his shell," an organizer grumbled.

Chapter Nine

A Matter of Taste

Scrape the rice pot, sample stir-fry at a kiosk, or devour a satay. Eating in Indonesia is a social occasion, regardless of the cuisine.

❁ **Mangan ora mangan, sing penting ngumpul** (Javanese)
"Whether we eat or not, the important thing is to be together"
= A saying about the bonds of communal living.

Traditional society in Indonesia revolves around the family, neighborhood or village. People share sad and happy moments, and milestones: a death in the village, a wedding party, a boy's ceremonial circumcision. On such occasions, everybody pitches in with food, cash or emotional support. Often, showing up is enough. The collaborative system also works in modern, urban settings. In residential complexes, tenants take turns cleaning the gutters, and the men share shifts on night patrol around the grounds.

Residents who are too lazy or busy bend the rules by paying someone else to handle their communal tasks. They can't ignore their duties completely or tongues will wag.

"Eat or not, we assemble."

Makan nggak makan, asal kumpul.

This was the Indonesian-language name of a hit love ballad released in 2000 by Slank, Indonesia's biggest rock band. Who cares if we don't have enough food on the table, the singer croons. The most important thing is to be together.

❀ Mengairi sawah orang
"Irrigate someone's rice field" = Do someone a favor.

Indonesians love rice, and have several words for it. The plant in the field is called *padi*. *Gabah* is unhulled, or unhusked rice; *beras* is hulled rice. Once cooked, it becomes *nasi*. Children linger in the kitchen, waiting to eat *kerak*, the blackened rice particles that stick to the bottom of a pan. Add salt, and the crunchy stuff tastes like crackers.

"Look for rice in someone else's country," is about pursuing a fortune far from home. *Mencari nasi di negeri orang.*

The expression comes from West Sumatra's Minangkabau people, who are known for traveling to distant lands. The region has produced many successful merchants, writers and statesmen.

"Have you eaten rice?" older Indonesians ask.

Sudah makan nasi? The expression can be shortened to *Sudah makan?*—"Have you eaten?"—and serves as a greeting akin to: "How's it going?"

They want to know whether you've eaten a full meal. In their view, anything short of rice—a heaping plate of spaghetti or a hefty sandwich—is a mere snack.

Indonesian Muslims feast on rice during Idul Fitri, the Islamic holiday at the end of the fasting month of Ramadan.

Ketupat (boiled rice cake), a traditional dish during the holiday, consists of a plaited packet of coconut leaves with rice inside.

Police step up highway patrols to safeguard the exodus of vacationers bound for their hometowns ahead of Idul Fitri.

Operasi Ketupat (Operation Boiled Rice Cake) is the name of the state campaign to keep the roads safe.

Nasi uduk is a tasty rice dish cooked with coconut, and served at street stalls with banners that read "Midnight uduk" in English. The stalls stay open until midnight to feed workers on the late shift and other nocturnal souls. Cooks wrap small portions of *nasi uduk* in banana leaves, and serve them with fried shallots and strips of omelette.

When Indonesia was a colony, Dutch plantation owners with big appetites elaborated on Indonesian cuisine, introducing a lavish meal called *rijsttafel* (rice table, in Dutch). It consisted of rice and dozens of side dishes: curried meats, fish, vegetables, fruits, relishes, pickles, sauces, condiments, nuts and eggs. The goal was to blend and balance salty, spicy, sweet and sour tastes

Rijsttafel faded in popularity after the end of Dutch rule in the 1940s. Today, some hotels dish up the feast to foreign tourists. They charge an arm and a leg.

Some Indonesians, including the Bugis of South Sulawesi, have traditionally paid homage to a rice god and a potato god. On Bali, farmers set up bamboo shrines in their fields, hopeful that the rice goddess, Dewi Sri, will grant a good harvest. They make images of the Hindu deity out of rice stalks. In Indonesian mythology, *Antaboga* is an underworld serpent that controls the production of rice.

Rice and Politics

Decades ago, impoverished Indonesia was the world's largest importer of rice. But subsidies, farmer training and high economic growth under President Suharto, a former army general, brought self-sufficiency by the mid-1980s. The achievement reinforced Suharto's authoritarian rule, bolstering his image as a benevolent provider. The rice plant is part of the emblem of the ruling Golkar party. Rice and the cotton plant were symbols of Indonesia's national ideology—Pancasila, a set of broad principles designed to unify a diverse nation.

The government encouraged Indonesians to view Suharto as *Bapak Pembangunan* (Father of Development), a slogan that appeared alongside a portrait of the president on banknotes issued in the early 1990s. The notes were pulled from circulation after Suharto quit in 1998.

When the Indonesian currency, the rupiah, plunged in 1997, prices of fuel and food staples soared. Some Indonesians had a hard time getting food. Riots broke out. People blamed their president for their misfortune, and demanded that he step aside. After Suharto resigned, Indonesia held its freest parliamentary elections in four decades. Some new political parties followed Golkar's lead, festooning campaign flags with a symbol of prosperity: the rice ear.

In recent years, rice production trailed consumption in Indonesia. The government resumed imports. Thailand and Vietnam are Asia's big rice exporters.

❈ Jangan jadi bangsa tempe
"Don't become a soybean cake nation" = Don't become a backward nation.

Indonesia's first president, Sukarno, loved to speak to huge crowds. The independence-era hero made the soybean cake remark after the struggle for nationhood that ended when the Dutch gave up claims to Indonesia in 1949. Suharto denounced colonialism, and urged Indonesia to become a proud voice for developing nations in a world divided by the Cold War. In his speeches, soybean cake represented poverty and stagnation because it had a reputation as cheap food for the masses. Those with enough money got protein from meat.

Sukarno's putdown irked soybean lovers, who pointed out that the food was nutritious. Sukarno was no snob when it came to food. He loved simple Indonesian fare of the kind eaten by construction workers and other laborers: steaming white rice, chili, raw carrots, aubergines and other vegetables. And even *tempe*, soybean cake. Though *tempe* once had bad connotations, magazine articles today praise its healthy qualities.

Sukarno's vision for Indonesia had some early success when he hosted Asian and African heads of state in Bandung, West Java, in 1955. Sukarno later leaned toward the left, and conflict and corruption plagued his tenure. His military commander, Suharto, edged him out of power in the mid-1960s.

✿ Nasi sudah menjadi bubur

"The rice has turned to porridge" = The damage is done. You can't turn back the clock.

A job candidate mutters this phrase after flubbing an interview in an office boardroom.

✿ Seperti ilmu padi, makin tua makin merunduk

"The older a rice plant, the lower it droops" = The older and wiser a person, the humbler he becomes.

The more diffident and down-to-earth you are, the better. A stereotypical master of Indonesian and other Asian martial arts is an old, tiny, stooped and even blind character. His strength lies in his mind.

❈ Apa boleh buat? Nasi sedap menjadi tawar

"What can you do? Delicious rice becomes tasteless" = If the heart changes, behavior changes.

You can't hide the way you feel. Sweet talk loses its spark when lovers shed their rose-colored glasses.

❈ Nasi sama ditanak, kerak sama dimakan

"Cook rice together, but only eat burnt rice together" = Everybody pitches in, but it's a thankless task.

The expression implies that someone takes all the credit, or runs off with the spoils—in this case, the cooked rice. The others are left to scrape burnt remains from the bottom of the pot.

❈ Nasi tak dingin, pinggan tak retak

The rice doesn't get cold, the plate doesn't break.

A commentary on competence.

A young wife struggles to take care of a baby and a household, and wonders how her older neighbor with two children gets on so well.

❈ Pepesan kosong

"Empty banana wrap" = Empty promise.

Pepesan is a steamed snack that is wrapped in banana leaves. A mix of tofu with fish, chicken or mushrooms lies beneath the folds.

❀ Pisang tidak akan berbuah dua kali

"Bananas won't yield a harvest twice" = Once bitten, twice shy.

You can't dupe someone a second time.

Or, luck and fortune come once in a lifetime. So don't miss out. A student who turns down a scholarship and plunges into the job market will never know what he/she missed.

❀ Bagai buah simalakama, dimakan Bapak mati, tidak dimakan Ibu mati

"It's like *simalakama* fruit. If you eat it, your father dies; if you don't eat it, your mother dies" = Damned if you do, damned if you don't. Things won't work out, regardless of the path you choose.

Simalakama is a small fruit with a maroon skin and white flesh that was cultivated in the vegetable gardens of the palaces of Javanese sultans.

Simalakama, also called goddess's crown (*mahkota dewi*), inspires mixed feelings. In some folktales, the fruit is sacred. A soldier who eats it will triumph on the battlefield. Plant it, and you will prosper. The fruit's detractors believe snakes lurk where the *simalakama* plant grows.

Simalakama is sometimes cut, dried and served with hot water as a medicinal tea. There's a catch. People fall ill if the preparation and dosage is wrong. Damned if you do, damned if you don't.

The expression about *simalakama* is common. But many Indonesians don't know what the fruit looks like; some claim it doesn't exist and compare it to *buah khuldi*, a forbidden fruit mentioned in stories about the beginning of Islam. The Quran,

Islam's holy book, says Adam and his mate, Hawa, succumbed to temptation and ate from a forbidden tree despite Allah's warning to stay away from it. The Quran does not mention the fruit of the "tree of immortality." Some Muslim scholars have speculated that the pair ate prohibited dates or grapes, a transgression for which they were expelled from paradise. Adam was Islam's first prophet.

❀ Asam di gunung, garam di laut, bertemu dalam belanga
"Tamarind in the mountain, salt in the sea, they meet in the cooking pot" = A couple that is destined to be together will unite, no matter what. Time and distance separate them, but they'll eventually meet.

The tamarind fruit traveled a long way to Indonesia. It is believed to have originated in Central Africa, and traders brought it from India to Southeast Asia. Tamarind trees yield a pod-shaped fruit that serves as a base for distinctive sweet and sour sauces in Javanese cooking.

In Indonesia, tamarind seeds sometimes serve as pieces in *congklak*, a game with African or Arab origins. The game is played on a wooden board with shallow depressions for the pieces, and has different names across the globe. *Congklak* is Indonesian for cowrie shell, the game's traditional playing piece.

"Tamarind in the mountain, salt in the sea" was the headline of a magazine article about an odd political couple in the 2004 presidential race. One candidate was Wiranto, a former military chief who was indicted by U.N.-backed prosecutors for human rights abuses in East Timor, a former Portuguese colony that was occupied by Indonesia until residents voted for independence in 1999. He teamed up with Salahuddin Wahid, an architect and former member of Indonesia's human rights panel.

Wiranto said his choice of Wahid as running mate would silence his critics and prove that he was sincere in pledging to uphold human rights. Wahid, a brother of former President Abdurrahman Wahid, said charges against Wiranto would be clarified if he teamed up with the former general, instead of fighting against him.

The unusual pair came in third in the election.

❀ Karena nila setitik rusak susu sebelanga

"Because of one dot of indigo, the milk in the earthen cooking pot is tainted" = One rotten apple spoils the barrel.

In the simmering pot, the color of milk represents the good while dark-blue indigo symbolizes the bad. Some Indonesians say the skin of poisoned people turns the color of indigo, a plant dye used in textiles, including *batik*, the fabric made from an Indonesian hand-printing method. Today, *batik* is part of the national costume.

❀ Air susu dibalas air tuba

"Give milk, get poison in return" = Stabbed in the back.

Tuba is a Malay word for a kind of root with toxic properties. Traditional fishermen take the roots, crush them and scatter them in lagoons or ponds around the roots of mangrove trees. The crushed roots inebriate the fish, which float to the surface, making it easy for fishermen to catch them. Ingredients in the roots also serve as a rat poison.

Poisoning is less destructive than so-called blast-fishing. Many fishermen lob bombs into the water, damaging coral reefs and killing large numbers of fish that float to the surface. The crude bombs usually consist of bottles filled with fertilizer and a wick. Sometimes, the bombs explode prematurely, and fishermen lose limbs. Indonesia bans blast-fishing, but the law is tough to enforce across the huge archipelago.

❋ Habis manis sepah dibuang
Throwing away pulp after the sweetness is gone.

You discard sugar cane after consuming its sweetness. The stalk is expendable. The expression refers to callous lovers who woo partners, then "discard" them when other temptations loom.

❋ Kecil-kecil cabe rawit
"Small as a hot chili pepper" = Small in stature, fiery in nature.

The spirit of the underdog. Small chilis are much hotter than the big green and red ones. The small ones are light green and turn orange when ripe.

Cabe rawit is the smallest chili pepper in Indonesia, but its size belies its firepower. Chomp on it at your peril. Many Indonesians love the taste and say a fiery, chili-like spark in one's character is a great asset.

In 2003, President Megawati Sukarnoputri addressed 800 Indonesian athletes before they left for Vietnam to participate in a regional sports contest.

"History has shown that Vietnam can defeat a powerful nation such as America. Can you imagine what their fighting spirit is like!" Megawati said.

"Be careful facing this chili pepper of a nation!" she declared.

Hati-hati menghadapi bangsa cabe rawit ini!

Indonesia finished third in the medals standings behind Vietnam and Thailand.

❀ **Warteg** (acronym)
WARung TEGal
Tegal food kiosk.

This street stall offers cheap eats. Most owners come from Tegal, a coastal town and region in Central Java. Tegal natives travel in search of work, and many operate stalls that offer a hearty meal at a low price.

Warung tegal serve stir-fried vegetables, soybean dishes, *nas-gor* (*NASi GOReng*, or fried rice) and *Internet* (*INdomie, TElor, koRNET*: Indonesia's most popular brand of instant noodles, egg and corned beef).

Tegal district has many tea factories. Tea producers promote their product on billboards along the highway that runs along the northern coast of Java. A popular brand is *teh poci* (pot tea), a mix of loose tea leaves and fragrant jasmine.

Tegal hosts the headquarters of the giant Sosro company, which produces the brand *Teh Botol* (bottled tea). Sales in Indonesia match those of Coca-Cola. These days, *teh botol* is a generic name for the sweet, cold black tea in bottles that is produced by a multitude of companies.

Tegal cuisine is less renowned than that of West Sumatra's Minangkabau people, who serve spicy dishes at restaurant chains across the country. In many parts of Indonesia, Manadonese from North Sulawesi run upmarket food houses with tangy, seafood-based recipes.

❇ **Perut keroncongan**

"Keroncong-playing stomach" = A rumbling stomach is a sign of hunger.

You're so famished that your stomach jangles like *keroncong*, an Indonesian music with Portuguese origins. The onomatopoeic *keroncong* comes from the sound of guitar-strumming. Indonesians pronounce the name quickly, so it loses a syllable and sounds like *kroncong*.

Portuguese mariners brought the music to Goa, India, and then to the Portuguese section of Batavia, Indonesia's colonial capital.

Keroncong musicians play the mandolin, violin, guitar and bamboo flute. Some lyrics include Portuguese phrases. A variation, *keroncong mourisco*, traces its routes to Cape Verde in West Africa, and forms the basis of some modern Indonesian music.

Gesang Martohartono, a *keroncong* composer, gained a big following among the Japanese who occupied Indonesia during World War II. Japanese soldiers loved his music, and his songs were broadcast on Japanese colonial radio. Today, Gesang's fans in Japan gather annually to sing his songs. In 1991, Japanese war veterans erected a statue of Gesang in the central Javanese city of Solo.

———————

Other places to eat and drink:

Warkop (*WARung KOPi*). These traditional coffee shops sell *kopi tubruk* (coffee complete with the grounds).

Amigos, or *Agak MInggir GOt Sedikit* (a little to the side of the sewer). Amigos is also a chain of Tex-Mex restaurants.

Balsem, or *BALik SEMak* (behind the bushes). These eating stalls are in out-of-the-way places on university campuses.

Sogo jongkok. Sogo refers to the smart Japanese department store, which has outlets in Indonesia. *Jongkok* (squatting) is a reminder of the seating arrangements. The pun contrasts the plush retail shopping experience with the roadside one at Sogo *jongkok*. Sellers squat on a straw mat, their wares laid out on the sidewalk. Buyers haggle before squatting to sample the food.

❀ STMJ (pronounced *ess-teh-em-jeh*)
Susu, Telor, Madu, Jahe
Fresh milk, raw egg, honey, and ginger.

The ingredients in *STMJ* make up an energy drink from East Java. Shake like a milkshake, or stir vigorously. Drink hot on rainy nights. Guaranteed to give you a boost.

❀ Torpedo

This has nothing to do with the lethal weapon on a submarine. It's a hot, spicy delicacy made with goat testicles that is said to enhance sexual prowess. The dish usually comes in the form of a soup.

❀ Soda gembira
Happy soda.

A Javanese drink of soda water, condensed milk and red syrup. It's also known as *susu soda* (milk soda) in West and Central Java.

The cheap, sweet drink became popular during the 1980s when street vendors served it in a zoo called *Gembira Loka* (Happy Place) in the city of Yogyakarta.

Soda pop arrived in Indonesia during Dutch rule, and it was known for a while as *air Belanda* (Dutch water).

❋ Bistik
Steak.

From the Dutch *biefstuk* (beef steak). *Bistik* refers to any type of meat fillet cooked in a Western style. Indonesia has *bistik daging* (meat steak, or beef steak) and *bistik ayam* (chicken steak).

The Indonesian version isn't much different from the original fare, with gravy, potatoes, and veggies on the side. Trains on long journeys serve a special *bistik* in their cafeterias: thinly sliced beef, or minced meat patties, along with sweet gravy, French fries, peas, carrots, and fried eggs.

❋ Kuku Bima
Bima's nail.

This herbal medicine is billed as an aphrodisiac. Bima is a warrior and the strongest of the five Pandawa brothers in the *Mahabharata*, an ancient story from India about a great war between two branches of a royal family. The tale encompasses myths, philosophy, theology and teachings, and plays a profound role in traditional Javanese culture.

Bima's long thumbnails, called *panca naka* (five nails), have extraordinary powers. Makers of the *Kuku Bima* brand of herbal medicine boast that it endows the buyer with sexual strength. *Kuku Bima* comes in liquid or capsule form and is available in markets and shopping malls.

Other over-the-counter stamina drinks are *Pil Kita* (Our Pill) and *Extra Joss*. *Joss* means spunk, or pluck.

Dozens of booths along a boulevard in North Jakarta sell *Kuku Bima* and other stamina pills made in Indonesia, as well as U.S.-designed Viagra. Some items, billed as brand-name goods, are probably fakes.

Most customers want a low profile. They drive up to the booths, lower their windows, hastily buy aphrodisiacs and zoom off without getting out of their cars.

❀ Meremas santan di kuku
"Like squeezing milk from a coconut with your nails" = An impossible task.

You need to use your palms and fingers to squeeze milk out of shredded coconut flesh. It won't work if you try it with your nails.

Use a grater to shave off coconut flakes, and pour water over the shreds. Take a lump of coconut chunks and squeeze with palms and fingers. Thick milk oozes out. Add more water, and squeeze the lumps to get thinner milk.

Or just chuck the coconut flesh in the food processor and flick the switch.

❀ Semar mendem
Drunken Semar.

A snack of glutinous rice and shredded chicken. It was originally served as a royal court snack, wrapped in an egg crepe. The downmarket version is wrapped in banana leaves.

Semar is a fat, drunken court jester who advises the royal Pandawa brothers in the *Mahabharata* tale. Abdurrahman Wahid, Indonesia's president from 2000 to 2001, was sometimes compared to Semar because of his ungainly appearance, frequent joking, and high social and religious rank. The Muslim cleric's official website listed his jokes, including one he told to a board meeting of his political party:

> Indonesian politics is like a tree full of monkeys. They are all on different limbs at different levels. Some are climbing up. Some are climbing down. The monkeys on the top look down and see a tree full of smiling faces. The monkeys on the bottom look up and see nothing but a bunch of assholes.

Wahid clowned around, and his leadership as president was erratic. But he commanded a big following over a long career as an advocate of political reform and religious tolerance.

❋ Bagai telur di ujung tanduk

"Like an egg at the tip of a horn" = On the precipice. In a tight spot, doomed to fail.

An egg balanced on the end of a horn stays there for an instant. Then it falls, and cracks.

Minutes before midnight on July 23, 2001, President Abdurrahman Wahid was an egg at the tip of a horn. His military chief and top security minister had just stormed out of the palace after arguing with him.

The dispute was over Wahid's last-ditch efforts to block lawmakers from impeaching him on charges of incompetence.

Earlier, Cabinet ministers had appealed to their hopping-mad president not to declare a state of emergency.

But Wahid announced on national television after midnight that he had ordered the suspension of the National Assembly.

Wahid's power was evaporating, and his onetime allies in government refused to back the decree. Wahid was impeached and forced to resign.

The egg had dropped and cracked.

Soon after this episode, *bagai telur di ujung tanduk* popped up in newspaper commentaries on Wahid and his desperate bid to stay in power.

❀ Ada ubi ada talas, ada budi ada balas

"Where there's cassava, there's taro; where there's a good deed, there's a reward" = One good thing leads to another.

The expression follows the *pantun* (rhyming couplets) tradition of Malay poetry. In the past, such poetry was widespread in ceremonies, and wedding rituals still feature it. The family of a bridegroom speaks in rhyming couplets when they greet the bride's relatives and request that the two families be joined through marriage.

Some farmers plant cassava, or sweet potato (*ubi*) in a field encircled with taro (*talas*). Cassava is an alternative to rice; the harvest time of both staples is about four months. Cassava is more resilient than rice, which falls victim to insects and other pests. Taro takes about a year to harvest.

Keladi is an uncommon word for taro, and *biang* means parent species. *Biang keladi* refers to the root of a problem, and also means brain, mastermind or ringleader.

The military accused the Indonesian Communist Party of being the *biang keladi*, or mastermind, of an alleged coup attempt in 1965. Mutinous junior army officers were involved. The extent of the communist party's role, if any, was unclear. The military seized the opportunity to crush the communist movement, enabling Maj. Gen. Suharto to sideline President Sukarno and become president in 1968.

❀ Pucuk dicinta ulam tiba

"Love the shoot/sprout, young leaves arrive" = Get more than you expect.

Ulam are the young leaves of edible plants. Many Indonesians, especially West Javanese, eat them raw. A favorite dish consists of steamed white rice, *ulam* and *sambal*, a blended sauce of chili peppers and spices.

Ulam also refers to a young woman. *Ulam-ulam* means mistress.

Ulam mencari sambal (young leaves looking for chili sauce) is a young woman who seeks a husband.

————————

Indonesians use *makan* (to eat) in many contexts:

❀ Makan daun muda

"Eat young leaf" = Rob the cradle.

A term for an older man who has a young mistress.

❀ Makan angin

"Eat wind" = Get some fresh air.

But another definition refers to someone who eats poorly, suffers from a gassy sensation and feels lousy.

❀ Makan asam garam
"Eat tamarind and salt" = To be experienced.

Most Indonesians cook without recipes. Someone who knows the right mix of salt and tamarind when flavoring a dish is said to have years of experience running a household.

Alah saasam sagaram (salted and soured) is a Minangkabau expression that indicates perfection. Nothing else needs to be added, like a fish that is salted and soured with tamarind before cooking.

Salt and tamarind play a role in childrearing rituals in Indonesia because women need experience to be a good mother. Rice also plays a part. During the fourth month of pregnancy, a Javanese woman holds a ceremony and guests feast on *nasi punar* (yellow coconut rice with buffalo meat) to ensure she will not have a miscarriage.

During pregnancy, a Javanese woman holds a ceremony and guests feast to ensure she will not have a miscarriage.

Javanese believe the soul of the baby arrives before birth. A pregnant woman has a special bath with flowers, and everyone eats elaborate cakes. Javanese have lots of baths to mark personal milestones such as marriage. They cleanse themselves for the next step in life.

Javanese have different rice dishes—coconut rice, saffron rice, red and white porridge and tapioca porridge—to mark a baby's birthday.

❋ Makan hati, berulam jantung
"Eat liver, sprout heart" = To become furious.

A failing liver can't break down sugar, alcohol and poisons in the blood. Indonesians sometimes put as much emotional emphasis on rising sugar levels and poison in urine as the pounding of the heart.

"Eat liver, sprout heart" describes someone who is so angry that emotion consumes him.

Jantung hati (heart's heart) and *buah hati* (the fruit of the heart) mean the same: the object of one's dearest attention, or a beloved child.

❋ Makan darah
"Eat blood" = To fret.

People who eat blood are always anxious. A more common expression is cry blood (*nangis darah*). It means you exert a lot of effort, or make a big sacrifice. You sweat blood and tears.

❋ Makan korban
"Eat victims" = Claim casualties; take, require, consume.

This phrase often applies to people who die in fires, flash floods, earthquakes and other natural disasters. It can also be literal. In 2003, police used the term in the case of a Javanese man who dug up a neighbor's body and ate parts of it. The man believed the flesh would give him supernatural powers. Indonesian law does not recognize cannibalism as a crime, but the man was jailed for theft and digging up a grave.

❈ **Makan gaji buta**
"Eat blind wages" = Get paid for doing nothing.

The wage is blind to the fact that the worker is doing nothing to earn it. When President Suharto was in power, radio show hosts sat idle while live broadcasts of his carefully staged conversations with farmers played on their stations. The hosts didn't know when his talk would finish, but they had to be ready to go back on the air when he stopped. They said they were getting paid to do nothing (*makan gaji buta*).

Less common expressions:

❈ **Makan sabun**
"Eat soap" = Fix (a game).

Soap is as slippery as a person who takes money and fixes the outcome of a game.

❈ **Makan sumpah**
"Eat a pledge or promise" = Break a promise.

Witnesses in a courtroom eat a pledge when they lie under oath.

❈ **Makan tanah**
"Eat dirt" = Starve.

You have nothing left to eat but the ground that you stand on.

Chapter Ten

Family Affairs

In the old days, parents selected spouses for their children, and couples were expected to have big families. Social change and government policy weakened those customs.

❊ Anak semata wayang
"One-eyed puppet child" = An only child.

Wayang kulit (*wayang* means shadow in Javanese, and *kulit* means leather) refers to the Javanese tradition of shadow puppet theater. A common type of arm-swiveling puppet is two-dimensional, with just one eye visible. In the phrase, the one eye of the puppet symbolizes the one child.

The status of an only child, translated literally as *anak tunggal*, is enviable in Indonesia, where Islamic inheritance law dominates.

If a couple has one child, the wife gets one-eighth of the wealth when her husband dies. If the only child is male, he inherits the rest. He is responsible for the female members of the family, sometimes covering expenses until they marry.

An only child who is female gets half when her father dies, while her mother gets one-eighth and the rest is divvied up among relatives. The daughter's share is her own and she has no obligation to fend for other people.

Suitors intent on marriage seek an only child from a well-to-do family because they anticipate a fat inheritance.

At a school contest or an office raffle, *gelar semata wayang* (one-eyed puppet award) is the sole/only award.

Some puppets portray mythical, demonic beasts and two eyes are painted on the side of their heads. West Javanese have puppets with three-dimensional, papier-mâche heads called *wayang golek*; in East Java, people (*wayang orang*, or people puppets) act the parts. The plots usually center on a struggle between good and evil and draw on ancient tales from India.

Some *dalang*, or puppeteers, use a single *wayang* to play the roles of several characters in one performance. Traveling puppeteers (*dalang keliling*) roamed the countryside without an orchestra, a singer, or even the screen and lamp that are mainstays of the shadow act. The puppeteer spread news and gossip from one place to the next.

✽ Anak gedongan
"A building child" = Rich kid.

Many years ago, most Indonesian homes were wooden, and a big building made of stone signaled wealth and modernity. *Anak* means child and *gedongan*, an offshoot of *gedung* (building), implies fraud or deception and is a derogatory reference to the rich.

Indonesia's newly rich made fortunes during an economic boom that began under President Suharto in the 1970s. Oil-rich Indonesia cashed in on the soaring price of oil on world markets. Profits in the timber industry yielded another bonanza at the expense of the environment. Corruption and close ties to Suharto's family helped tycoons get ahead. Today, their children get business degrees in the United States and speak English with

American accents. They are called *anak OKB* (*Orang Kaya Baru*, or newly rich people).

Indonesians with old money inherited wealth from Dutch colonial times. Some speak Dutch, and have distant relatives in the Netherlands. They tend to avoid the nitty-gritty of business deals, and mix in elite political circles.

Their children are called *anak menteng*.

Menteng is a wealthy neighborhood in the center of the capital that was built by Dutch colonialists. The wide, tree-lined avenues skirt spacious houses surrounded by lush gardens and high walls and fences. Menteng is home to government officials, ambassadors and business executives.

Obama anak Menteng, a 2010 biopic of Barack Obama, is a fictionalized account of the early years of the U.S. president, who resided in Menteng from 1967 to 1971. It wasn't as affluent then as it is now.

Another wealthy Jakarta neighborhood is Pondok Indah, which means "beautiful home." Many houses have ostentatious columns in Greco-Roman style and sweeping balconies, hallways and grandiose staircases that recall the plantation house in the 1939 movie *Gone with the Wind*.

Menteng is also the name of a marble-sized fruit with pink or white flesh that has a sweet and sour taste. Eating too much of it causes diarrhea.

"The menteng fruit has yet to ripen, but excrement is already everywhere," goes a Sumatran expression. *Tupak elum masak, kincit lah beramburan.*

It could mean that the writing is on the wall. Or: don't believe the hype—success has yet to be achieved.

❀ Air dicincang tiada putus
"Chopped water won't break" = Blood is thicker than water.

An upbeat view of the relationship between husband and wife, brother and sister, father and son. The family or blood tie endures, regardless of separation, argument or other strains. Another expression about family loyalty is *bagai api dengan asap* (like fire with smoke). You can't separate the two.

❀ Tak kenal maka tak sayang
"Not to know is not to love" = Understand before you judge. Don't jump to hasty conclusions.

Parents said this to a daughter in the days when arranged marriages were common. The idea was to persuade her that she shouldn't be too hard on a suitor. Even if he doesn't leave a good impression, she'll warm up to him over time. Or so the parents hope.

❀ Tumbuhnya cinta karena sering bersama
Love grows because you are often together.

The original expression in Javanese is: *Tresno jalaran seko kulino*.

Many Javanese parents teach this expression to their children. They tell their children that they didn't love each other at first because their families arranged their marriage, as was often the case in the old days. But love evolved after years of enduring the good and the bad together. Now only death can separate them.

The custom of arranged marriages ranked prospective sons-in-law and daughters-in-law according to their *bibit*, or heredity; *bebet*, social standing; and *bobot*, or wealth, morality and education.

Agony aunt columns in magazines refer to these Javanese terms if a reader writes that her boyfriend has failed to win the family's approval. *Cosmogirl Indonesia* and other hip magazines for young people refer to a modern version of this rating system:

Bibit, once a measure of aristocratic pedigree, now refers to a family with riches or political connections.

Today, you have high *bebet* if you're mentioned in *Indonesian Tatler* or *A+* magazine for socialites, or named *Matra* Man of the Month. *Matra* is a men's magazine similar to *Esquire*.

Education is an important factor in modern *bobot*. The more academic titles, the better. A wedding invitation boasts the degrees of the betrothed. For example, Dewi Ratih BA MSc. The titles declare that the couple has finished studying and is ready to marry.

The concepts apply to business. Newspaper columnists debate whether the merger, or marriage, of two companies will succeed. They analyze the companies' *bibit* (management background), *bebet* (standing in the industry) and *bobot* (financial stability).

❈ Mati seladang

"Being dead in the same field" = A husband and wife remain faithful until the end, and are buried together. Even in death, they do not part.

Many folktales explore the idea of love in death. In Bali, plague struck down a family. Only a boy named Jayaprana survived, and he was adopted by the King of Buleleng. When he grew up, Jayaprana chose a beautiful bride called Ni Nyoman Layon Sari. Her beauty bewitched the king, who ordered the execution of Jayaprana. But the king never married because the distraught bride killed herself to join Jayaprana in death.

Some Indonesian villagers don't bury their loved ones in a big cemetery. Residents of many hamlets reserve a small burial plot in front of their homes. Children get up in the morning and look out the window at the graves of their grandparents. The graves are part of the landscape, but some people don't like to walk past them at night.

❀ Datang bulan
"The month/moon has come" = I'm menstruating.

Indonesians think open talk of menstruation is vulgar or awkward, so they choose a euphemism. *Datang bulan* refers to the whole time of menstruation.

In predominantly Muslim Indonesia, women who are menstruating don't fast during the fasting month of Ramadan, and don't enter a mosque to pray. Similarly, menstruating Hindus cannot enter a temple on Bali.

Men have no qualms about asking women if they can eat or pray, an indirect way to learn whether it's that time of the month.

Besides *datang bulan*, a menstruating woman can reply, in order of politeness:

Saya lagi halangan (I have an obstacle).

Saya lagi haid (I have my period). *Haid* is Arabic for menstruation. The term appears in written form, but is rarely used in conversation.

Saya lagi mens (I'm menstruating). *Lagi* means "in the process of" when it comes before a verb. It means "again" when it comes after a verb.

Sometimes a woman jokes: *Oh, lagi M.* (Oh, I am M). *M* stands not only for *menstruasi*, but also *malas* (lazy). The woman really means: I'm lazy, so I'm not praying or fasting.

The impact of menstruation depends on the day that the menstrual period begins, according to the *Primbon*, a Javanese philosophy influenced by Islam and Hinduism:

Monday—there will be good luck; Tuesday—there will be happiness; Wednesday—a fight/argument; Thursday—sadness; Friday—happiness; Saturday—a surprise; Sunday—a meeting with an old acquaintance.

In the Javanese calendar, the days of the week fall into categories based on the position of the moon as it rotates around the earth. Javanese consult these categories to decide when to pray, travel, get married and do other important things. Like menstruation, the moon is believed to influence luck, emotions and future events.

❀ Seperti bulan dan matahari
"Like moon and sun" = A perfect match.

Bagai bulan kesiangan (like an overslept moon) refers to a bleary-eyed, young woman.

Bagai bulan empat belas (like the moon on the 14th day) is about the beauty of a young woman, curvaceous and glittering.

❀ Pisang raja
Banana king.

In Javanese and South Sumatran wedding traditions, the groom brings a dowry and the stem of a bunch of bananas. The stem is called *pisang raja*. The banana season runs all year, and the fruit is a symbol of abundance and constancy, fitting qualities for marriage.

A long time ago, the bride's parents or family decided on the contents of a dowry, based on the social status, beauty and intelligence of the bride. The dowry might consist of gold, jewelry, party handbags, sandals and clothes. There was also the *songket*, a traditional fabric handwoven with gold and silver thread, and worn as a headcloth by a groom, or more often as a sarong or stole by a bride.

The *songket* usually numbered from three to seven pairs, meaning they could be passed to the couple's offspring for three to seven generations. Today, the groom decides the dowry most of the time, and his financial situation is taken into account. Sometimes, the bride shares the cost.

Mas kawin (marriage gold) or the Arabic word *mahar* are the most widely used terms for dowry in Indonesia. Other dowry names are *uang jujur* (honest money) and *uang jemputan* (collected money).

❀ Seperti pinang dibelah dua

"Like an areca nut cut in two" = You can't tell one from the other. Twins.

The areca, or betel nut, and its leaves are props in traditional weddings. The areca nut is *pinang* in Indonesian, and proposing marriage to a woman is *meminang* (to give areca nut).

In a wedding ritual, the groom offers a brass box containing the areca nut, along with its leaves, chalk and tobacco to his father-in-law to symbolize the union of two separate bodies.

The nuts stand for the flesh, the leaves are the veins, the chalk is blood and tobacco is the hair.

Chewing the nut, tobacco, and chalk creates a black film on the teeth, and the chewer spits out a reddish juice. It has a mild stimulative effect. The areca nut is a treatment for tapeworm, and is also applied to bleeding gums and ulcers, as well as cuts and burns.

❀ Kawin lari
"Runaway marriage" = Elopement.

A tradition in some parts of Indonesia, including Bali, Lombok and areas of Sumatra and Sulawesi islands.

A young man runs away with his lover because her family rejects his marriage proposal. After a while, the couple seeks the family's blessing through elders or other relatives, and the family eventually relents. In some cases, the couple pays a fine to the bride's family.

Indonesia's founding president, Sukarno, was born from parents who married through *kawin lari*. His mother, Idayu, was a Balinese from the Hindu Brahmin class, a high caste. Sukarno's father was a Muslim Javanese school teacher descended from an aristorcrat in East Java. In those days Balinese women, especially aristocrats, never married outside their caste or religion. So the couple eloped, and had to pay a big fine.

These days, elopement is usually a charade: the couple runs away to spare the expense of a big wedding for the bride's father, who is aware of the supposedly secret scheme and feigns anger.

❀ Kawin bawah tangan
Underhanded marriage.

Polygamy is rare, but a man who wants a second wife despite the objections of his first wife sometimes resorts to the option of *kawin bawah tangan*. A Muslim preacher (*penghulu*) presides over an "underhanded marriage" to lend it legitimacy. The newly-weds do not register their union with the state. *Kawin bawah tangan* is legal, but many Indonesians disapprove of it.

Indonesian law says polygamy is illegal unless it is "desired by the concerned parties."

If a husband marries a second woman without the permission of the first, the latter can seek an annulment. But financial dependence and social and religious pressure make it hard to pursue this option.

Siti Suhartinah, the late wife of former President Suharto, was instrumental in pushing through a regulation called *P10*, which bars civil servants from having more than one wife.

The law is still in place, though it was not applied to former Vice President Hamzah Haz, who had three wives.

In 2003, Puspo Wardoyo, the owner of a franchise chicken restaurant named *Wong Solo*, held an awards ceremony for dozens of polygamists at a Jakarta hotel. Wardoyo, who has four wives, said polygamy was man's biological instinct and referred to Quranic verses that say a man can have several wives if he treats them fairly. Women's groups protested the event. Wardoyo won an award at his own show.

The most prominent polygamist in Indonesian history was the late President Sukarno, whose wives included Fatmawati, Hartini, Dewi and Inggit.

Indonesia only recognizes marriages sanctioned by the faith of the couple. Mainstream Islam in Indonesia bars interfaith marriages, though one liberal branch of Islam in Indonesia, Paramadina, has been open to such marriages.

To sidestep the problem, some people convert to their partner's religion. Some non-Muslims say they become Muslims solely in order to marry. At their weddings, they recite the *syahadat*, an oath of induction or reaffirmation into the Muslim faith. The oath is in the five daily prayer recitations and other important prayers:

"I bear witness that there is no god but Allah and Muhammad is his prophet."

Saya bersaksi bahwa tiada Tuhan selain Allah. Dan saya bersaksi bahwa Muhammad (saw) adalah utusan Allah.

Other people go abroad—to Australia, Singapore or Hong Kong—to tie the knot.

❀ Ada uang Abang sayang, tidak ada uang Abang melayang
If there is money, I love you, Abang. If there's no money, bye bye, Abang.

A materialistic girl says this. *Abang* is a term for a boyfriend, or a title of respect for someone older. It's common in Sumatra. Similar honorific terms are *mas* in Java, *uda* in West Sumatra and *kakak* in other parts of Indonesia.

Piala bergilir (alternating trophy) is a woman who juggles boyfriends. She is a trophy who awards herself to a different winner each year.

Plin plan and *plintat plintut* mean: now this way now that, swaying with the wind. They refer to people who drift from one romantic liaison to the next. The terms apply to fickle behavior in any scenario, including politics.

❀ Kapan janur kuningnya?
"When will you raise yellow coconut leaves?" = When are you getting married?

A frequent question for single women, and a favorite at family gatherings during holidays such as Lebaran at the end of the Muslim fasting month of Ramadan.

The phrase refers to *janur kuning*, a coconut leaf decoration that is hoisted atop a large bamboo pole in front of a house to signal that a wedding party is underway. The coconut leaf is twisted into the form of a lamp with long tassels.

Janur is a special name for young coconut leaves, which are yellow. *Daun kelapa* are mature green leaves of the coconut.

Some women respond to the coconut leaves question with a joke:

"I am waiting for the yellow flag."

Aku tunggu bendera kuningnya.

Most Indonesian families raise a white flag outside their house as a sign of mourning after the death of a relative. The cheeky retort means that the woman wants to wait for marriage until her lover's mother dies. That way, the woman doesn't have to win the blessings of her suitor's mother, or deal with a meddlesome mother-in-law, but still inherits the old woman's fortune.

A single woman might also say she's waiting for the white flag if she is involved with a married man. Cruelly, she yearns for his wife to die.

❧ Sudah isi?

"Are you filled yet?" = Are you pregnant yet?

A newlywed fields this question from relatives soon after taking the vow. Sometimes the question surfaces after the wedding night. Traditional Indonesians think women should get married, maintain the home and perpetuate the family line. *Macak, masak, manak*, they say. "Dressing up, cooking, giving birth."

———————

In a Sundanese folktale, a king urinated while hunting in a forest, and a hog licked up the liquid and became pregnant. Nine months later, the king discovered his baby in the woods and named her *Dayang* (girl) *Sumbi* (the wood for a loom). One day, Dayang Sumbi was weaving when the wood fell out of the loom. Too tired to pick it up, she said she would marry the boy who retrieved it. Her dog picked it up and made love to Dayang Sumbi while she slept, impregnating her.

The king was furious when he learned Dayang Sumbi was pregnant and banished her from his palace. She gave birth to Sangkuriang, who at the age of 11 killed the dog because it refused to kill a boar: the same boar that gave birth to Dayang Sumbi.

Dayang Sumbing was distraught that Sangkuriang had unknowingly killed his own father, the dog. She struck his head and told him to leave.

Sangkuriang returned to his hometown when he became a man. He fell in love with an older woman, and asked her to marry. One afternoon before the wedding, the woman offered to pluck lice from his hair. While doing so, she found a mark on his head. It was the scar from her blow when she found out that he had killed his father.

Dayang Sumbing committed suicide rather than marry her own son.

❈ MBA
Married by Accident.

To most people, an MBA is a degree in business. The English acronym has other meanings in modern Indonesian slang. A couple that weds because of an unplanned pregnancy is Married by Accident. MBA also stands for Married But Available, or someone who has tied the knot but still plays the field. Urban Indonesians sprinkle conversation with English words.

❋ Di mana bunga yang kembang, di situ kumbang yang banyak

"Where there are flowers in bloom, there are lots of bumblebees" = Wherever there are beautiful women, there are plenty of young men. Like bees to honey.

A man who flirts shamelessly in the company of women invites the sarcastic remark:

"Huh! There's a goat in the midst of flowers."
Dasar kambing di antara kembang.

❋ Bandot tua makan lalap muda

"Old goat eating young leaves" = An old man who tries to seduce young women.

The expression once referred to an elderly man who married a young woman, but now it has a harsh meaning. It implies the old man is a lewd skirt-chaser. Goats have a reputation as creatures with a strong sexual desire.

Bandot means a fat goat with a long beard; a married man who is infatuated with a young, attractive woman; and a playboy.

Lalap are salad leaves, eaten raw. The Sundanese in West Java love this food, and people joke that they will eat any type of leaf, including *daun jendela* (window leaf, or frame).

❋ Dua anak cukup

Two children are enough.

A slogan of the state campaign to curb population growth that began in 1970.

The slogan appears on the base of crude, cement statues

of parents with two children that still stand in many parts of Indonesia. These sculptures sit in front yards of district offices or community clinics called *posyandu*, short for *Pos Pelayanan Terpadu* (Integrated Service Post).

Some statues depict heroes with bamboo sticks and head-bands of red and white, the national colors. This is a typical image from the fight for independence from the Dutch, and the statues are seasonal. They mushroom during celebrations around the anniversary of the August 17, 1945 declaration of independence. Some are modeled on a town mascot or symbol such as an animal or flower. One town commissioned a life-size statue of a short, portly policeman with a mustache. It's a frightful sight at night if you drive around a corner and come upon it.

―――――――

The *posyandu* clinics are the backbone of Indonesia's health services, providing vitamins and immunizations to children and advising mothers on breast-feeding. A bigger version of *posyandu* is *puskesmas*, a community health center.

Indonesian couples once tried to have as many children as possible. A big brood tended the fields, performed other chores and looked after elderly parents. People also had a lot of children as a safeguard against the high child mortality rate.

"Lots of kids, lots of fortune," an old saying goes. *Banyak anak, banyak rejeki.*

Family planning under Suharto weakened the tradition behind this expression. His birth control program curbed the growth rate, and was hailed as one of the most successful in the developing world.

The government pulled subsidies for cheap contraceptives after the onset of the economic crisis in 1997, and experts feared that the birth rate would soar. The population explosion never happened, though overcrowding remains a problem. Indonesia has at least 235 million people and is the world's fourth most populous country after China, India, and the United States. About half of Indonesians live on Java, one of the most densely populated areas in the world.

Another government slogan urging reproductive restraint was *catur keluarga* (family of four)—two parents and two children. *Catur* is a Sanskrit word that means four.

Dia sedang berbadan dua (she has two bodies) means she is pregnant. *Buah hati* is "heart fruit," an expression for a child or children.

❀ Kumpul kebo
"Buffalo gathering" = Living together out of wedlock.

This Javanese expression became popular during the 1980s, when more university students lived with their partners without getting married. They rented a house near the campus or lived in a *kos* (one-bedroom digs).

The custom shocked Indonesians for whom extramarital sex was taboo. Buffaloes are associated with sexual activity.

Another popular saying for cohabitation is *samenleven*, or living together in Dutch. Indonesians say Westerners, viewed as sexually uninhibited, exported the custom to Indonesia. Financial independence and the loosening of family ties made it easier for unmarried couples to live together, though many keep it a secret from their relatives.

❀ Sastra wangi
"Fragrant literature" = Also known as *sastra bunga*, or flower literature.

These are terms for the works of young female writers who

became prominent in literary and media circles after the fall of Suharto. Female authors were rare in Indonesia, but the new writers made a splash with bold novels about sex, marriage and unconventional relationships. They thrived as social and political freedoms took hold after decades of authoritarianism, though their reach was limited because relatively few Indonesians read novels.

Some writers objected to the term *sastra wangi* because it suggested their work was a female fad. At the same time, the label helped market their books. The authors didn't hold back on once-taboo subjects. In 2004, a publishing house released a compilation of short stories by writer Djenar Maesa Ayu. The book title: *Jangan main main (dengan kelaminmu)* or *Don't play about (with your genitals)*. The red glossy cover shows a blurred photograph of a woman's breasts, her nipples covered by computer keys.

❈ Kebebasan pribadi

"Personal freedom" = The dictionary definition of privacy in Indonesia.

There is no Indonesian word for privacy. Many topics that are largely considered private in the West—money, love life, family decisions—end up in the public domain in Indonesia.

A highly publicized case of divorce involved elderly television producer Eddy Sud and his wife, a singer of the Indonesian *dangdut* music who was half his age. Eddy's wife asked him for a divorce, and he responded:

"I have to consult my extended family about what decision I should take. This is a private matter."

A week later, Eddy appeared on television and said: "I have talked it over with my family and have decided to accept my wife's request."

His weeping wife then changed her mind.

True to form, Eddy said he had to consult his family. The couple reconciled several times before finally divorcing.

Under Islamic law, a Muslim man can say "I divorce you" three times to validate a divorce. This practice is rare in Indonesia because a man has to make the declarations in front of a judge in a religious court. A couple can reconcile after the first two times, but they have to hold another wedding ceremony if they want to remarry after the third time. The repetition of the phrase is supposed to ensure that a man really means it when he says he wants a divorce.

Usually, estranged couples hand in their *buku nikah* (marriage book) and get a certificate of divorce in return. The paperwork helps them separate joint bank accounts and sort out other details.

❀ Diam seribu bahasa

"Quiet in a thousand languages" = So angry that you're in shock. You can't say a word.

A furious father expresses his feelings toward his son without a word. Silence carries a powerful message. Javanese traditionally brood over a problem, rather than confront it.

The term also refers to a rebuffed suitor. He declares his love, but the target of his affection is quiet in a thousand languages.

Chapter Eleven

Wisdom

Old expressions about wisdom appear in print, but rarely turn up in conversation. Axioms about knowledge, perseverance and good deeds hold true today.

❉ Sekali merengkuh dayung, dua tiga pulau terlampaui

"In one rowing, two, three islands were passed" = Killing two birds with one stone.

Indonesia has some 17,000 islands. In 2005, the maritime affairs minister, Freddy Numberi, urged local officials to come up with names for more than 9,000 nameless islands. He made the call in response to a request from the United Nations. Indonesia has had territorial disputes with neighbors including Malaysia and the Philippines. Numberi hoped that stamping names on islands, especially uninhabited ones, would avoid more border quarrels.

Skull Island, the jungle home of dinosaurs, giant insects, bloodthirsty warriors and a big ape in director Peter Jackson's movie King Kong, is said to be west of Sumatra in the Indian Ocean.

Fantasy aside, scientists declared in 2004 that they had found the skull and bones of a member of a previously unknown human dwarf species in a cave on Flores, an island in central Indonesia. Villagers recalled tales passed down the generations of tiny, human-like creatures with big appetites that were known as *Ebu Gogo*, or the "Grandmother who eats everything."

The reports drew comparisons to the fictional hobbits in *The Lord of the Rings* by J.R.R. Tolkien, a series brought to the screen by Jackson. But some experts were skeptical, saying the bones could have belonged to a human with a disability.

Another island with a rich history is Run, part of the Banda island group. Run was rich in nutmeg and a vital part of the lucrative spice trade that flourished in the 17th century. The English and the Dutch laid claim to the island amid war between the two colonial powers. Under a treaty, the English abandoned claims to Run, and the Dutch agreed to let them keep the American island of Manhattan.

Indonesia's sea area accounts for four-fifths of the total area of the nation. In ancient times, people from the archipelago are believed to have sailed as far as Madagascar in the Indian Ocean. A couple of centuries ago, traders in vessels moved easily along the Javanese coastline instead of transporting goods along the island's rough roads.

Indonesia's name comes from *indos nesos*, Greek words that mean "Indian" and "islands."

✤ Malu makan perut lapar, malu berkayuh perahu tak laju

"Shy to eat, get hungry; shy to row, the boat stays still" = If you don't get up and go, you will never amount to anything in life, or get rich.

✤ Kapal satu, nakhoda dua

"One ship, two captains" = Too many cooks spoil the broth.

❀ Air pun ada pasang surutnya

"Even water has its ebbs and tides" = You can't predict which way the wind will blow. One day, you're on top of the world. The next, you're down and out.

❀ Berjalan sampai ke batas, berlayar sampai ke pulau

One walks to the border, one sails to an island.

It was that simple in the days when there were no cars or airplanes. This expression recalls the benefits of common sense.

❀ Hujan emas di negeri orang, hujan batu di negeri sendiri, baik juga di negeri sendiri

"Golden rain in another country, stony rain in one's own country, it's still better in one's own country" = There's no place like home.

Sometimes the phrase is shortened to *hujan emas di negeri orang*.

❀ Gantungkan cita-citamu setinggi langit, tetapi dalam menjangkaunya hendaknya tetap berpijak tanah

"Hang your dream above the sky, but keep your feet on the ground when you wish to fulfill it" = Be realistic.

Have lofty goals, but don't lose your head while trying to achieve them.

The full phrase is unwieldy, but adults commonly tell children: *gantungkan cita-citamu setinggi langit*. Teachers like to write it on report cards. President Sukarno made it famous decades ago when he urged the young nation to match ambition with a clear head.

❀ Bibit yang baik di mana saja ditanam, niscaya tumbuh

"Fine seed will grow anywhere it's planted" = A talented person will succeed anywhere.

❀ Menepuk air di dulang terpecik muka sendiri

"Splash water in the bucket, and it splashes your own face" = Hoist with your own petard.

A petard was a gunpowder-filled device used to blow up walls and gates during European conflicts centuries ago.

❀ Tidak ada rotan akar pun jadi

"When there's no rattan, roots will do" = Make do with what's available.

Harvested in the jungles of Kalimantan, Sumatra and Sulawesi, rattan is a climbing palm that is ideal for making furniture because its stems are durable and can be bent into shapes without splintering. It is not hollow like bamboo, and less susceptible to moisture. Indonesia is a major exporter of rattan canes, baskets, furniture and other wickerwork.

A major rattan trading center is the West Javanese port of Cirebon. An alternative name for this city is Carubaw, which comes from *caruban*, or mixture in Javanese, an apparent reference to the cultural blend that includes Sundanese, one of the island's main ethnic groups.

In *ujungan*, an ancient martial art practiced on Java, adversaries whip each other with pieces of rattan.

❀ Emas dan permata walaupun terbenam dalam lumpur takkan hilang kemilau cahayanya

"Though buried in mud, gold and jewelry won't lose their shine" = Someone who has done a good deed will be respected, regardless of the circumstances.

❀ Tidak ada gading yang tak retak

"There is no ivory that is not cracked" = Nothing's perfect.

❀ Di mana bumi dipijak, di situ langit dijunjung

"Where the earth is stood on, there the sky is respected" = When in Rome, do as the Romans do.

❀ Berakit-berakit ke hulu, berenang-renang ke tepian; bersakit-sakit dahulu bersenang-senang kemudian

"Travel by raft upriver, swim to the edge; get sick first, have fun later" = Work hard to achieve your goals.

This is part of a traditional four-line poem, or *pantun*. Indonesians understand the reference if you just say one phrase of the *pantun*. For example, *berakit-rakit ke hulu*.

"You are so successful now," the admirer says.

"Yes, well, travel by raft upriver, you know. It was hard at first."

The Malay verse form of *pantun* captures the wisdom of the elders and passes it to the younger generation. Ethnic Malays on

Sumatra island say *pantun* in marriage ceremonies, and the custom has spread to Java, Kalimantan and other areas. Older people sometimes speak in *pantun* in daily conversation.

✸ Ke mudik tentu ke hulu, ke hilir tentu ke muara

"If you go upstream, you will get to the spring; if you go downstream, you will reach the estuary" = Life must have a purpose or a destination.

Hilir mudik (upstream, downstream) describes someone who anxiously paces up and down. Teenagers sometimes say:

"Always pacing back and forth, you're like a heating iron."
Bolak balik terus, kayak setrikaan!

✸ Biar tekor, asal nyohor (Betawi)

"Even though I'm broke, at least I'm famous" = Spend every cent, give it all you've got.

Reckless Indonesians say this when they do something that flies in the face of common sense. Two-bit celebrities typically say it on television chat shows.

Traditional Javanese prefer to show humility, and view flashy conduct as vulgar. They frown on people who flaunt their wealth, or strive to give an appearance of affluence. *Pakaian keren, kantongnya kosong*, the Javanese say. "The clothes are nice, but the pockets are empty."

✸ Berjalan peliharakan kaki, berkata peliharakan lidah

"When you walk, take care of your feet; when you talk, take care of your tongue" = Be cautious in actions and words.

❈ Arang itu jika dibasuh dengan air mawar sekalipun, tiada akan putih

"Even if doused in rose water, charcoal will not turn white" = A villain never changes.

❈ Menang jadi arang, kalah jadi abu

"Winner becomes charcoal, loser becomes dust" = There's no winner in a dispute. Both parties suffer.

❈ Sehari selembar benang, lama-lama jadi sehelai kain

"A length of yarn one day, eventually it becomes a piece of fabric" = Slowly, but surely. Persevere, and your efforts will bear fruit.

❈ Menegakkan benang basah

"Erect wet yarn" = Do the impossible.

❈ Benang jangan putus, tepung jangan berserak

"Don't break yarn, don't scatter flour" = Don't rock the boat. Be discreet.

❈ Guru kencing berdiri, murid kencing berlari

"The teacher stands when he pees, the pupils run when they pee" = If a leader sets a bad example, his followers will do something even worse.

Teachers demand obedience at thousands of Muslim boarding schools called *pesantren*, most of which are on Java. Supervisors expect students to be disciplined and follow instructions. The pupils pray five times a day, recite the Quran and study other religious books. They live in spartan surroundings in compounds, and engage in sports, cooking and other activities. The teachers oversee the lives of the students throughout the day.

❈ Keris panjang berbelok, ke mana dibawa ke sana elok

"A *keris* curves, it's beautiful wherever it is" = A smart person will be always be able to figure out how to do a job well.

The *keris* is a knife with a curved, double-edged blade that kings and aristocrats carried. It was as much a status symbol as a means of defense, and inspired tales of supernatural exploits, including *keris* hurtling out of sheaths and attacking a foe. Some house owners attached *keris* to the roof beam to protect their homes. Even today, some Javanese view *keris* as sacred and magical, able to generate luck or fend off misfortune.

Berkeras tidak berkeris (insist on not using a *keris*) pays tribute to one courageous enough to fight without a weapon.

❈ Mulut bawa madu, pantat bawa sengat

The mouth carries honey, the posterior carries a sting.

People resemble bees. At first, they say things as sweet as honey. Later, they deliver a sting.

❈ Mengambil langkah seribu

"Take 1,000 steps" = Run fast to escape a problem.

❀ Buang arang ke laut
Throw coal into the sea.

You have to do a good deed to recover your reputation after a bad deed. Coal is associated with bad deeds.

❀ Ilmu lebih berharga daripada harta
Knowledge is more valuable than treasure.

Elders advise youths to seek knowledge rather than money because the former begets the latter. Unlike cash, wisdom never runs out.

"Seek knowledge as far away as China," is an expression attributed to the Prophet Muhammad. *Cari ilmu sampai ke negeri Cina.*

PART IV
Modern Life

Chapter Twelve

Around Town

Oil profits spurred an economic boom in the 1970s, and cities swelled with job-seekers from the countryside. Some people made fortunes. Urban living was gritty for most.

❀ Jakarta

Indonesia's capital grew out of *Sunda Kelapa*, a port controlled by a Hindu kingdom. It became *Jayakarta* (City of Victory, in Sanskrit) after a Muslim sultan, Fatahillah, defeated the Portuguese there in 1527. In 1619, Dutch colonizers torched the place and renamed it Batavia, a name that derives from an ancient Germanic tribe which once lived in what is now the Netherlands. Batavia became the administrative center for the Dutch East Indies, which later became Indonesia.

Cholera, typhoid and malaria raged in Batavia, a swampy outpost known to some colonizers as *het graf der Hollanders* (the grave of the Dutch). The first recorded epidemic of dengue fever in Batavia was in 1779. The Dutch called it *knokkelkoorts* (joint fever) because of the intense joint pain.

The Dutch built canals in Batavia. They dredged them with the help of laborers who dived into the filthy water and filled baskets with dirt from the bottom. Each time, they wriggled deeper into the mud.

Eventually, colonizers moved inland to a plantation area called *weltevreden* (very pleased, or happy, in Dutch). They built tree-lined avenues and walled mansions in spacious, salubrious surroundings.

The Japanese occupied Indonesia during World War II. Eager to win local sympathies, they restored the city's old name, though in shortened form: *Djakarta*. That name was officially adopted after the Dutch gave up claims to their former colony in 1949 following armed conflict. Indonesia introduced a new spelling system in 1972, dropping Djakarta in favor of Jakarta.

Indonesia's first president, a former architecture and civil engineering student called Sukarno, commissioned grandiose monuments in the capital. The Soviet Union built a sports stadium. Japanese reparations from World War II funded the nation's first international hotel, Hotel Indonesia.

In *The Year of Living Dangerously*, a novel set against the backdrop of upheaval in 1965, Australian author C.J. Koch compared the Hotel Indonesia to "a luxury ship in mid-ocean." Five-star hotels and gaudy shopping malls eclipsed the hotel's one-time grandeur.

Much of Jakarta's affluence hugs the main arteries of the city, south of the old port. Gaudy mansions with pillars and limos in the driveways line upscale streets. Other neighborhoods have narrow alleys and tightly knit, one-storey dwellings that resemble *kampung*, or rural villages. They are poor and overcrowded. Some people live in *pondok*, traditional rooming houses. Sewage-laden canals sometimes flood in the monsoon season. Public health programs have curbed disease, but rats and refuse abound.

Indonesia's biggest garbage dump sits in Bekasi on the outskirts of Jakarta, where hundreds of beetle-like scavengers, many of them children, swarm over mounds of rubbish. They spear plastic bottles and other recyclable items with metal spikes and tuck them into wicker baskets slung on their backs.

The dump closed for a week in 2001 because of a dispute with local residents. The *Jakarta Post*, an English-language daily newspaper, declared in a headline: "Jakarta may sink under mountain of garbage."

Traffic is a grind. Millions of cars, buses, motorbikes, motorized tricycles weave through the gridlock. Migrants swarm daily into the densely-populated city. The city is running out of space to bury people, as most Muslims eschew cremation.

In 2004, Jakarta launched a bus-based, rapid transit system similar to a model implemented in Bogota, Colombia. Reviews are mixed. Progress on plans for a monorail is slow.

In many areas, buses still stop anywhere to pick up passengers, snarling traffic. Vehicles break down and drivers repair them in the middle of the road. Exhaust fumes invade eyes, noses and throats.

Jakarta has few green areas to offset the heat and smog. Some urban planners say Jakarta needs a modern version of *alun-alun*, a central space where kings meted out punishment, or allowed citizens to voice grievances. A huge spire topped with gold coating sits near the presidential palace in a square with lawns and fountains. The area is more bleak than inviting. An enclosed section was set aside for spotted deer, an incongruous sight to passing motorists. The deer population has soared.

Indonesia's second-largest city, Surabaya, is said to be named after an epic, mythical battle between a shark (*sura*) and a crocodile (*buaya*). The two creatures adorn the city emblem, and curl around each other on a large monument at a traffic circle.

❀ Jalan Malioboro
Malioboro Street.

A thoroughfare in the central Javanese city of Yogyakarta that draws shoppers, tourists, street musicians and rickshaw drivers.

Vendors sell jewelry and textiles on the sidewalks, sharing space with diners at low, roadside tables.

The street was reputedly named after Britain's Duke of Marlborough, a visitor to the city. The British administered Indonesia from 1811 to 1816 after France occupied Holland during the Napoleonic wars. Britain returned Indonesia to the Dutch after the fighting ended.

Generations ago, Javanese didn't need street names because most towns were small. Everybody knew everybody. They just pointed a traveler in the direction of a town district such as Yogyakarta's *kraton*, the palace quarter. Once in the district, a traveler mentioned the name of his host, and someone showed him the way.

❈ Jam karet

"Rubber time" = Indonesian time = The hours can be as elastic as rubber. Punctuality is optional.

One word works as a foolproof excuse if you're late for an appointment: *macet*. Traffic jam. Anyone who has endured the smog-clogged gridlock of city streets will understand, or is unlikely to call your bluff.

Doing business in Indonesia can frustrate foreign executives. *Besok* (tomorrow) doesn't mean the deal will be sealed tomorrow. It can refer to some undefined time in the future.

Centuries ago, Javanese royal courts dominated other cultures in the archipelago. Javanese aristocrats frowned on haste, and their taste for grace was evident in the refined, languid movements of their court dances.

In the 17th century, Dutch merchants arrived and turned the archipelago into a supplier of resources to Europe. They ordered farmers to plant crops and toil on rubber plantations, surrendering yields to the government. Farmers had a tough time coping with the rigorous rhythm of fixed hours and forced labor.

Malaysian historian Syed Hussein Alatas criticized the colonial stereotype of the lazy local in his 1977 English-language book, *The Myth of the Lazy Native.*

Alatas speculated that the term *jam karet* emerged during colonial times because Indonesian workers worked sluggishly on rubber plantations to protest the harsh conditions.

In 1915, a West Sumatran newspaper alluded—in the spelling of that era—to the heavy workload that the Dutch imposed on plantation laborers:

"If we pay close attention, the clock is shouting another kind of time. Listen to it: 'Work! Work! Work!'

Djika kita hati-hatikan benar ada lagi jang diteriakkan djam itoe: dengarkanlah oleh moe: 'Kerdja! Kerdja! Kerdja!'

Today, managers and urban dwellers view *jam karet* as a national handicap, and reprimand staff and friends when they turn up late.

Janji Belando is a "Dutch promise." This defunct expression from colonial days was a pledge of punctuality.

———

In the early 19th century, thousands of laborers under the supervision of Dutch colonizers constructed a road along the coastline of Java island. Conditions were hard, and many workers died of disease and deprivation. The man who conceived the idea for the road was Herman Willem Daendels, governor of what was then called the Dutch East Indies. His harsh methods earned him the nickname *Tuan Besar Guntur* (Thunder Boss).

✻ Jalan tikus
"Rat road" = A shortcut.

A blessing to car and motorcycle drivers who avoid the crush of traffic on main roads at rush hour. Enough nooks and crannies for an army of rats line cluttered byways. The car- or motorbike-bound traveler scurries through the warren, gaining a few extra minutes on commuters jammed on the thoroughfare. Or maybe, like a flimsy bug in a spider's web, he gets into a new jam.

✻ Belok kiri, boleh langsung
Turn left, can go straight.

This traffic sign at intersections seems to say two things at once, but it means drivers who want to turn left can do so on a red light.

Indonesians chop up sentences and still understand each other. Crammed onto a small sign, the traffic directive is short for:

"If you want to turn left you can go straight ahead on a red light."

Kalau mau belok kiri boleh langsung saat lampu merah.

The ruling makes sense because Indonesians drive on the left. Authorities sometimes remove these signs without warning. One-way signs and other road rulings also come and go because Jakarta and other major cities are always changing. Police struggle to keep up with the ebb and flow of traffic. Many Indonesian drivers don't know much about traffic rules, and chaos ensues. The variety of vehicles, including the *bajaj*, or motorized rickshaw, makes things worse. Motorcycles are known as *laler* (flies).

The highlands city of Bandung in West Java is notorious because the streets are one-way. South of Jakarta, the public minivans in Bogor seem like thousands of ants crawling around the city streets. Medan, a noisy, industrial center in North Sumatra, is another motorists' nightmare.

✱ Joki

From the English jockey, or horse rider. A *joki* is a stand-in, usually in some dubious, or illegal activity.

In Jakarta, *joki* helped drivers get around the restrictions of a three-in-one, car-pooling system. During rush hour and other busy periods, only cars with three or more passengers could travel on major roads to reduce traffic congestion.

Some drivers paid a few thousand rupiah to *joki*, unemployed bystanders who hopped in a car at a traffic light so the driver could take the faster, three-in-one route. Some *joki* dressed like office workers and dodged the scrutiny of city inspectors. *Joki* disappeared from the streets after the morning rush hour, and returned for the late afternoon shift.

Students hired another kind of *joki* to take their driving tests or university entrance examinations. Exams are a huge affair, with thousands of youths filling up sports stadiums to answer multiple-choice questions. Some students figured they can get away with sending someone smarter in their place.

Komplotan joki (gang of cheats) are "professional" students who move from university to university, taking exams for money.

Many Indonesian students are relaxed about cheating. They risk becoming outcasts if they don't let others look at their test papers.

"Your position will determine your fortune" (*posisi menentukan prestasi*) is a common saying among youths. It sounds serious and career-oriented, but it's tongue-in-cheek. In the classroom, it means: hours of study won't get you good marks. But you will get high grades if your desk is next to that of the class genius.

✿ Ketok magic

"Magic knocks" = An automobile garage that fixes dented cars for low prices.

The mechanics don't use high-tech tools, and instead bang away with hammers wrapped in cloth. Labor is cheap in these places.

An urban myth in Indonesia says *ketok magic* employ genies to remove dents. Secretive mechanics perpetuate the myth, asking customers not to peep around the garage door while they're working.

Many of these closely guarded workshops are enclosed by cheap, corrugated metal sheets spraypainted with huge signs reading *ketok magic*.

The most famous auto workshops of this kind are in Blitar, a small town in East Java where the first *ketok magic* opened in the late 1950s.

Believers swear by the mechanics, who supposedly cast spells on their cars. Others say mechanics just knock the metal back into place and smooth the body with putty.

Indonesian youths who dent the family car while out for a joy ride depend on *ketok magic*, which are cheaper than regular garages and hassle-free. You don't need to show an ID as long as you pay upfront or leave a large deposit.

Some people say you shouldn't drive past a *ketok magic* where your car has been fixed. If you do, you'll end up turning it in for repairs again and again.

———

These days, some conventional garages call themselves *ketok magic* to attract customers.

Bekleding means upholstery in Dutch. It refers to small shops that sell seat coverings for cars and motorcycles.

Tambal tubles (tire repair) is a sign on many garages. *Tubles* is a bastardization of "tubeless"—the tire without an inner tube. The expression looks funny if you understand both Indonesian and English; how can you patch or repair holes if there's no tube?

Small stalls also offer to fix tires, with or without tubes. You can tell by the buckets of water lying around. They dunk the inner tires in water and look for the bubbles of air that float to the surface. That's how they find the punctures.

❀ Wartel & Warnet

Wartel are *warung telepon*, telephone stalls that offer fax and telephone service. *Warung Internet* are a step up because you can go online as well.

These places let cent-scraping students or factory workers call mobile phones or long-distance at a decent price. They are easy to find in small towns or on main thoroughfares of big cities.

Wartels have three to a dozen booths, each furnished with a stool and a meter box with bright red lights that keeps track of the cost of the call. It's easier to chat because you don't have to frantically feed coins into a box, or buy expensive calling cards.

Most *wartel* booths have thin walls that make it hard for a dashing, college-bound Casanova in the big city to woo his sweet girlfriend back in the home village. It's not the best place to negotiate a sensitive business deal, unless you want the whole neighborhood to hear.

Warnet have clusters of cubicles with computers and Internet for millions of Indonesians who can't afford to buy a computer, or sign up to a service provider. It's a step down from more expensive cyber cafes, where cappuccino replaces bottled tea (*teh botol*) on the menu.

Some *warnet* and *wartels* are open all night, filling with zombie-like customers who surf the web, join multiplayer, shoot-em-up games or craft that perfect e-mail. Hackers and makers of false IDs and other forged cards and documents are known to frequent the *warnet*.

Imam Samudra, an Islamic militant executed for the deadly bombings in Bali in 2002, said he visited *warnets* to check messages when he was on the run. Logging on from his hideouts would have made it easier for investigators to track him down, he said.

❧ Komputer Jangkrik

"Cricket computer" = A locally assembled personal computer.

The cricket, or grasshopper, computer owes its name to low-quality components. When the hard disk broke down, the computer would emit a shrill cricket-like "creeeeeek, creeek." The term spread in the 1980s when PCs became more widely available in Indonesia.

Today, workshops, many of them catering to university students, cobble together computers that look second-hand but have all the latest features. These miracles of technology are *komputer rakitan* (assembled computers). Indonesia is a haven of hackers and pirated software.

The government-run Indonesian Language Center tried to introduce several computer terms. Mouse is *tetikus*, from *tikus* (mouse). *Laman* (page), a Malay term, is a Web page. Wizard became *wisaya*, the Javanese term for a net.

Most were clunky, direct translations, and tech-savvy youths didn't think they were catchy enough. The center's terms didn't generate much interest, and English remains the language of computers. Carder, hacker, USB port, hub, router and switch are all commonly used by Indonesians familiar with computers.

❦ Sesama bus kota dilarang saling mendahului
City buses are prohibited from passing one another.

A sticker with this warning adorns the back windows of many buses in Jakarta. It urges drivers not to race with colleagues or other competitors, though many motorists ignore the edict. The goal of speeding is to collect more fares to cover the vehicle rental fee (*uang setoran*), and have a leftover profit.

Some people use the expression to encourage fair competition in whatever field, and discourage pushing and shoving, literal or otherwise.

❦ Rokok kretek
Clove cigarettes.

Indonesia is home to *rokok kretek*, or clove cigarettes; a blend of tobacco, cloves, and flavoring, wrapped either in ironed corn husk (*kelobot* or *klobot*) or paper. Clove cigarettes were originally conceived as medicine for sore throats and asthma in Kudus, Central Java, in 1880.

Rokok comes from the Dutch *roken* (to smoke). *Kretek* is onomatopoeic, referring to the crackling sound of cloves when they burn.

Today, hundreds of *kretek* manufacturers operate in Indonesia, and the tobacco industry is the government's biggest source of revenue after oil, gas and timber.

Well over half of Indonesians smoke. Despite imports of Marlboro, Pall Mall and other brands, many Indonesians prefer local *kretek* blends such as HM Sampoerna and Gudang Garam.

Many elderly women smoke *klobot* in the countryside even though a lot of Indonesians think only men should smoke.

Indonesia's most famous author, Pramoedya Ananta Toer, said in media interviews: "I smoke two packets of *kreteks* a day; it's best for my lungs. If I smoke, I'm still living."

Pramoedya was born in 1925, and died in 2006.

A simple way to make friends in Indonesia is to offer a *kretek*. The gesture shows thanks for a small service rendered.

Spectators at traditional shows sometimes reward a performer by throwing cigarette packs onto the stage. A note inside the box tells the performer where to look for the giver after the show. In one case, a Chinese puppet master met a woman that way and they later married.

Tobacco cigarettes, or *rokok putih* (white cigarettes), first appeared in the Dutch East Indies around 1850. The term distinguishes the cigarette filter of white paper from the traditional *kretek* wrapping of yellowish corn husk.

Rokok ting-we is a cigarette that you roll yourself. It comes from the Javanese phrase *linting dhewe* (to roll your own).

Road stalls called *warung rokok* sell cigarettes, as well as sodas, snacks, sweets, lightbulbs, detergent and soap. Peddlers at street intersections offer single cigarettes, or *ketengan* (by the stick). The vendors are called *asongan* (*asong* means to carry).

In Jakarta, cigarette sellers on the street enjoy raunchy jokes based on inside acronyms. If one vendor runs out of stock, he asks a colleague for more. He shouts the brand name, and both sellers share a private laugh.

In the cigarette seller's world, Ardath, a brand that is cheaper than Marlboro, means:

Aku Rela Ditiduri Asal Tidak Hamil.

"I don't mind sleeping with you as long as I don't get pregnant."

The Kansas brand name means:

Kami Anak Nakal Suatu Saat Akan Sadar.

"We are naughty kids, but we'll come to our senses one day."

❀ Pecinan
Chinatown.

The word is a short form of *pe-cina-an*, a place where Chinese congregate. Many Indonesian towns have *pecinan*, sectors originally reserved for ethnic Chinese during Dutch colonial times. Some cities also have *pekojan*, areas that were originally reserved for Indian and Arab merchants. *Koja* was a name for immigrants from Gujarat in India, and Arabs lived in *pekojan* after Indian influence ebbed. The districts were also called *kampung Arab* (Arab village).

The terms *pecinan* and *pekojan* live on today, although many of those areas have more of an ethnic mix.

Resentment towards ethnic Chinese in Indonesia goes back to the colonial era, when the Dutch government gave trading privileges to the Chinese. Chinese, *peranakan* (children of Chinese–Indonesian parentage), Arabs and other foreigners had a higher social status than indigenous Indonesians, who were called *pribumi*. At first, *pribumi* were not allowed to trade with overseas merchants. Arabs, Chinese and *peranakan* were go-betweens for indigenous people who wanted to interact with the Dutch.

In 1740, economic rivalries were high and Dutch efforts to control the number of Chinese in Batavia led to the slaughter of thousands of Chinese.

In the 1960s, Gen. Suharto crushed the Indonesian Communist Party. China had supported the party, and many ethnic Chinese in Indonesia were accused of being communist and killed or jailed for years without trial. Much of the slaughter had roots in ethnic and economic tensions.

Under Suharto's rule, ethnic Chinese had to use Indonesian names instead of their Chinese ones. The government banned Chinese-language publications, as well as the use of Chinese characters in writing.

Tionghoa is a traditional Indonesian term for people from China. They come from *Tiongkok*, which means Middle Country or Middle Kingdom in Chinese. The Chinese traditionally considered themselves as being at the center of culture, while barbarians lived on the fringes.

Under Suharto, *Tionghoa* was replaced with *Cina*. Depending on the tone, *Cina* can be a neutral or derogatory term.

At the same time, Indonesia benefited from the commercial savvy of the Chinese, who make up only a few percent of the population. Suharto granted monopolies and other business privileges to Indonesian Chinese tycoons. The Chinese were resented for links to the government, their economic power, and a perception that they hoarded wealth at the expense of the community. They made convenient scapegoats, and rioters attacked their homes and businesses as Suharto's rule collapsed. Many people died in the chaos.

After Suharto's fall in 1998, Indonesia launched a campaign to remove restrictions on ethnic Chinese. In 2002, the government designated Chinese New Year as a national holiday.

❀ Si manis jembatan Ancol
The pretty girl on Ancol bridge.

It is said that a young woman was raped and murdered at the end of the 19th century at Ancol bridge in North Jakarta, and that her white-clad ghost still haunts the place. The body of the woman, Ariah, was never found, and neither was the culprit.

Ancol at that time was a monkey-infested marshland. Until the 1950s, the area was empty. Nobody built on it, reputedly because its reputation scared away prospective buyers.

The ghost was said to turn cold with fury when men tried to seduce her. Motorists passing over the bridge honked in a ritual greeting to Ariah, but they do so rarely now.

In the 1960s, President Sukarno had a grand plan to build a tower in his name in the area, but he lost his job and the scheme fell through. Eventually, an amusement park was built there.

Ariah's legend was the subject of several movies in the 1970s and 1980s, as well as a television series in 2000 that mixed horror with comedy. The story was popular because Ariah was a stunner. Besides, Indonesians love ghost stories.

❀ Pedagang kaki lima
"Five-footed trader" = A peddler who sells pens, knives, sunglasses, stickers and other knick-knacks from a three-wheeled cart.

These traders work on sidewalks, hindering pedestrians and spilling into the roads. They perch on pedestrian bridges.

Some *kaki lima* roam residential areas, advertising their wares with distinctive sounds. The most prominent are the call, *te... sate...* for satay; the knock of wood upon wood for fried rice; the *tek tek* sound of spatula on wok for noodles called *mie tek-tek*; a high-pitched steam whistle for *putu*, steamed rice cakes filled with brown sugar; Portuguese-inspired *keroncong* music for *gethuk*, sweet cassava cakes eaten with shredded coconut; and the jingle of a bell for bread.

Pedagang kaki lima is said to have originated in the time of Sir Thomas Stamford Raffles, a British administrator in Indonesia in the early 19th century. Raffles decreed that all buildings have a five-foot-wide sidewalk in front of them for pedestrians. Traders used to park carts on the pavements, so the five-foot moniker stuck, according to the theory.

Singapore's Chinatown has similar, covered sidewalks in front of shops. An entire subculture revolved around these five-foot-wide paths, little strips where life in shops, offices and homes tumbled onto the streets.

Kaki means both foot and leg in Indonesian. Another belief about the origin of *pedagang kaki lima* says a vendor's legs as well as the two wheels and balancing stick in front of his cart make up the *kaki lima* (five legs, or feet).

Today, *pedagang kaki lima* means anyone who sells on the street: a woman with a carton of cigarettes, or a stick with two hanging baskets balanced on her shoulder.

———————

Another familiar figure on the street is *ahli kunci* (key expert, or locksmith), who duplicates keys for a living and sets up shop on roadsides near markets and other crowded places. Walk down any main road, and you'll find *ahli kunci*. *Tukang kunci* is another name for this character. *Tukang* is a handyman. A man who sells meatballs is *tukang bakso*. The guy who makes rubber stamps for sealing documents, *tukang stempel*, is also a common sight on the streets.

Indonesians love rubber stamps, a mainstay of the national bureaucracy. A neighborhood that organizes a street celebration on the August 17 Independence Day requires a committee and *stempel*, the custom-made rubber stamps.

Committee members make dozens of photocopied proposals. They stamp the documents and then canvass the neighborhood looking for donations to fund the party.

✺ Dolly

A red–light district in the eastern Javanese city of Surabaya. Dolly comprises eight alleys and hundreds of buildings where about 3,000 prostitutes work.

The area was well known for prostitution in the 1940s, and the clientele consisted of Dutch soldiers stationed at a nearby army base. Tante Dolly (Aunt Dolly) was a pioneering madam who provided prostitutes in the same district after World War II. According to one account, Dolly married a Dutch sailor. Her name stuck.

Today, residents mix with prostitutes in their humdrum daily lives. The brothels have cheap living quarters, and a "show room" where girls line up so clients can take their pick. A mosque and a Christian church sit amidst the brothels. Children of some prostitutes study in a kindergarten in Dolly.

✺ Harga mati
"Dead price" = The lowest price available when bargaining grinds to a halt.

You can bargain the price down in many Indonesian shops, but not in modern department stores and supermarkets.

Harga miring (slanted price) is a discount offer.

Paku Belando (Dutch nails) is an expression from the colonial era that means "fixed price." In those days, Dutch nails were expensive and you couldn't bargain down their price. Forget about a discount if an item for sale was *harga paku Belando* (Dutch nail price).

✻ Cuci gudang
"Wash the warehouse" = A clearance sale.

This modern term is common in department stores. Linguists say it came from salesmen who studied marketing textbooks in English, and botched the translation of clearance sale. They assumed that clearance was a reference to cleaning the warehouse, not clearing it.

✻ Layar tancap
"Screen stuck on the ground" = Outdoor cinema.

This mobile movie house was for poor Indonesians. Companies with national chains promoted their business by sponsoring a truck, equipped with a generator, projector and a screen. The crew unloaded the movie gear in open-air, communal areas. Crowds gathered in the evenings to watch the free entertainment. Dozens of street vendors camped out, selling refreshments, cigarettes as well as mosquito coils, sprays or lotion.

Advertisers paid for the films, and received on-screen publicity that was sometimes as long as the film.

Layar tancep were the most common way to watch films in rural areas in the 1970s and 1980s. They were an effective tool for the government to deliver its messages to remote regions. Much of the fodder on *layar tancep* consisted of flicks about government policies.

Layar tancep disappeared in the 1980s as more people moved to the cities, and television and other modern diversions became more accessible.

A common name for outdoor cinema in West Java was *misbar*, short for *geriMIS buBAR* (a drizzle, pack up). When the rain comes, the outdoor cinema has to close up shop.

The drive-in cinema never caught on in Indonesia. In the 1980s, Jakarta's only drive-in was in Ancol, the northern neighborhood by the harbor. It has closed.

❀ Nongkrong

"Hanging out" = The national past time, which usually involves crouching or squatting in the street to chat.

Nongkrong is not a fleeting pause. It's long and aimless, and those who do it are *nyantai* (chilled out). A veteran of the custom wears flipflops (*sandal jepit*) and takes long drags from clove cigarettes (*ngisep kretek*, or sucks *kretek*).

Men who *nongkrong* squat on the roadside, sit in front of house porches, or lounge on a row of parked *ojeks* (motorbike taxis). Some might be jobless youths with nothing better to do than hang out on the roadside, or near a kiosk selling drinks and cigarettes. But some Indonesians do it after work, or on their day off.

Nongkrong went upmarket in the mid-1980s. A hit radio drama, *Catatan si Boy*, made it cool for brat packs to loll at flashy shopping malls in Jakarta.

Atong is short for *anak tongkrongan*, which translates roughly as "hangout spot kids." If ever a member of a gang of *atong* goes off to the United States to study, chances are good he'll find one of his buddies hanging out in the usual spot when he returns on vacation to Indonesia.

Chapter Thirteen

Insults and the Underground

Yams, canaries and kneecaps are fodder for insults. Television is a rich source of putdowns. Vice is easy to find, depending on the definition.

❀ **Ndasmu njeblug!** (Javanese)
"Your head blew up!" = Give me a break. You're talking bull.

Ndasmu (your head) is an insult on its own that suggests you don't know how to use your brain.

Ndasmu njeblug is an expression of disbelief that takes it one step further: you can't use your head because you don't have one any more. The insult is potent because the head, as the highest part of the body, should be respected.

"Revenues are up because I've managed to scrimp and save on our budget," a department head says at a meeting.

"Save? Revenues are up because we've been slaving away," a worker grumbles. "Your head blew up."

Ndasmu njeblug.

Gundulmu (your bald head) is a lighthearted insult. Bald people portray bumbling clowns in street shows. *Gundul* also means bare. *Bukit gundul* is a barren hill, the kind of landscape that alarms farmers.

❦ Kurang ajar, lu
"You lack learning" = You're out of line.

This harsh reprimand means you are rude, uncouth and sneaky. You're impolite to elders and don't know your place in society.

Kurang ajar, screams a woman whose boyfriend has cheated on her or stood her up. She really means: "You're a lying bastard!"

A mother admonishes her unruly child: *Kamu anak kurang ajar.* (You are a child who has no manners.)

An exasperated office worker sighs and shakes her head when her office mate shows up late for work. *Kurang ajar.*

The expression is also said in jest, as a gentle form of mockery. Some say it in admiration for someone who challenges an unpopular boss or figure of authority.

❦ Dengkulmu (Javanese)
"Your knee" = Idiot. Think before you talk.

"Use your brain, not your knee," is a common epithet on Java. *Pake otak jangan pake dengkul.*

"Your knees are falling down," is a similar putdown. *Dengkulmu anjlog.*

You're stupid and rash if you can't keep your knees in place. Javanese comedians hurled these feisty insults on television shows, and the terms spread among non-Javanese.

❋ Udelmu bodong (Javanese)
"Your belly button sticks out" = You're ugly.

A convex belly button is considered funny and fair game for childish banter.

No matter if the target of this insult is ugly or not. Say it when you're fed up and in a mood for mockery.

"You think you can charm her? In your dreams. And you're ugly!" a sister tells a brother who dreams of wooing a girl.

Kamu pikir bisa gaet dia? Mimpi kali! Udelmu bodong lagi.

For the same impact, you can also say:

"Your belly button is on fire."

Udelmu kobong.

Puput puser (dropping off of the navel) is a Javanese ritual conducted when the stump of the umbilical cord falls off. People say prayers and slather a healing potion on the baby's belly. The Javanese think a concave navel is a good sign.

Some people, though, have a convex belly button, or outtie (*bodong*), a navel with a protuberant lump of scar tissue. This is a source of amusement among Javanese.

After the baby is born and the cord is cut, a husband heads home with the unwashed afterbirth. He washes it in tamarind-scented water and wraps it in white cloth.

The parcel is equipped with a pencil and paper to ensure the baby becomes a diligent student; a sewing needle to ensure the baby stays healthy; a handful of rice for wealth and good luck; an old coin to help it earn money easily in the future; flowers for a sweet and healthy environment; and a prayer to ensure that it becomes pious.

The entire kit is sold in markets.

The husband buries the whole lot by the door in front of the house, where it decomposes. He covers the spot with an umbrella, which protects the burial site from the elements for 34 to 40 days, as well as a light bulb that is permanently switched on to ward off the darkness.

❀ Kulit badak
"Rhino skin" = An oaf. Ignoramus.

No amount of advice gets into his skull, which has a hide as thick as that of a rhinoceros.

Indonesians say such people are *muka tebal* (thick face): humorless and pokerfaced.

❀ Telo (Javanese)
"Yam/cassava" = Numbskull.

Telo means tuber. *Telo rambat* is yam, and *telo pohong* is cassava.

Yams or cassava are food of the poor. Javanese believe they can make a person dumb because they aren't as nutritious as rice.

❀ Otak bunglon
"Chameleon brain" = A fickle character.

A flip-flopper, someone who changes opinions as often as a chameleon changes its color.

❀ Anjing! (Dog!)
"Babi! (Pig!)" = Scum. Filth.

"Dog! Pig!" a man thunders with a withering look and a quivering, pointed finger. *Anjing! Babi!*

Pigs and dogs are unclean and the lowest of animals, according to Muslim beliefs.

Their saliva is considered unholy and adherents who come into contact with it must wash the "contaminated" body part seven times with water, and rub it once with earth before prayer.

Kunyuk (a Sundanese word for monkey) is slang for idiot.

❄ Bangsat

"Wood louse" = Rascal. Scoundrel.

This insult is as harsh as calling someone a bastard or son of a bitch. Indonesians hate the destructive wood louse, which emits a stench as pungent as that of a skunk and burrows into the foundations of houses.

Bangsat also means bedbug. It is considered malevolent in contrast to *kutu* (louse), which is odorless and widely viewed as harmless.

❄ Lemot (acronym)
LEMah OTak
Weak brain. A sluggish thinker.

A frustrated passenger sneers *lemot!* at a taxi driver who has lost his way.

Otak (brain) usually precedes an adjective. It comes second in *lemah otak* because the acronym *lemot* rolls off the tongue easily.

Otak udang (shrimp brain) has the same meaning as *lemot*.

Someone who doesn't pay attention is *telmi*, short for *TELat MIkir* (late to react/think).

The Betawi people of Jakarta like to cuss, and many of their insults are known nationwide. Salty-tongued characters on television comedies reinforced the image of the Betawi as a foul-mouthed lot. They included Bajuri, the driver of a *bajaj* (three-wheeled taxi) who bemoans his misfortune.

A character on another show is Dul, an earnest young man who is eager to get ahead and please his parents. He works his way through university and gets a job. Dul's sidekick is Mandra, a dumb, happy-go-lucky fellow who spouts Betawi phrases about animals and household objects.

The first comedy series to hit it big on Indonesian television was *Lenong Rumpi*, featuring mostly Betawi comedians. *Rumpi* is slang for gossip, and *Lenong* is an old form of Betawi folk theater in which the actors banter with the audience.

The theater form started generations ago as a series of jokes accompanying the Betawi traditional music, *gambang kromong*. *Gambang* is a xylophone and *kromong* is a gong, and flutes and a kind of violin accompany those instruments. It's an off-the-wall music that originally developed in the outskirts of Jakarta. The music's funky rhythms, rap-style male vocals and female wailing have strong Chinese roots.

There were no plotlines in *Lenong Rumpi*, but the performance evolved into an all-night, comic act in villages. *Lampu colen* (fire torches) on the four corners of the stage were a trademark of the *lenong* set.

In the early 1990s, *Lenong Rumpi* aired on RCTI, a fledgling, private television station. The show injected modern pizzazz into the old theater form. It was lively and irreverent. Urban audiences loved the banter about tough city life and attitudes toward sex, marriage, neighbors, jobs and money. Indonesia's conservative set loathed the slapdash mix of Indonesian and the Betawi language on *Lenong Rumpi*. Some found it lowbrow because a pop singer, a fashion designer and other celebrity guests turned up.

Still, *Lenong Rumpi* was a relief after years of staid, state-run programming. Indonesians had been hungry for something different. In the 1980s, state-run TV broadcasts ran from 3 p.m. to midnight during the week. On Sundays, they started at 9 a.m. The menu comprised ribbon-cutting ceremonies, military choruses, stodgy comedies and special broadcasts of Suharto talking to farmers. Some Western television series started at 11 p.m., an inconvenient hour for teenagers. The programs were heavily censored. Not a smidgeon of kissing or nudity.

❀ Pantat kutilang kuning (Betawi)
"Yellow ass canary" = Miser.

A miser displays the yellow backside of a canary because he doesn't want you to see the bird upfront, or hear how nicely it sings.

"You miser! Who wants to be friends with you?"

Dasar pantat kutilang kuning. Siapa yang mau temenan sama lu?

Dasar is used for emphasis in Indonesian insults, and a negative adjective often follows. *Dasar* means base, or most basic (of traits). When it precedes a noun such as miser, it can mean you, or typical. It implies that the lousy behavior of the accused person is to be expected.

❀ Kamu dodol!
"You're a coconut fudge!" = You're slow on the uptake. How foolish of you!

Dodol is a gooey fudge made from coconut, rice flour and unprocessed date palm sugar. To prepare it, you need a sturdy arm to stir the pot vigorously and avoid burning the contents. It takes several hours to cook.

Another common expression is *Dasar dodol!* The long meaning is: "That's typical of you, fudge-brain!"

❈ **Dasar tobangke gile** (Betawi)
You dirty, crazy old man.

One theory says *tobangke* (slang for crazy, old man) comes from *tua bangka* (old wood from Bangka island).

Dutch colonial reports said Bugis sailors from South Sulawesi had reached an island on the east coast of Sumatra in the 17th century.

The Bugis reportedly found *wangka* trees, whose sturdy timber was perfect for building houses. Carpenters concluded that the older the wood, the greater its strength. This trait came to describe men. The wood became famous across Indonesia.

The theory goes that the pronunciation of *wangka* changed over generations, and the island where the wood was found became known as Bangka.

The link between age and strength eventually faded, and old and strong became old and nasty. Today, *tua bangka* refers to lewd, old men who prey on young women.

Kampung Bangka (Bangka Village) is a neighborhood adjacent to Kemang, an upmarket, residential area in South Jakarta.

The neighborhood got its name because many trees from Bangka were planted there.

Despite the fame of its wood, Bangka is best known among Indonesians for tin production.

❈ **Lagu lu kayak nenek-nenek keilangan sisik** (Betawi)
"You act as if you are a grandmother losing her chewing tobacco" = You're out of your mind. You've lost the plot.

Some old women chew tobacco to cleanse the palette and teeth after a meal, or because they think it's more polite than smoking. The custom is common among the rural poor. A grandmother who loses her chewing tobacco goes nuts. Try this expression on someone who fusses over a trivial matter.

❈ Kalu begini terus-terusan, lama-lama gue bisa mati berdiri (Betawi)

"If this goes on, I could die standing up" = You're killing me.

A father rolls his eyes and says this if his son asks for cash or makes other grating demands. To die standing up is considered unnatural because it happens quickly and without warning. No time for a slow, bedridden decline.

❈ Mak dirodok (Betawi)

"Oh mother, I've been speared" = Oh damn.

"Yuck! Oh damn! This coffee is so bitter. You haven't put any sugar in it."

> *Puih! Mak dirodok. Nih kopi pait banget. Elo belon kasih gula.*

Sir Thomas Stamford Raffles, the British lieutenant-governor of Java in the early 19th century, wrote in his book *The History of Java* that *dirodok* means "to spear from beneath."

Betawi people used spears or long wooden sticks with sharpened ends to pluck mangoes and other ripe fruit from tall trees. A thief hiding among the leaves and branches might get speared from beneath and cry *mak dirodok!*

Today, the expression sums up an awkward situation. Anyone caught in the act, especially a sexual one, might say or think: *Mak dirodok!*

Mak is short for *Aduh emak* (Oh mother!) and the connotation is: "I do despair!" Blurt this out if you are confronted with incompetence.

Another common Betawi expression is *mak dikipe* (Oh mother, it's got flaws). This also means, "Oh damn."

❀ Kambing congek (Betawi)
"Deaf goat" = Someone who might as well be a part of the furniture on social occasions.

He doesn't know how to take part, and has to accept he won't be included. He's like a third wheel, the unwanted companion tagging along behind a romantic couple.

This Betawi expression is so widespread that it appears in Indonesian-language dictionaries.

A scapegoat is *kambing hitam*, or black goat.

❀ Bujug buneng (Betawi)
"There's nothing left" = You can't top that.

Bujug means "It's all gone" or "There's nothing left."

Buneng has no meaning, and is linguistic decoration. The *boo* sounds are funny and emphatic.

Betawis say the whole phrase if there's nothing left that can top or beat something. It can be negative, or denote admiration.

"Oh my, what a surprise, he's finished a full plate of rice."

Bujug buneng, nasi ulam sepiring bengkak ludes dia gegares.

This is an indirect criticism of greed.

But you can also exclaim in admiration:

"Oh, fantastic. That's a really great piece of writing."

Bujug buneng. Keren banget tulisannya.

❀ Gertak sambal

"Chili bluff" = An empty threat.

Chilies burn your throat and the searing sensation is unbearable. But they won't kill you.

"Don't be afraid. He's only making empty threats."
Jangan takut. Dia cuma gertak sambal.

❀ Dhuwite mbokdemu tah! (Javanese)

Your auntie's money!

❀ Dhuwite mbahmu!

"Your grandfather's money!" = Really? You don't say. You're kidding.

Javanese turn to the family for good-natured ribbing. Roll these phrases out when shocked or skeptical.

❀ Musik ngak-ngik-ngok

An onomatopoeic term for the vexing din of bad music.

In the early 1960s, President Sukarno condemned Western music as a contaminating influence. He accused the Indonesian band Koes Bersaudara, five brothers who modeled themselves on the Everly Brothers, of playing *musik ngak-ngik-ngok.*

The brothers were jailed for three months in 1965, allegedly because Sukarno loathed their music. But in 2004, one of the brothers claimed they were imprisoned as part of an elaborate counterintelligence plot. The goal, he said, was to publicly appear out of favor with Sukarno and be expelled to Malaysia, where they would gather intelligence. At that time, Indonesia was trying to undermine Malaysia, which it viewed as a puppet of Western colonial aggression.

The band later changed its name to Koes Plus after replacing one of the brothers with a musician from outside the family. It recorded 17 albums to become Indonesia's most prolific rock band. Their tracks had innocent titles: *Bis Sekolah* (School Bus), *Dara Manisku* (My Sweet Girl), *Angin Laut* (Sea Wind), *Pagi Yang Indah* (Beautiful Morning).

Today, buskers play Koes Plus songs on city buses. The elderly, grizzled band members routinely appear on rock shows to receive honors.

✺ Goyang ngebor
Drilling dance.

The erotic dancing style of Inul Daratista, a hip-grinding singer of *dangdut*, a music with strong Malay, Indian and Arabic rhythms. *Dangdut* is an onomatopoeic name based on the sound of a drum beat. Flutes enhance the languid pace of *dangdut*, which burst onto the scene decades ago. Some people say it's monotonous.

Inul's style is brash and high-tempo. Swinging her hips, she squats and swivels upward, drill-like. Inul performs the maneuver a couple of times during a song, her breath never faltering as she sings.

Inul's extra-sexual style won her foes and fans. Her critics included Rhoma Irama, the so-called king of *dangdut* who barred her from performing his songs, saying she was an affront to traditional *dangdut*. Irama also aligned himself with Muslim groups, which said Inul was a threat to morality.

Inul's supporters include artists, scholars, office workers and village folk. In private houses, mothers ask toddlers to dance like *ratu ngebor* (the drilling queen). At family gatherings, one contest is *goyang Inul* (Inul dance). The literal definition of *goyang* is move, or shake.

Other female *dangdut* singers are not in Inul's league, but can still grind a hip. Some appear at campaign events to give politicians a boost.

❀ Musik rap tidak berseni
Rap is not art.

Former President B.J. Habibie made this statement when he was a technology minister in 1995. He objected to plans to hold a national rap festival in Jakarta, saying the lyrics were crass. But rap thrived during Indonesia's authoritarian rule.

Indonesian rap bands poke fun at the elite. Sound Da Clan's *Anak Gedongan* (Rich Kid), Neo's *Borju* (Bourgeois) and Black Skin's *Cewek Matre* (Material Chick) and *Nyontek Lagi* (Cheating Again) slam the wealthy as corrupt and indifferent to the plight of Indonesia's poor.

Top rapper Iwa K blasted the indifference of middle-class youths to the country's problems in his chart-buster *DMMT*, short for *Di mana... Mata... Mulut... Telinga.*

"Where are... your eyes... mouth... ears."

Iwa K's fans are middle-class youths.

❀ Apotik jalanan
"Walking drugstore" = Drug dealer.

Drug abuse has a long history in Indonesia. Opium dens thrived in Java centuries ago, and the Dutch colonial government later licensed stores that sold the drug. Today, clandestine factories churn out tablets of the drug Ecstasy for export. The government is trying to crack down, but state corruption slows the campaign.

Perangi Narkoba means: Wage war on drugs. It's the Indonesian version of the anti-drug slogan made famous by Nancy Reagan in the United States: "Just say no!" *Narkoba* is a catch-all term for *NARKotika dan OBAt-obatan* (narcotics and drugs). Another term is *Napza* or *narkotika dan zat adiktif* (narcotics and addictive substances).

On the streets, abusers refer to illegal drugs as boat, a reversal of the first two letters in *obat* (drugs). To take drugs is *ngeboat*.

Pop in, inhale, inject, and puff on the drugs to get *lagi on* (switched on, or high). *Konak* is slang for *ketagihan*, or addicted. *Sakau* is when you shiver with withdrawal symptoms.

You get drugs from a *bandar* (dealer). *Joki* (jockey) is one cog in the distribution chain. They usually become dealers to feed their own addiction.

Heroin (*putaw*) and cocaine (*salju*, or snow; *srepet*, or sniff; and *charlie*) were once confined to the well-off who could afford the prices. Heroin has had a presence on university campuses since 1970, and later entered poor, urban neighborhoods. It became more widely available in the free-for-all atmosphere that followed the 1998 fall of Suharto.

Morphine is *bedak setan* (devil's powder) or *bedak mayat* (corpse powder). The stuff sold on the street is *kain putih* (white sheet). The dealers call it *kain panjang* (long sheet). *Kipe* is to inject drugs.

Marijuana is favored by university students and self-styled bohemians who call it *ganja*, *cimeng*, *gress* (from grass), *daon* (*daun* is a leaf) or its slang *dogel* or *doggi*. *Ngaben* is light up a joint. On Bali, *ngaben* is a high-society cremation.

A common measurement is *se-am*, short for *seamplop* (one envelope). A bigger stash is *bantal* (a pillow), *batu* (stone) and *balok* (block).

The verb *ngecak* describes divvying up *ganja* into *amplop*, or envelopes. *Betrik* describes the process of getting every bit of the weed out of the sachet.

Ecstasy, also called *E* or *inex*, is the designer drug of choice for Indonesian clubbers and ravers who dance on its euphoric wave at all-night parties.

Cheap pills on the market include Pil BK, a reverse play on Pil KB, a birth control tablet. Pil BK is sometimes called Pil Bung Karno, the nickname of Indonesian President Sukarno.

Crystal methamphetamine is *sabu-sabu* or a reverse version, *ubas*. Some workers take it to stay awake if they work long shifts or more than one job.

Ngelem (to sniff glue) is the cheapest option for getting high and is popular among street youths in the cities. One well-known brand is Aika Abon, the orange, heavy-duty adhesive for wood and ceramics. It comes in a yellow can.

Anti-drug activists say drug abuse has surged and fear Indonesians could become *generasi pil koplo* (the stupid pill generation). *Koplo* means stupid in Javanese.

Anti-drug slogans hang on banners at crossroads and entrances to many neighborhoods and communities:

Basmi pengguna narkoba (Destroy drug users and dealers)

Narkoba: Musuh utama Indonesia (Drugs: Indonesia's number one enemy)

Hukuman mati untuk pengguna narkoba (Death to all Drug Users and Dealers)

One Jakarta university missed the mark with an anti-drug banner in English. It said: We take drugs seriously.

The government formed special task forces to fight drugs and introduced the death penalty for some drug offenses.

❀ Saya hanya orang biasa, hidup hanya sekali
I am just a normal man, I can only live once.

Some of the last words of Ayodhay Prasad Chaubey, a convicted heroin smuggler from India who was executed by a police firing squad in August, 2004.

Chaubey, who was on death row for a decade and converted to Islam in prison, said those words in fluent Indonesian. Two Thais arrested in the same case as Chaubey were executed two months later.

Dozens of people are on death row in Indonesia. Many are also foreign drug traffickers. Some were convicted in terrorist bombings.

❀ Hidup segan, mati tak mau
"Reluctant to live, don't want to die" = Beyond caring.

A sick, poor or heartbroken person laments dismal circumstances, but can't or won't do much to change them.

The expression also referred to companies on the wane during the 1997–98 economic crisis. Directors were unable or unwilling to revive the firms with fresh funds or austerity measures. At the same time, the managers were reluctant to shut them down. The enterprises limped along, neither dead nor alive.

❀ Kijang baru
"New mousedeer" = Jailhouse slang for female prisoners.

Police usually transport them to jail in a Toyota *Kijang*, the name of a popular family car in Indonesia. Male prisoners are *kambing* (goat) because they supposedly smell like the animal.

Police who prepare a dossier of charges question suspects in a *proses verbal* (polite report).

Hierarchy rules among prisoners in Indonesia's prison system.

Kepala blok (block head) or foreman is an inmate in charge of several deputies called *palkam*, short for *kePALa KAMar* (room head). Each *palkam* appoints a *korve*, a prisoner who handles his superior's needs outside the cell block. *Korve* is from *corvee*, a French word that means forced labor. That came to mean a tiresome duty.

Brengos, or bouncer/guard, provides security for the prisoners in power. *Brengos* is Javanese for mustache, and mustachioed men are said to be fearsome.

In the women's cell block, the chief prisoner is *mami* (mommy).

Prisoners who don't follow orders are *digulung* (rolled up). That means the guards shout at them, or beat them up.

Inmates who remain unruly are locked in *sel tikus* (rat's cell), so named because of its small size. A prisoner eats, sleeps and defecates in the same place.

Everything has a price in jail, whether it's getting a bar of soap, or an extra portion of meat for lunch. Each prisoner pays *uang toll* (toll fee) to guards or prisoners in order to walk from one cell block to another.

❧ **BF** (pronounced *beh-eff*)
"Blue Film" = A pornographic movie.

BF spawned other terms for porn films such as *Botol Fanta* and *dua-enam*, which is Indonesian for the number 26 (B is the second letter in the alphabet, and F is the sixth). Another term is *Jakarta Bogor*: the letter on car number plates in Jakarta is B, and license plates in Bogor always have F.

Pornografi and *pornoaksi* are terms for pornography that appear in conservative Muslim newspapers and periodicals. *Pornografi* refers to photographs, while *pornoaksi* is the "action" version, or porn films. Pornography is forbidden under a broadly worded law that bans anything offensive to public morality. Efforts to curb access to online pornography have largely failed.

Pirated DVDs and VCDs are available at stalls in a warren of shops and alleys in Jakarta's Chinatown.

Mau BF? the vendors ask. "Do you want blue?"

Police occasionally sweep the area, but the purveyors of smut are back in business before long.

Chapter Fourteen

Hanging Out

Indonesian slang sounds anarchic, and that's where the fun lies. Chop up syllables or get rid of a vowel. Grammar isn't a big concern.

❀ Mau ke mana?

"Where are you going?" = What's up?

This casual greeting sounds intrusive, but don't take it literally. No need to reveal your destination. *Mau ke mana?* is a conversation opener, an attempt to grab your attention for a breezy chitchat.

It's OK to give a non-committal reply: *Ke sana* (Over there). You can also try *mau main* (want to play). *Main* means a lot of things for different people in different situations: to play, to have fun, to meet friends, to hang out, to have sex.

❀ Bahasa Prokem

Thug language.

Slang of the 1970s and 1980s, largely based on syllable patterns. *Prokem* comes from *preman* (thug), which evolved from *vrijman*, the Dutch word for free man.

Linguists believe the roots of *bahasa prokem* lie in an underworld language of Jakarta thieves who spoke in code while planning robberies. For example, police in ocher-colored uniforms were *rumput* (grass).

———————

"Watch out for the grass," a thief warned his accomplice. *Awas ada rumput.*

The slang spread when city youths picked it up from fictional street toughs in books and on television. The trend was to distort a word by taking its first syllable and sticking "OK" in the middle.

That's how the term *pr-OK-em* was born.

Other examples:

Bapak (father) boils down to *bap*, which becomes *bOKap*.
Duit (money) – *du* – *dOKu*.
Siapa (who) – *siap* – *siOKap*.

Jumbling consonants was also fun. *Mobil* (car) became *bo-il*. This wordplay is still around, but a lot of people think it's old-fashioned.

Slang artists in the 1970s sliced off syllables and replaced them with *se*:

kowe (you) → *kowese*.
Genit (flirtatious) → *gense*
Babi (pig) → *babse*
Sombong (snob) → *somse*.

People added a second consonant in the second syllable of a word, and sandwiched it between o and e:

Saya (I) → *sayOyE*

Kamu (You) → *KamOmE*

Or they added *fa* at either end of the second syllable:

Saya → *saFAyaFA*
Kamu → *kaFAmuFA*

Things really got out of control in the 1980s.

People added *in* to everything. The addition was a prefix if the word started with a vowel, and fell in the middle of a word beginning with a consonant.

Here's an example:

A formal sentence such as *Anda tidak bisa bicara begitu* (you can't say that) sounds cold and stiff. It's a social blunder to say that to a hip, young crowd. A casual way of saying it for the Jakarta bunch is: *Elu gak bisa bilang 'gitu. Elu* is *Anda*, *gak is tidak*, *bilang* is *bicara* and *'gitu* is *begitu*.

But that isn't enough. The in-crowd made it more complicated with the in pattern.

The sentence ends up:

INelINu—gINak—bINisINa—bINilINang—bINegINitINu.

Maestros of this language rattled off long sentences without effort. Simpler transformations reached the mainstream and survive today.

Banci, a derogatory term for gays that sprang up in the 1980s, became *bINancINi* in the corrupt form. That was shortened to *binan*, an inoffensive term for gay.

Banci had started out as an insult or stereotype because it associated gays with effeminate behavior and unsavory nightlife. Over time, the stereotype faded and *banci* now refers only to transvestites.

Bule is a white foreigner. In *bahasa prokem*, it becomes *bINulINe*, and then *binul*.

Novels, comic books and radio plays made *bahasa prokem* popular among trendy youths. The tough-talking hero of one set of novels, Ali Topan, wore sunglasses, flared jeans and a leather jacket and roamed the streets on a motorbike. Youths took after Ali and called themselves *anak jalanan* (street children), the Indonesian version of homeboys.

A radio program named after its lead character, *Catatan Si Boy*, narrated the adventures of a pious Muslim kid who prayed five times a day, and carried a prayer mat and worry beads in his luxury sports car. Directors made four high-grossing movies about *Catatan Si Boy*. Some of the action was shot in Los Angeles, where the kid stays with his wealthy uncle. The character helped turn *bahasa prokem* into an institution.

Another fictional icon of the 1980s was Lupus, a joke-cracking schoolboy in Jakarta whose life was serialized in a magazine for teenagers. Lupus failed his tests because he was too lazy to study, squeezed inside crammed buses to go to school and coped with little pocket money.

The popularity of these characters dipped with the spread of television and the surge of American shows for teenagers. Hawaii Five O, Starsky and Hutch and Beverly Hills 90210 distracted Indonesian teenagers from their local heroes.

———

Jakarta was the cradle of street slang, and its young sophisticates dismissed linguistic trends in other cities. Still, other places made their mark.

The newspaper *Suara Merdeka* in Semarang, a steamy, coastal city in Central Java, generated and disseminated youth talk in the 1980s. One expression was *wakuncar*, short for *wajib kunjung pacar*. It means "obligatory sweethearts' visit," or date. In the 1990s, the term became popular after Camelia Malik, a respected singer, dancer and actor in her 40s, made it the title of a pop song.

Snobbish Jakartans said the expression was clumsy.

✤ Bahasa gaul
Hanging out language.

Hip, urban slang of the 1990s until today. *Gaul* means to make friends, or hang out with them.

The insertion, reversal and chopping of syllables stays, but the novelty wears off and people turn to word substitution. This fad is fun and radical because there is no pattern to decipher. The words chosen as substitutes are glamorous and bombastic, and bear little resemblance to the original words. Only the first syllable stays.

Pusing (confused, or getting a headache) became *puspita* (the Sanskrit word for flower).

Bahasa gaul has a cosmopolitan flavor, with heavy doses of English vocabulary. The slang is more widespread and flashy than its precursor, *bahasa prokem*. Some trendy Indonesians say things that even native speakers can't understand. A lot of the slang revolved around the gay, showbiz and fashion worlds.

"There's a cute one," a hairdresser says. *Yang itu cakrawala!*

The phrase is discreet because *cakrawala* (horizon) is slang for *cakap* (cute guy).

Some words worked with insertions or substitutions. *Lambat* (late) became *Lambretta*, an old Italian-designed scooter, or *Lamborghini*, the Italian sports car.

Lapar banget (very hungry) became *laprida banget* (chop off the second syllable and add the meaningless suffix -*rida*), or *lapangan bola* (soccer field).

The soccer field conveys an image of vastness to describe how ravenous you are.

You can have a conversation with both types of slang— insertion and substitution—at the same time. Cool people understand.

The spread of private television gave the slang more exposure. Viewers soaked up *bahasa gaul* on teenage dramas, comedies, reality TV shows, celebrity gossip news and game shows. The invasion of cable and satellite television, and the Internet, gave it an international flair.

Bahasa gaul creates a shared identity among those who speak it. It defines a sexual, professional or generational lifestyle, and is a comfort and refuge for people outside the mainstream.

Prostitutes developed their own secret language to talk privately in case they were arrested, or in unwanted company.

Heterosexuals picked up some *bahasa gaul* from gays. The English acronym *ML* (make love) was popular among gays, but the straight crowd liked it too:

"Tanti was sleeping with a guy who wasn't her boyfriend."

Si Tanti ML sama cowok lain yang bukan pacarnya.

The following slang is strictly gay: *kucing* (cat)—a young, male, cheap prostitute; *GI Joe*—a gigolo, a male, older prostitute who caters to wealthy clients; *belok* (turn, or anomaly)—gay; *brondong* (young corn)—a cute boy.

Many gay terms end in *-ong*. Homophobes borrow the *-ong* ending, and describe gays as *sekong*. *Sekong* is a variation on *sakit* (illness), a reference to the stereotype of gays as deviants.

Some gays don't use much homosexual slang and think it's unsavory. Although night clubs set aside gay nights and transsexual performers appear regularly on television, many gays don't tell their families or employers that they are gay, and some succumb to social pressure and get married. They pursue a double life.

In 1999, a former model and television comedian, Debby Sahertian, published a 66-page dictionary of slang. She called the book *Kamus Bahasa Gaul* (Hanging Out Language Dictionary). The slang title was *Kamasutra Gaul*.

Sahertian talks fast, smiles a lot, laughs loudly and loves to make up words. She coined quite a few of the terms in her dictionary. She first learned the slang while waiting to be made up before catwalk shows and photo shoots in Medan, North Sumatra in the mid-1990s.

Sahertian absorbed the chitchat of gay hairdressers with heavy lipstick who flirted with each other while administering hair rinses, cream baths and other treatments. Sahertian claims to have invented the term *bahasa gaul*, a spinoff of *tenda gaul* (hanging out tents). She researched the slang in these makeshift cafés, which sprouted during Indonesia's economic crisis in the late 1990s.

Many middle-class office workers lost jobs when the economy collapsed. They opened cafés in front of their houses or in a park. A tarpaulin served as cover for clients. The most successful cafes were funded by celebrities, who loved to gossip.

Bahasa gaul is always evolving. Sahertian invented *mawar* (a rose) as a replacement for *mau* (want). By the time her book came out and hip celebrities were saying *mawar*, she had replaced *mawar* with *kebun bunga* (flower garden).

2000 and onward

The intonation and gestures that accompany expressions are the big things. Celebrity news and gossip shows spread the trends.

❊ Kasiaaaaaaaaaan deh lu
I pity you.

Break my heart, I can already hear the violins playing. I feel sorry for you because you are so behind the times. You're not with the in-crowd.

Say this sarcastic phrase with a cheery yet dismissive tone. At the same time, lift your right hand and make a long zigzag in the air from top to bottom with your index finger.

A celebrity presenter, Eko Patrio, made this expression popular. In 2001, Eko hosted a celebrity gossip show called *KISS*, or *Kisah Intim Seputar Selebrity* (Intimate Stories About Celebrities).

He was such a hit that in 2004 he hosted his own show called *E' Ko Ngegosip* (Oh! Gossip!) The name of the show was a pun on his name.

Such shows enthrall Indonesia. Many of them hit record high ratings. Flick through all the TV channels on prime time from 4 p.m. to 7 p.m., and watch a barrage of gossip news that dissect the career flops, secret loves and shock marriage shake-ups of the stars. It's repetitive stuff, but viewers laugh or cry in mockery at their idols' misfortune and say: *Kasiiaaan, deh!*

———————

Nowadays, urban Indonesians mix English with *bahasa gaul*, and weird patterns emerge. The trend comes from MTV programs that were screened on Indonesian television, at first through privately owned stations, and later with the spread of cable television.

In the 1990s, one radio station, KISS FM, mixed English and Indonesian in broadcasts. Now, it's hard to find a station for young people that doesn't use a heavy dose of English in programs. MTV Radio and Hard Rock FM stations lead the way. Many television advertisements have also borrowed English. Some wacky tag lines:

❀ Bahasa Indonesia yang baik dan benar
Proper and correct Indonesian language.

This phrase encourages Indonesians to speak a "proper" form of their language, untainted by slang and other deviations. But some people say it as a sarcastic poke at brainy nerds and geeks.

"He's a know-it all. He speaks good and proper Indonesian language."

Dia sok tau. Dia ngomong bahasa yang baik dan benar.

❋ Nge-clear-in rambut seperti Nge-clear-in pikiranmu
Clear (your dandruff) out of your hair and clear your mind.

From the makers of Clear, an anti-dandruff shampoo. Indonesian slang easily makes a verb by adding the prefix *nge-* and the suffix *-in* to a noun. Some urban Indonesians tack these terms onto English words.

❋ Pleeze, deh!
"No way. Oh, c'mon..." = A dismissive putdown.

Two girls gossip about the new boy in class:

"He asked me out to see this old boring 80s singer. Can you believe it? No way. Oh c'mon please."

Dia ajak gue nonton penyanyi tahun 80an itu. Percaya nggak? Pleeze deh.

Another common practice was the use of English with an Indonesian sentence structure. Indonesians know it isn't proper English, but they're just fooling around.

"Can you speak English?"

Bisa bicara bahasa Inggris?

"Little-little *sih* I can."

The reply matches the original sentence structure for *Sedikit, sedikit sih bisa* (Oh, I can speak a little bit). *Sih* adds emphasis.

"My body is not delicious," a sick Indonesian says. The expression is a direct translation from *aku nggak enak badan* (I don't feel well).

Want to know, aja! someone snipes at a busybody. You just want to be nosy.

Aja comes from *saja*, which means just. Indonesians drop the s when they say *saja* quickly.

Baik (good) and *benar* (correct) turn up often in government campaigns to get people to speak good Indonesian. The rules were spelled out in the government term *EYD* (pronounced eh-yeh-deh), short for *Ejaan yang disempurnakan*, which means perfected spelling, or system. Despite the efforts of linguists, there is a big difference between *EYD-style*, or written Indonesian, and the spoken version. Another expression that mocks anything serious or conventional: *EYD sekali*. Very Eh-yeh-deh.

Some writers seem to pride themselves on breaking every *EYD* rule. As a result, Indonesians have a carefree attitude to their language.

One example is the variety of name spellings. One senior government official had several different versions of his name on his business cards.

Travel out of Jakarta for two hours and you'll see a couple of different ways to write the name of a village in West Java. First, it's Cukangleles and a sign further down the road says Cukangleuleus. (*Eu* and *e* can be interchangeable). The Central Javan towns Sala, Salatiga, Wara can be Solo, Solotigo or Woro (the short *o* is spelled most of the time).

Indonesia has had three different spelling systems, which further explains the confusion.

Dutch scholars codified the Malay-based Roman alphabet, which replaced the Arabic script in 1896.

Djakarta with a silent D came during this time. President Soekarno spelt his name with *oe*. The system lasted half a century.

In 1948, the education minister in Indonesia's newly independent cabinet, Soewandi, said the old system was clumsy and needed to be streamlined. *EYD* was born in 1972 as the government, in cooperation with Malaysia, tried to make the spelling simpler, and more practical, consistent and flexible.

You can tell when people were born by the spelling of their names. Soekarno and Soeharto were born before 1947, and Susilo Bambang Yudhoyono was born in 1949.

❀ Curhat corner
"Corner to pour your heart out" = Indonesia's Agony Aunt.

Curhat is short for *CURahan HATi*, the heart's outpouring. *Curhat* is teenage lingo that has been adopted by older, urban Indonesians. It can also be a verb:

"C'mon, pour your heart out!"
Curhat, dong! Dong adds emphasis.

Curhat corner was the name of a high school psychology program that invited children to unload their private burdens.

"Now is the time for you to pour your heart out on any topic: family, school or relationships," said a flyer on the walls of a South Jakarta school.

"Don't be paranoid. Come to *curhat corner*," it said.
Gak usah Parno. Datang saja ke curhat corner.

Parno is slang for paranoid. It implies negativity, or a bad attitude to life.

The casual language on the flyer mixes English with teenage, Indonesian slang.

❀ BeTe (pronounced *beh-teh*)
"In a bad mood, or temper" = Boring.

"How was the meeting?" a colleague asks. *Gimana meetingnya?*

BT, you reply. Boring.

Some Indonesians say *BT* is an acronym of the English bad temper, or bad time. Young people use this expression, but its meaning is lost on the elderly.

❀ TP (pronounced *teh-peh*)
Tebar pesona
Spread around enchantment. Look pretty.

"Let's TP," a young woman crows and she and her friends doll up before a night out. *TP yuk!*

❀ Ke laut aje
"Go to the sea" = Forget it! Go to hell!

This Jakartan slang came from a song by NEO, an Indonesian rap band that peaked in the late 1990s. The subject of the lyrics is *cewek matre*, or material girl, who has fallen out of favor. *Ke laut aje!* the singer raps. "Throw her into the sea!"

In the context of a romantic breakup, the expression also means: It's history.

Or, it snaps someone out of a funk:

"Don't have a negative attitude! Throw it into the sea!" *Jangan parno. Ke laut aja.*

❀ Tau ah gelap
"I don't know, it's dark" = My mind is blank.

Hari Harry Mau, a character on a 1990s television comedy, said this if he couldn't answer a question, or was too lazy to do so. The show was a series of unrelated skits. For example, a night security guard lounging at a crowded food stall yawns and starts to gossip about the neighborhood. An argument breaks out. Hari steps in as the humorous arbiter who settles things. But sometimes he shrugs off an awkward situation by saying: *Auh ah gelap*. Or if the banter veers into sexual innuendoes, he says: *Auh ah gelap*.

End of conversation.

✿ **Gaptek** (acronym)
GAgaP TEKnologi
"Stuttering/stammering with technology" = Techno illiterate.

Someone who can't operate a digital camera, a cellular telephone with the latest features or any other high-tech gadget.

B.J. Habibie, a research and technology minister who succeeded Suharto as president, loved the term *iptek*, short for *ilmu pengetahuan* (science). He wanted Indonesia to make technological strides like those of its neighbors, Malaysia and Singapore.

"Indonesians shouldn't fall behind in science," Habibie said repeatedly. *Bangsa Indonesia jangan ketinggalan iptek.*

People mimicked the president whenever a frustrated friend fussed over a new computer or DVD player:

"So, don't stutter with technology."

Makanya, jangan gatek.

✿ **Jomblo** (Sundanese)
Single.

Single Indonesian adults fear a barrage of questions about their private life:

"Are you still alone?" *Masih sendiri?*

"Do you have a family (husband) now?" *Sudah berkeluarga?*

Jomblo is a derogatory word for single, a status that is sad and eccentric to many Indonesians. Those who face the questions say *masih jomblo!* (still single!) with tired smiles. They are bored with the endless probing about their personal life.

The Sundanese slang term became popular after an Indonesian pop band, GIGI, came out with a mournful song in 2001 called *Jomblo*. Angst-ridden teenagers loved it. The last two verses:

> *Semua itu mimpi* (Everything was a dream)
> *Hanyalah bualan* (Only lies)
> *Semua itu bohong* (Everything was a lie)
> *Aku tetap saja* (I am still)
> *Tetap sendiri* (Still alone)
>
> *Bila ku diterimamu* (If you accept me)
> *Bintangpun ku berikan* (I would give the star to you)
> *Bila kau menerimaku* (If you accept me)
> *Ku berikan pelangi* (I would give you the rainbow)

❋ Jayus
Unfunny.

People say this derisively when someone tells a bad joke. It refers to Jayusman Yunus, a member of a dance troupe established in 1977 by Guruh Sukarnoputra, the youngest son of Indonesia's first president, Sukarno. The group was called *SM*, or *Swara Mahardika*, which means Voice of Freedom in Sanskrit. It was a hit, and many young members of *SM* enjoyed successful careers in show business long afterward.

Jayusman Yunus danced and became an accomplished photographer. But he told lousy jokes, showed up late for appointments, and broke promises. He agreed to develop a photograph for a friend at a cost of 100 rupiah, only to raise the price after the deal was done. After a while, dancers who showed up late at *SM* rehearsals were greeted with catcalls of *Jayus lu.*

Lu or *elu* is Jakartan slang for you.

SM shows were musical extravaganzas of fur, feathers and teased hair reminiscent of Le Lido, the famed Paris cabaret.

❧ Airnya diobok-obok
"The water has been stirred up" = It made quite a splash.

Obok-obok is Javanese for stirring up ripples.

The expression became popular in 1997 when six-year-old singer Joshua burst onto the music scene. He captivated Indonesians with quips and comments in heavily accented Javanese. He performed in a trademark snow hat or back-to-front cap, his bangs peeking out cheekily.

His album, *Air* (Water) was Indonesia's most successful ever, selling one million copies. Fans called it the *obok-obok* album from a phrase in the hit single:

Diobok-obok air diobok ada ikan ikannya kecil-kecil pada mabok.

"Stir up the water, and the little fishes will get drunk."

It became popular among people of all ages to say:

Jangan diobok-obok ya.

"Don't stir up problems."

For years, Joshua appeared in TV ads and sitcoms and hosted quiz shows. But he rarely releases records.

Other popular expressions came from children's songs. Ria Enes, a singer and ventriloquist, notched a hit—*Cita-citaku* (My goal in life)—just before President Suharto quit in 1998. Her doll, Susan, sang that her goal was to be president.

Cynics applauded the song, saying only a lifeless doll had the audacity to declare that it wanted to replace Indonesia's authoritarian leader. The song was popular with anti–government activists, and it was viewed as politically subversive. But enough change was afoot in 1998 that the song didn't attract government scrutiny.

Susan also appeared in TV ads, including one for a floor cleaner in which she screamed *Bedes! Bedes!* (Monkey! in Javanese). People seized on the expression and said it while screwing up their noses and eyes at anything distasteful: a smell, objects or people.

A 1999 song *Si Komo* tells of a purple Komodo dragon that jams up traffic in Jakarta.

Frustrated drivers, stuck in bumper-to-bumper traffic, sang the refrain with clenched teeth:

Macet lagi, macet lagi! Gara-gara si Komo lewat.

"There's a traffic jam again because the Komo is passing by."

The komodo dragon's cry in the song, *weleh-weleh-weleh*, also expressed fury and helplessness.

The singer was Kak Seto (Brother Seto), a respected children's psychologist who hosts TV shows on how to raise children.

❀ Ngecap
To blab.

From the root *kecap*, or soybean sauce.

Indonesians add *kecap* liberally to most foods and a person whose tongue wags out of control is like someone who drowns his plate in *kecap*. Don't let him go on, he's *ngecap*.

Many Indonesian regions advertise their local *kecap* as the most popular brand in Indonesia. Commentators say political parties are like *kecap*: they all make wild promises and claim to be No. 1 in Indonesia.

English-language dictionaries say ketchup comes from *kecap*, a Malay word dating to the late 17th century that means fish sauce.

❅ ABS (pronounced *ah-beh-ess*)
Asal Bapak Senang
Whatever makes the boss happy.

An expression of cynicism about business or government culture. An underling doctors the results of a bad report to please his superiors, or an insincere deputy compliments his director on a run-of-the-mill presentation.

❅ Dugem (acronym)
DUnia GEMerlap
"Shining world" = To go clubbing, or have a wild night out.

"Let's party!" *Dugem yuk!*

❅ Ember (Dutch)
"Bucket" = Blabbermouth.

Ember can't be trusted with secrets because a bucket leaks if there is a hole, or spills water if it's full to the brim.

Ember is also an Indonesian acronym that means *EMang BenER*, or so right. It's an exclamation of wholehearted agreement.

"It's really far!" a friend says. *Jauh banget ya!*

"So true!" another replies. *Ya, ember!*

✻ **Cengdem** (acronym)
CeCENG aDEM
"A thousand cools" = Cheap sunglasses.

Ceceng is 1,000 in the Chinese Hokkien language; *adem* is Javanese for cool. The expression refers to 1,000-rupiah sunglasses that provide instant coolness.

———————

Indonesians love acronyms. There are tens of thousands, many originating in the vast government bureaucracy. The idea is to make things simple and concise, but the jumbled sea of letters often confuses. People add to the alphabetic clutter by inventing parodies of official acronyms. They also borrow foreign acronyms. Sometimes they pronounce them the English way, like VCD (vee-see-dee) and DVD (dee-vee-dee). At other times, the pronunciation becomes haphazard.

AC is used more often than *penyegar ruangan* (room freshener), the Indonesian term for air conditioner. But the pronunciation is erratic: a mixture of the Indonesian *ah* and the Dutch consonant *seh* (in Indonesian, *C* is pronounced as a hard *cheh*).

Indonesians refer to a cellular telephone as *telepon genggam*, or hand phone. The popular abbreviation HP is pronounced *ha-peh*.

This is probably because the English sound, *eich-pee*, is difficult for the Indonesian tongue.

Students at the Universitas Islam Indonesia in Jakarta insist they study at UII, pronounced *you-ee-ee* (a mixture of the English U and Indonesian double I). Anyone who tries it with a pure English version, or the Indonesian way—oo-ee-ee—is uncool.

This fluid mishmash of acronyms, jumbled pronunciations and foreign influences upsets a small but vocal group of Indonesian linguists. They believe modern trends show a lack of confidence, and inconsistency in Indonesian culture. The language's young trendsetters, however, pick up whatever they deem cool.

✽ Dari Hong Kong!
"From Hong Kong!" = Not likely!

Indonesians view Hong Kong as a luxury destination, a place to splurge. Shopping, shopping, shopping. Rich Indonesians flock to Hong Kong, but it's out of reach for most Indonesians.

"Your wallet must be thick!" *Pasti dompetnya tebal! Dari Hong Kong!*

"From the moon!" has the same meaning. *Dari bulan!*

———

Indonesians pluck one-syllable terms from some ethnic languages as a way to express feeling (*rasa*) through nuance rather than precise language. The Betawi of Jakarta say *dong, sih, deh, nih* and *nah*. These terms spread around Indonesia via the media and entertainment industries, which are based in the capital.

Dong! means the person with whom you are talking should know better, or should have done something already. *Dong* usually follows a verb, and sometimes emphasizes an order or a warning. It also stresses the obvious, so it has the same meaning as "Of course!" Sometimes, it denotes resignation to circumstances.

"Come with me (you know you should)." *Ayo ikut, dong!*

"You should eat!" *Makan, dong!*

"Are you coming?" "Yes, of course." *Kamu ikut? Ya dong.*

Be careful with *dong*. Some Indonesians associate it with pickup talk in sleazy nightclubs. They joke that foreigners pretend they speak fluent Indonesian by saying *dong*, when it only shows that they learned a pidgin version of the language from bar girls.

Indonesians outside Jakarta sometimes deride people who say *dong*. The term is unpopular in Riau, Sumatra, where pride in Islam and the Malay ethnicity is very strong. *Sih, deh, nih* and *nah* don't inspire such rejection.

Sih softens a question if you want to bring up a sensitive subject and aren't sure what reaction you will get.

"Hmmm, what's wrong?" *Ada apa, sih?*

"Why?" *Kenapa, sih?*

A speaker also says *sih* to acknowledge or accept an explanation.

"Well, it's true that he IS smart." *Memang betul dia pintar, sih.*

––––––––––––

Gimana sih? Gimana dong!

"What's happening?"

Indonesians say *gimana* in place of *bagaimana*, which means how. *Sih* and *dong* give different meanings to *gimana*. The terms are best said with heavy intonation on the vowels, along with a scowl, raised eyebrows or other exaggerated facial expressions.

Sih is the best option for a frustrated person who wants to lash out at the world.

"What the heck is going to happen!" *Gimana, siiiiih!*

A speaker who is resigned to defeat or a dismal fate says:

"Oh…what on earth is going to happen?" *Gimana, doooong…*

An answer is not expected.

Deh is a term that urges and pleads. It isn't forceful like *dong*. It also signals acceptance.

"C'mon, let's eat!" *Ayo makan deh.*

"Ok, I'll try it!" *Ok deh, aku coba.*

Nih is a slang version of *ini* (this). It is used to point out a nearby object, or make a point in a discussion. It's a neutral term.

"This is the money." *Nih… duitnya.*

"There are many problems, see, that Indonesia faces." *Memang banyak, nih, masalah yang dihadapi Indonesia.*

Nah marks an action or the start or end of an explanation. It also implies acceptance of a fact, opinion or common knowledge.

"Here! Take it, here are your wages." *Nah! Ambil. Ini gaji kamu.*

Some Javanese exclamations—*loh, kok* and *wah*—are well known in Indonesia.

Loh emphasizes a surprising or positive statement:

"I already bought that book!" *Loh, aku sudah beli buku itu.*

Kok emphasizes a question:

"What, really? Is that right?" *Kok begitu? Emang benar?*

Wah serves when the element of surprise is far bigger:

"Wow! Amazing! Did you really finish it?" *Wah! Hebat! Kamu benar-benar sudah selesai?*

Some Sundanese terms of emphasis—*euy, atuh* and *mah*—appear often on television shows, but other ethnic groups don't use them much, if at all.

❀ MLM (pronounced *em-ell-em*)
Mulut Lewat Mulut
"Mouth to mouth" = Through the grapevine.

"They must have heard it mouth to mouth," says a woman whose life is the subject of gossip.

Mereka pasti dengar em-ell-em.

It's hard to keep a secret in Jakarta, where your nasty divorce, failed business or family feud is fodder for chat among total strangers.

MLM is a pun on Multi-Level Marketing, a freelance sales phenomenon that mushroomed during the 1997–8 economic crash. People who lost jobs sought other forms of income. A financial consultant at a big bank became a taxi driver. Former white-collar workers opened *kafe tenda* (tent cafés) in front of their homes.

Some turned to MLM, collecting catalogues of products, buying them from warehouses and delivering them to buyers at a discount. These entrepreneurs are known as *konsultan* (agents, or sellers). Some are trained to promote the products, while others are teenagers whose clients are family and friends. They flog whatever sells: bags, medicine, cosmetics, food supplements and herbal medicine. A lot of the goods are knockoffs. Bottles of cheap "essence of perfume" are brand name ripoffs.

High school graduates soak up most low-paying jobs in shops and restaurants, so MLM is a decent alternative for someone with verve.

❀ Cabut dulu!
"I'm extracting myself, first!" = I'm leaving. I'm out of here.

You pluck or extract yourself from your friends or family. *Cabut* is slang for leaving (extracting yourself).

Pergi dulu (leave first) is a casual but proper way of saying goodbye. People also say *pamit dulu* (ask permission to leave first). You have to say farewells three or four times before the crowd lets you out of its clutches. Sometimes, leaving a social or family gathering entails elaborate gestures: kissing hands and cheeks, and putting your hands together and touching your host's hands with the tips of your fingers.

Now, in the cities, it is enough to say:

Cabut dulu.

I'm off. Bye. Later.

Chapter Fifteen

Tech Talk

Technology and a love of gossip make an explosive match. Chatter buzzes on blogs and other social media websites, spinning off a new vocabulary for the Internet age.

❀ Cekidot Gan!
Check it out, Boss.

This is an invitation to read or see or comment on a post or a thread in KASKUS, Indonesia's biggest Internet forum with over two million active users in late 2010.

Cekidot (pronounced check-ee-dot) is how some Indonesians would pronounce the phrase "check it out" in an oh-so-cool drawl. *Gan* is short for *juragan*, an old term for a plantation master, an owner of an enterprise or a captain of a ship. To the digital generation, it means "boss."

KASKUS stands for *kasak-kusuk*, which means gossiping, or literally, influencing others through whispers or subtle means. Entrepreneur Andrew Darwis and two other twenty-something friends studying in the United States developed KASKUS for a university project as a forum for overseas Indonesians to keep in touch. The other two dropped out but Darwis turned his venture into a profitable business.

KASKUS spawned dozens of online chat rooms that discuss politics, hobbies, parenting tips, music and the latest computing trends. It's a bazaar, too. KASKUSers peddle USB sticks, Iphones and high-end apartments in buy and sell forums similar to the U.S.-based Craigslist model.

Some KASKUS expressions don't venture beyond the domain of computer geekdom. *Cendol* is a rating system. If an online item tweaks interest, a user punches in one or more green commas resembling a *cendol*, or a wormlike, flour-based green jelly, or dessert. The origin of the term *cendol* is open to debate: Thailand is one possible source, though *jendol*, or "bump" in Indonesian, suggests a more domestic origin. Under the latter theory, jelly fragments bump through the mouth when one drinks *es cendol*, a refreshing ice and jelly drink.

Trit, which sounds a bit like "thread," is the Indonesian version of that term for an online discussion series. *Main tenis* (play tennis) is how an Indonesian ear might pick up the word "maintenance," as in web repairs. *BB17* is an abbreviation for *buka-bukaan 17* (taking off clothes, for those older than 17). This risque forum was closed down following a 2008 ban on online pornography in Indonesia.

Sundul, Gan! (Do a header, boss) is a football-inspired call to forward an online article to others.

KASKUS helped popularize phrases that languished in other online forums. Indonesians love to compete to be the first to post a comment on a great article published online. Those who do so triumphantly slap in the word *pertamax*, which combines "the first" (*pertama*) and "time" (literally *kali*, but in this case the letter X stands for the multiplication symbol, as in five "times" five).

The term was used a lot in a now-defunct website for car aficionados. Pertamax already sounded familiar to Indonesians. It's a lead-free, high-octane gasoline available from the state-owned energy company, Pertamina.

Some online terminology is seeping into daily talk:
Sedih nih, gue bukan yang pertamax. Tapi gak papa. Yang penting dapat bonus.

I'm a bit sad that I wasn't the first. But that's ok. At least, I got a bonus.

✳ Cicak dan Buaya
Gecko and crocodile

In 2009, a high-ranking police officer, Gen. Susno Duadji, was targeted for alleged graft by Indonesia's Corruption Eradication Commission, which has chipped away at the impunity of powerful political and business interests suspected of illegally amassing fortunes.

Duadji, compelled to resign his post and on trial in late 2010, said he was clean but infuriated the public with a folkloric reference to the saga. In an interview with Tempo news magazine, he implied that the police force was like a crocodile, bigger and stronger than a gecko, a symbol of the anti-corruption panel.

"Does a gecko want to attack a crocodile? The crocodile won't be angry but only disappointed by the fact that, apparently, the gecko could be so stupid," Duadji said.

Cicak kok melawan buaya. Apakah buaya marah? Enggak, cuma menyesal. Cicaknya masih bodoh saja.

The perceived arrogance was too much for Indonesians, even in a country accustomed to corruption long after the excesses of the Suharto era. Hundreds staged protests, screaming: "I am a gecko!" Pictures of the small lizard were emblazoned on posters and T-shirts. The populist campaign really took off on the Internet; a Facebook campaign attracted more than 1.3 million members within days. Allegations of a smear campaign against anti-corruption officials only whipped up more Internet activism.

Appearing before parliamentary investigators, Djuadji tried to shrug off his reptilian remark. He joked that he might end up defending his rights to the notorious "gecko and crocodile" phrase if someone else tried to hijack it for their own purposes.

Internet penetration in Indonesia is still low compared to a developed country but the number of Facebook and Twitter users is surging at one of the fastest rates in the world.

Social media networks do more than gossip or buy and sell. The public mobilized financial support by collecting *Koin untuk Prita,* or "Coins for Prita" for Prita Mulyasari. The housewife was prosecuted after a hospital sued her for alleged slander because of her complaints about bad service. She was found not guilty. The case triggered other campaigns to collect coins for different causes.

In July 2009, Indonesia passed a law regulating the status and use of the national flag, language, symbols and anthem. Many bloggers applauded, saying they hoped it would clarify and standardize the use of the Indonesian language. Soon enough, though, doubts emerged.

The law said state officials must use the Indonesian language in official speeches and other formal communication. One blogger wistfully noted that while failure to uphold the dignity of the Indonesian flag, state symbols and anthem can lead to a maximum of five years in prison or a heavy fine, the law remained mum about penalties for those who didn't follow its stipulation on language. Another blogger cheekily suggested that President Yudhoyono broke the law while delivering his state of the nation's address in parliament, three months after the law passed.

In that speech, Yudhoyono said his administration would represent "Change and Continuity," strive for "De-bottlenecking, Acceleration, and Enhancement" and called for "Unity, Together We Can." He delivered those phrases in English.

❀ Bahasa alay
The language of the kite runner kids.

Alay is short for *Anak LAYangan* or "kite runner kids." On the one hand, it's a disparaging label for uneducated *kampong* or village kids who play hooky from school and spend hours flying kites. Alternatively, it's a liberating term for an edgy bunch of youths who delight in flouting the linguistic rules. The second interpretation became popular in 2010.

Some say technology-bound bahasa Alay is more anti–establishment than the bahasa Prokem of the 1970s and 1980s and the bahasa Gaul of the 1990s and 2000. Bahasa Alay came to prominence along with the rise of mobile text messaging and micro blogging. The young and trendy have to convey their feelings in 140 characters or less, Twitter-style. They communicate with emoticons and a whirlpool of capital letters, numbers and special characters. At times, users of bahasa Alay seem to be trying to speak in code so that already discombobulated adults don't interfere with the world of teenagers.

Some examples of Bahasa Alay:

—The Islamic greeting of Arabic origin—*Assalamu Alaikum*, or "Peace be upon you"—is often used in a non-religious setting by many Indonesians, regardless of their faith. This is written down in many tweets or blogs as *Chamleeqummbh*, which is how an Indonesian might hear the phrase when it is said very quickly.

—"Add" turns into *Et* or *Ett*, as in "can you add me as a friend" on Facebook, Friendster or another social media network.

—House is spelt *Hoz*—

—Whatchadoing is *Lagi apa nih*. *Lagi* is further short-ened into *gi*. *Apa* becomes *paa* and *nih* is made into *nich* because of an idea that it sounds like an Indonesian speak-ing English with an accent. So the whole phrase becomes: *gipaanich*.

To make things more confusing, teenagers will spell this in text messages with capital and small letters: *gi Paa NicH*,

—h4b15 is a typical mix of numbers and letters. The number 4 looks like an "a" while 1 and 5 look like "i" and "s." The combination spells out the word *habis*, which spells an end to things.

We're done. Finished.

Sources

Kamus Besar Bahasa Indonesia, Pusat Bahasa, Edisi Ke-4. Departemen Pendidikan Nasional, Jakarta 2008

100 Tokoh Yang Mengubah Indonesia, Hamonangan Simanjuntak, Tim Narasi, Yogyakarta, 2009

Kamus Peribahasa, Sarwono Pusposaputro, Gramedia Pustaka Utama, Jakarta, 2001.

Kamus Bahasa Betawi–Indonesia, Bundari, Pustaka Sinar Harapan, Jakarta 2003.

9 dari 10 Kata Bahasa Indonesia adalah Asing, Alif Danya Munsyi, Kepustakaan Populer Gramedia, Jakarta, 2003.

Kamus Bahasa Prokem, Prathama Rahardja, Henri Chambert-Loir, Pustaka Utama Grafitti, Jakarta, 1990.

Kamus Bahasa Gaul, Debby Sahertian, Jakarta, Pustaka Sinar Harapan, Jakarta, 1999.

Peribahasa Minangkabau, Anas Nafis, Intermasa, Jakarta 1996.

Kamus Indonesia-Inggris, John M. Echols and Hasan Sadily, PT Gramedia Jakarta, 1989.

A Short History of Indonesia: The Unlikely Nation, Colin Brown, Allen & Unwin, Crow's Nest NSW, 2003.

Kamus Ungkapan Indonesia-Inggris Hadi Podo Joseph J. Sullivan, Gramedia Pustaka Utama, Jakarta, 2000.

Kamus Gestok, Hersri Setiawan, Indonesia Tera, Magelang 2003.

Soeharto: pikiran, ucapan dan tindakan saya, Citra Lamtoro Gung Persada, Jakarta, 1989.

The Year of Living Dangerously, C.J. Koch, Vintage Books, Random House Australia, 2001.

The History of Java, Sir Thomas Stamford Raffles, Oxford University Press, 1979. [1st edition 1817, tcv. edn 1830]

Indonesian Heritage Language and Literature, Archipelago Press, 1998.

Krakatoa: The Day the World Exploded, Simon Winchester, Penguin Books, 2004.

INDEX

3
3-M, 84

5
5-D, 84

A
abang, 196
abdicate. *See* **lengser keprabon**
Abdurrahman Wahid. *See* Gus Dur
ABS, 267
abu, 210
Acang, 136
Aceh, tipu, 130
advice. *See* **wejangan**
agitator. *See* **provokator**
air, 160, 163, 166, 173, 186, 206, 207, 210, 216
akar, 207
alamat, 159
alap-alap pengadilan, 99
albino, 37
Ali Sadikin, 34
ali-ali, 71
alis, 55
alon-alon, 77
aman, 140
Amigos, 178
anak
  dua anak cukup, 199
  gedongan, 187, 245
  menteng, 188
  rejeki, 200

semata wayang, 186, 187
Ancol, 228, 232
angin, 24
anjing, 23, 148, 163, 236
ants. *See* **semut**
apel bendera, besar, paripurna, 135
api, 44, 189
apotik jalanan, 245
Aqua, 54
arang, 46, 210, 212
areca nut. *See* **pinang**
Arjuna, 42, 43
arrow. *See* **panah**
asam, 172, 182
attack, 83
auntie. *See* **tante**
aur, 57
axis tengah, 86
ayam, 16, 17, 18, 20, 23

B
babi, 77, 236, 252
bad luck. *See* **celaka**
badan, 57, 201, 259
bahasa, 5, 203
  alay, 277
  gaul, 255, 256, 257, 258
  prokem, 251, 252, 253, 254
bajing loncat, 11, 12
balsem, 176
bamboo. *See* **aur**
banana, 171
  heart, 129

king, 192
wrap, 170
banci, 253
bandot, 199
bangsat, 237
Banser, 138
bantal, 49, 247
bapak pembangunan, 70, 168
barisan, 138, 151
barrel, 44, 173
basah, 96, 210
Batak, 36
batas, 206
batu, 247
  bakar, 136
  hujan, 206
  lempar, 112
beard. *See* **jenggot**
bebet, bibit, bobot, 189, 190
bedil, 43
Belanda, 41
Belando
  air, 178
  janji, 218
  paku, 230
belanga, 172, 173
benang, 210
bencong, 34
bendera, 135, 138, 197
bersatu, 106
Bete, 261
betis,
  paha balalang, 55
  pagar, 119

Bhinneka Tunggal Ika, 106
biawak, 43
bibir
   buah, 51
   delima, 55
bibit, 189, 207
bird. *See* **burung**
bistik, 178
BKO, 136
blanket. *See* **selimut**
blood. *See* **darah**
boat, 205
bobot, 189, 190
bodohisasi, 81
body. *See* **badan**
bolo, 83
bon, 131
bones. *See* **tulang**
border. *See* **batas**
bribes, 98
bridal well. *See* **sumur pengantin**
bridge, 228
brow. *See* **alis**
buaya,
   darat, 16
   keroncong, 107
   lidah buaya, 14
   mulut buaya, 13, 16
bubur, 169
bucket. *See* **dulang**
budi, 57, 99, 181
buffalo. *See* **kerbau, kebo**
bug, 17, 237
bulai, bule, 37, 253
bulan, dari bulan, 269
   datang, 191
   empat belas, 192

kesiangan, 192
pungguk, 21
bull, 233
bumblebee *See* **kumbang**
bumi, 208
bungkamisasi, 81
Buru, 65, 66, 67, 68
burung, 59
bus kota, 224
busuk, 24
Buto Cakil, Ijo, Kala, 48

C
cabe rawit, 174, 175
cabut, 114, 272
cacing, 19, 26
canary. *See* **kutilang**
candle. *See* **lilin**
captain. *See* **nakhoda**
caravan, 153. *See* **khafilah**
carmuk, 45
cart. *See* **pedati**
cassava. *See* **ubi**
cat. *See* **kucing**
cekal, 76
celaka, 161
cengdem, 268
central axis. *See* **axis tengah**
cerai, 166
cermin, 46
Ceylon, 65
charcoal. *See* **arang**
chicken. *See* **ayam**
child. *See* **anak**
chili bluff. *See* **gertak sambal**

Chinatown. *See* **pecinan**
churches. *See* **gereja liar**
ciduk, 131
Cina, 212
cinta, 21, 94, 182, 189
cita-cita, 206
civet. *See* **musang**
cleric. *See* **kyai**
coal. *See* **arang**
coblos moncong putih, 88
cockroach. *See* **cunguk**
coconut,
   milk. *See* **santan**
   fudge. *See* **dodol**
   leaves. *See* **janur**
collusion. *See* KKN
confrontation. *See* **konfrontasi**
cooking pot. *See* **belanga**
coreng, 46
corruption. *See* KKN
cow. *See* **sapi** *or* **lembu**
cracked. *See* **retak**
cradle, 182
cricket computer. *See* **komputer jangkrit**
crocodile. *See* **buaya**
cuci gudang, 231
cunguk, 127
curhat, 261

D
dagu lebah, 55
dari Hong Kong, 269
Darma Wanita, 74
dayung, 204
debt. *See* **utang**
deed. *See* **budi**

deer. *See* **kijang**
demo
    kampung, 102
    masak, 101
dengkulmu, 234
Detachment, 144
development,
    father of. *See* **bapak**
      Pembangunan
diam, 5, 84, 203
dibalikpapankan, 125
dirt, 57, 185
disekolahkan, 124
disukabumikan, 125
dodol, 239
dog. *See* **anjing**
Dolly, 230
domba, 18
dragon. *See* **ular naga**
dream. *See* **cita-cita**
drilling dance. *See*
    goyang ngebor
dry. *See* **kering**
duck. *See* **itik**
duduk, 84, 99
dugem, 267
dukun. *See* **shaman**
dulang, 207
durian, 160
dust. *See* **abu**
Dutch. *See* **Belanda**
dwi fungsi, 103, 139

E
eat. *See* **makan**
earth, 208
egg. *See* **telur**
ekor, 23, 163
elephant. *See* **gajah**
emas, 98, 99, 206, 208

ember, 267
enemy. *See* **musuh**
envelope. *See* **amplop**
estuary. *See* **muara**
EYD, 260, 261
eye. *See* **mata**

F
face. *See* **muka**
fate. *See* **nasib**
Fatima, 129
feet on the ground.
    See **pijak tanah**
fence of shins. See **betis,**
    pagar
fire. *See* **api**
fish. *See* **ikan**
floating mass. *See* **masa**
    mengambang
flour. *See* **tepung**
flower. *See* **bunga**
fly. *See* **laler**
frog. *See* **katak**
fry. *See* **kelas teri**
frying pan, 13

G
gading, 25, 208
gains. *See* **sabetan**
gajah, 23, 24, 25, 66
gaji, 96, 184
gall bladder. *See* **empedu**
gaptek, 263
garam, 24, 174, 184
gelanggang, 112
gereja liar, 155
germ. *See* **kuman**
gertak sambal, 243
Gestapu, 62
Ghufron, 12

gigi, 53
gigit, 23, 53, 100
goat. *See* **kambing**
    old goat. *See* **bandot**
gold. *See* **emas**
Golkar, 40
Golput, 85
Gotong Royong, 73
goyang ngebor, 299
GPK, 122
grave, 99
gugur, 105, 106
gula, 91, 172
gunung, 110, 172
guru kencing, 210
Gus Dur, 158
Gusmao, 14, 120, 121

H
Haatzaai Artikelen,
    76
hadis, hadith, 150
hair. *See* **rambut**
hand. *See* **tangan**
harga mati, 230
harimau, 13, 25
harta, 212
hati, 49, 51, 57, 261
    buah, 61, 183, 201
    jantung, 183
    makan, 183
    mati, 47
    panas, 58
hay. *See* **sekam**
head. *See* **kepala**
heart. *See* **hati**
heaven. *See* **surga**
hen. *See* **ayam**
henna, 55
hero, 71

hidung, 18, 50, 51
  belang, 16
hidup, 126, 163, 248
hilir, 209
hole. *See* **lubang**
hom, 123
Honda, 54, 67
honey. *See* **madu**
horn. *See* **tanduk**
horse-trading. *See*
  dagang
hujan batu, **emas**, 206
hulu, 208, 209
hungry. *See* **lapar**
husband. *See* **suami**

I
ibu, 108, 116, 150, 159,
  171
ikan, 12, 68, 160
ilmu, 169, 212, 263
indigo. *See* **nila**
Inggit, 116, 117, 195
inong bale, 130
intel, 114
invisible troups. *See*
  pasukan silam
Islam KTP, 147
Islamic Community. *See*
  Jemaah Islamiyah
island. *See* **pulau**
itik, 17
ivory. *See* **gading**

J
Jakarta, 214
jalan, 206, 209, 216,
  219, 254
jam karet, 217
jantung, 58, 219, 183

janur, 196
jayus, 264
Jemaah Islamiyah, 12,
  143
jempol, 56
jenggot, 20
jewelry. *See* **permata**
jihad, 148
jin, 158
joki, 220, 246
jomblo, 263, 264
juklak, 135

K
Kabayan, 41, 42
kacang, 129, 164
kafilah, 148
kain, 210
kaki, 150, 209, 228,
  229
kambing, 199
  congek, 242
  hilang, 91
  hitam, 242
  kampung, 124
  kelas, 33
kampung, 133, 226
kancil, 24
kandang, 98, 99
kapal, 205
karet
  jam, 217, 218
  pasal, 76
karung, 81
katak, 20
kawin
  bawah tangan, 194
  lari, 194
kebo kumpul, 206
kekaryaan, 139

kelas
  kakap, 12
  teri, 12
kelekatu, 16
kembang, 199
kenal, 189
kepala
  blok, 249
  batu, 46
  sayur, 66
kerak, 170
kerbau, **kebo**, 18, 98,
  99
kerikil, 120
kering, 96
keris, 211
ketok magic, 221
kijang, 248
KKN, 93
klenteng, 155
knowledge. *See* **ilmu**
komputer jangkrik,
  223
konfrontasi, 118
Kopassus, 136, 137
korlap, 102
kos, 115
Krakatoa, 15
kucing, 20, 81, 82, 256
KUHP, 92
kuku, 56, 57, 178, 179
kulit, 59, 121, 169
kulit badak, 236
kuman, 24
kumbang, 199
Kumpeni, 38
kuningisasi, 79
kuntilanak, 158
kunyuk, 237
kurang ajar, 234

kutilang, 239
kutu. *See* louse
   buku, 13
   loncat, 12
   mati kutu, 12
Kyai mbeling, 44

L
ladder. *See* **tangga**
lalap, 199
laler ijo, 68
langit, 206, 208
langkah seribu, 211
languages. *See* **bahasa**
lari, 210
laut, 24, 172, 212, 262
layar, 206, 231
leak, 158
lembu, 21, 129
lemot, 237
lengan, 55
lengser keprabon, 113
lidah, 14, 43, 53, 209
lip. *See* **bibir**
literature. *See* **sastra**
little people. *See* **wong cilik**
liur jilat, 54
liver. *See* **hati**
lizard. *See* **biawak**
long life. *See* **panjang umur**
louse. *See* **kutu**
love. *See* **cinta**
lubang, 54, 95
ludah, 53
lullaby. *See* **ninabobok**
lumpur, 208
Lutung Kasarung, 22

M
madu, 177, 211
makan
   angin, 182
   asam garam, 183
   buah simakalama, 171
   darah, 184
   daun muda, 182
   gaji buta, 185
   hati, 184
   lalap muda, 199
   kerak, 170
   kumpul, 165
   korban, 184
   mula, 205
   sabun, 185
   sumpah, 185
   tanah, 185
makelar, 100
Malang, 36
malaria, 67
maling, 95
Malioboro, 216
mangan ora mangan, 165
manis, 174, 228
manusia, 25
marriage. *See* **kawin**
massa mengambang, 83
mata, 12, 17, 24, 25, 41, 94, 99, 108, 171, 190, 197
matahari, 192
mati, 190, 230, 241, 248
Maubere, 120
MBA, 198
menang, 83
mengadu nasib, 159

merpati, 21, 52
mikul, 115
milk. *See* **susu**
mirror. *See* **cermin**
misbar, 232
MLM, 271
money. *See* **uang**
Monkey. *See* **monyet**
monyet, 21
moon. *See* **bulan**
mosquito. *See* **nyamuk**
mother. *See* **ibu**
mountain. *See* **gunung**
mousedeer. *See* **kijang**
mouth. *See* **mulut**
muara, 209
mud. *See* **lumpur**
muka, 13, 51, 267
mulut, 13, 16, 51, 211, 271
mupeng, 47
musang, 6, 16, 17
musik ngak-ngik-ngok, 243
musuh, 43

N
nail. *See* **kuku**
nakhoda, 205
nasi, 166, 169, 170, 242
nasib, 5, 159
ndasmu njeblug, 233
neonisasi, 81
nepotism, 93
New Order, 69, 70, 71, 74, 75
ngadeg pandita, 113
ngasorake, 83
ngecap, 266
ngeluruk, 83

ngono, 114
nila, 173
ninabobok, 100
nongkrong, 5, 232
nose. *See* **hidung**
Nusakambangan, 65
nyamuk, 25, 100

O
Obet, 132
obok–obok, 265
ocean. *See* **laut**
Odol, 54
OKB, 188
oknum, 140
Old Order. *See* Orde
    Lama
omen. *See* **alamat**
operasi, 167
Orde Baru, 126
Orde Lama, 126
organik, 136
otak, 234, 236, 237
overdo, 114
owl. *See* **pungguk**

P
P4, 74
padi, 17, 166, 169
pagar betis, 119
paha, 51
pahlawan devisa, 71
panah, 134
Pancasila, 73
pang bayak, 127
pangan, 83
panjang umur, 163
pantat, 211
papan, 83
pasang surut, 163, 206

pasukan siluman, 141
PBB, 137
peanut shell. *See* **kacang**
pebble. *See* **kerikil**
pecinan, 226
pedagang kaki lima, 228
pedati roda, 163
pembangunan, bapak,
    70
penis, 59
pepesan, 170
perahu, 205
permata, 208
perut, 205
    keroncongan, 176
peti, 98
Petrus, 142
pig. *See* **babi**
pigeon. *See* **merpati**
pijak, 206, 208
pillow. *See* **bantal**
pinang, 193
pinggan, 170
pisang, 171
    raja, 192
plate. *See* **pinggan**
plin plan, 196
plintat plintut, 196
pocong, 158
poison. *See* **nila**
porridge. *See* **bubur**
posyandu, 200
Pramoedya, Ananta
    Toer, 65, 66, 225
prison, 65, 66, 67, 68
prostitution, 37
protes, 102
provokator, 111, 112
pucuk, 182
pulau, 204, 206

pulp. *See* **sepah**
pungguk, 21
putra daerah, 90

Q
quiet. *See* **diam**

R
rain. *See* **hujan**
raja, 39, 192
rambut, 55, 259
rat. *See* **tikus**
    in a suit, 11
    in a tie, 11
    office rat, 10
    rat road, 219
    state rat, 10
reformasi, 104
repot, prek, 87
retak, 208
revolusi, 108
rhino. *See* **badak**
rice, 17, 166, 167, 169,
    170
rokok, 98, 224
roll call. *See* **apel**
rotan, 207
rubber articles. *See* **pasal
    karet**
rubber time. *See* **jam
    karet**
runtuh, 106

S
sabetan, 96
sabun londo, 67, 186
sack, 81
sage. *See* **ngadeg
    pandita**
salam tempel, 98

salary. *See* **gaji**
saliva. *See* **ludah** *or* **liur**
salt. *See* **garam**
sandang, 83
santan, 179
sapi, politik dagang, 85
SARA, 72
sastra, 201, 202
Satan, 151
satgaskam, 138
sawah, 161, 166
sayang, 49, 58, 183, 196
sayur, 66, 67
scales. *See* **timbangan**
school. *See* **sekolah**
scoop out. *See* **ciduk**
sea. *See* **laut**
seed, 207
sekam, 44
sekolah, 124
selimut, 43
Semar mendem, 179
semut, 71, 91, 111
sepah, 174
sepatu, 120
September 30th
    Movement, 62
Serambi Mekkah, 149
serigala, 18
setan, 151
shaman. *See* **dukun**
sheep. *See* **domba**
shield. *See* **tameng
    hidup**
shins. *See* **betis**
ship. *See* **kapal**
shit. *See* **tahi**
Shock and Awe, 126
shoe, 98, 120
Silat, 52

silaturahmi, 153
simalakama, 171
sit. *See* **duduk**
skin. *See* **kulit**
sky. *See* **langit**
snapper class. *See* **kelas
    kakap**
soap, Dutch. *See* **sabun**
soda gembira, 177
Softex, 54
Sogo jongkok, 172
sole. *See* **telapak**
sons of the region. *See*
    putra daerah
soup. *See* **sup**
spit. *See* **ludah**
spring. *See* **hulu**
sprout. *See* **pucuk**
spy, 127
squirrel. *See* **bajing** *or*
    tupai
stable. *See* **kandang**
steps. *See* **langkah**
sticky handshake, 99
STMJ, 177
stomach. *See* **perut**
stones. *See* **batu**
Suara, 89, 108
subjugation, 83
sugar. *See* **qula**
Sukabumi, 125
sumur pengantin, 163
Supersemar, 64
surga, 150
susu, 173
syaf, 151

T
tahi, 20
tail. *See* **ekor**

take off. *See* **tinggal
    landas**
talas, 181
tamarind. *See* **asam**
tameng hidup, 126
tanduk, 180
tangan, 51
    dingin, 56
    **kawin bawah
        tangan**, 194
    sembunyi, 112
tangga, 161
tante girang, 35
tapioca, 66
Tapol, 68
taro. *See* **talas**
tau ah gelap, 262
tawar, 170
teacher. *See* **guru**
teeth. *See* **gigi**
teguh, 106
tekor, 209
telapak kaki, 150
telo, 236
telur, 17, 19, 180, 181
tempe, 168
tempurung, 20
tepian, 208
tepung, 210
thigh. *See* **paha**
thumb. *See* **jempol**
tiger. *See* **harimau**
tikus. *See* rat
    berdasi, 11
    berjas, 11
    jalan, 219
    kantor, 10
    negara, 10
timbangan. *See* scales
Timun Mas, 48

tinggal landas, 70
tip, 92
tipu Aceh, 130
titian, 152
TKI, 72
TKW, 72
tobangke, 240
Toer. *See* **Pramoedya**
tong, 44
tongue. *See* **lidah**
tooth. *See* **gigi**
toothpaste. *See* **odol**
TOPP, 113
torpedo, 117
TP, 262
trader. *See* **pedagang**
transsexual, transvestite.
    See **banci**
treasure. *See* **harta**
troops. *See* **pasukan**
tuba, 173
tujuh, 152
tulang,
    manis mulut, 51
    banting, 57
    lidah, 52
tupai, 23
turunkan harga, 108
tut wuri handayani,
    113
tuyul, 158

U
uang,
    jemputan, 193
    jujur, 193
    kopi, 98
    KUHP, 92
    minum, 98
    pelumas, 98

rokok, 98
sirih, 98
taxi, 98
transpor, 98
ubi, 181
ulam, 242
ular naga, 25
undercover agent, 111
united, 106
Unity in Diversity. *See*
    **Bhinneka Tunggal
    Ika**
unjuk
    gigi, 53
    otot, 102
    rasa, 101, 102
untung, 161
utang, 99
UUD, 92

V
Veranda of Mecca. *See*
    Serambi Mekkah

W
Wahid Abdurrahman. *See*
    Gus Dur
walk. *See* **jalan**
wall face. *See* **muka
    tembak**
warkop, 176
warnet, 222
wartawan
    amplop, 98
    Bodrex, 97
warteg, 175
wartel, 222
water. *See* **air**
wejangan, 82
wet, 96

White dove. *See*
    Merparti Putih
widow. *See* **inong bale**
wolf. *See* **serigala**
womanizer. *See* **hidung
    belang**
wong alit, 89, 90
    cilik, 89, 98
    elit, 89
worm, 13, 19, 26
WTS, 97

X
Xanana, 121

Y
yarn. *See* banana
yellowing. *See*
    kuningisasi